JOHN
SAUL

John Saul. Photograph by Michael Sack. Used by permission of the photographer.

JOHN SAUL

A Critical Companion

Paul Bail

CRITICAL COMPANIONS TO POPULAR CONTEMPORARY WRITERS
Kathleen Gregory Klein, Series Editor

Greenwood Press
Westport, Connecticut • London

36137

Library of Congress Cataloging-in-Publication Data

Bail, Paul.
John Saul : a critical companion / Paul Bail.
p.   cm.—(Critical companions to popular contemporary
writers, ISSN 1082–4979)
Includes bibliographical references and index.
ISBN 0–313–29575–1 (alk. paper)
1. Saul, John—Criticism and interpretation.   I. Title.
II. Series.
PS3569.A787Z55   1996
813'.54—dc20   95–39492

British Library Cataloguing in Publication Data is available.

Library of Congress Catalog Card Number: 95–39492
ISBN: 0–313–29575–1
ISSN: 1082–4979

First published in 1996

Greenwood Press, 88 Post Road West, Westport, CT 06881
An imprint of Greenwood Publishing Group, Inc.

Printed in the United States of America

The paper used in this book complies with the
Permanent Paper Standard issued by the National
Information Standards Organization (Z39.48–1984).

10 9 8 7 6 5 4 3 2 1

For my parents, Roderick and Jeanne Marie, who instilled an early love of books, and for Romeo Grenier, pharmacist turned bookseller, whose fine Odyssey Bookshop provided countless hours of adolescent exploration.

And for my children, that the romance of literature may lay claim to their youthful hearts and steal their leisure hours.

By definition, horror cannot be surmounted. This is because horror implies *boundlessness*—the never-ending potentialities of the objects of our dread. Hence, it is not womb fantasies or castration complexes per se but the constrictive and expansive implications of those standpoints—their chaotic or obliterating possibilities—that concern us so.

Kirk J. Schneider, *Horror and the Holy* (1993)

Contents

Series Foreword

The authors who appear in the series Critical Companions to Popular Contemporary Writers are all best-selling writers. They do not have only one successful novel, but a string of them. Fans, critics, and specialist readers eagerly anticipate their next book. For some, high cash advances and breakthrough sales figures are automatic; movie deals often follow. Some writers become household names, recognized by almost everyone.

But novels are read one by one. Each reader chooses to start and, more importantly, to finish a book because of what she or he finds there. The real test of a novel is in the satisfaction its readers experience. This series acknowledges the extraordinary involvement of readers and writers in creating a best-seller.

The authors included in this series were chosen by an Advisory Board composed of high school English teachers and high school and public librarians. They ranked a list of best-selling writers according to their popularity among different groups of readers. Writers in the top-ranked group who had not received book-length, academic literary analysis (or none in at least the past ten years) were chosen for the series. Because of this selection method, Critical Companions to Popular Contemporary Writers meets a need that is not addressed elsewhere.

The volumes in the series are written by scholars with particular expertise in analyzing popular fiction. These specialists add an academic focus to the popular success that these best-selling writers already enjoy.

The series is designed to appeal to a wide range of readers. The general reading public will find explanations for the appeal of these well-known writers. Fans will find biographical and fictional questions answered. Students will find literary analysis, discussions of fictional genres, carefully organized introductions to new ways of reading the novels and bibliographies for additional research. Students will also be able to apply what they have learned from this book to their readings of future novels by these best-selling writers.

Each volume begins with a biographical chapter drawing on published information, autobiographies or memoirs, prior interviews, and, in some cases, interviews given especially for this series. A chapter on literary history and genres describes how the author's work fits into a larger literary context. The following chapters analyze the writer's most important, most popular, and most recent novels in detail. Each chapter focuses on a single novel. This approach, suggested by the Advisory Board as the most useful to student research, allows for an in-depth analysis of the writer's fiction. Close and careful readings with numerous examples show readers exactly how the novels work. These chapters are organized around three central elements: plot development (how the story line moves forward), character development (what the reader knows about the important figures), and theme (the significant ideas of the novel). Chapters may also include sections on generic conventions (how the novel is similar to or different from others in its same category of science fiction, fantasy, thriller, etc.), narrative point of view (who tells the story and how), symbols and literary language, and historical or social context. Each chapter ends with an "alternative reading" of the novel. The volume concludes with a primary and secondary bibliography, including reviews.

The Alternative Readings are a unique feature of this series. By demonstrating a particular way of reading each novel, they provide a clear example of how a specific perspective can reveal important aspects of the book. In each alternative reading section, one contemporary literary theory—such as feminist criticism, Marxism, new historicism, deconstruction, or Jungian psychological critique—is defined in brief, easily comprehensible language. That definition is then applied to the novel to highlight specific features that might go unnoticed or be understood differently in a more general reading of the novel. Each volume defines two or three specific theories, making them part of the reader's understanding of how diverse meanings may be constructed from a single novel.

Taken collectively, the volumes in the Critical Companions to Popular Contemporary Writers series provide a wide-ranging investigation of the complexities of current best-selling fiction. By treating these novels seriously as both literary works and publishing successes, the series demonstrates the potential of popular literature in contemporary culture.

Kathleen Gregory Klein
Southern Connecticut State University

Acknowledgments

A former colleague from the Houston Independent School System kept telling me, "Someday you've got to write a book." Well, here it is.

I would like to thank John Saul for graciously consenting to be interviewed for this book, his partner Michael Sack for providing a photograph, and their assistants Lori Dickinson and Rob Miller for facilitating both of these transactions.

I also must acknowledge the efforts of Patsy Taucer, Deidre Taucer, Eric Nivala, Wayne Grey, and Sylvia Vellino, whose assistance with child care, minor research chores, and proofreading made this project possible. My colleague Chuck Carroll provided support and understanding. The editorial guidance of series editor Kathy Klein was very valuable.

Two excellent independent bookstores were a source of consistent inspiration and refreshment. The staff of the Raven Used Bookstore in Northampton and the Odyssey Bookshop in South Hadley were more than tolerant of my browsing through their treatises on literary theory between book-buying binges.

Finally, large sections of this book could not have been completed without the generous research assistance of the librarians at the Leominster and Fitchburg public libraries. Those who were most called upon to demonstrate forbearance with my many requests were reference librarians Ann Finch, Ed Bergman, and Amy Ricciuti of Leominster and Joanne McGuirk, Kathy French, and Sandy Cravedi of Fitchburg and youth librarian Diane Sanabria of Leominster.

1

The Life of John Saul

> I don't mean just a figure of speech. This is what comes of trying to
> talk about deep things. . . . I mean that I really did see myself, and
> my real self, committing the murders. . . . I realized I really *was* like
> that, in everything except actual final consent to the action.
> Father Brown, in G. K. Chesterton, *The Secret of Father Brown* (1927)

John Saul in conversation is a gregarious and engaging storyteller with
a ready wit, frequently giving way to contagious laughter, more likely
than not when recounting his own foibles. He was born John Woodruff
Saul III on February 25, 1942, so that his astrological symbol is, appropriately, the mystical and water-loving Pisces. His father, John W. Saul,
worked in an oil refinery and was a staunch trade unionist. His mother,
Elizabeth Lee Saul, worked at home raising the children.

John Saul has one sister who is two years older than he. Born in Pas-
adena, California, he grew up in Whittier, a short drive from Los Angeles
and the Pacific seacoast. His love of the ocean is reflected in the fact that
a third of his published novels are set by the sea; these include *Suffer the
Children, Cry for the Strangers, Comes the Blind Fury, The Unwanted, The
Unloved*, and *Second Child*.

Saul was raised in the Swedenborgian Church, a tiny Christian de-
nomination sometimes known as the New Church. Emanuel Swedenborg
was a scientist who wrote several books of theology based on his mys-

tical experiences. These books influenced poet Ralph Waldo Emerson and Henry James, Sr., father of the novelist who wrote the psychological ghost story *The Turn of the Screw*.

Saul says, "Both sides of my family were Swedenborgians for several generations back. My father's grandfather was a Swedenborgian minister whose name was also John Saul. Every time I wander into a Swedenborgian church or reading room anywhere in the country, everyone knows exactly who I am and knows all my cousins. In fact, they turn out to *be* my cousins!" (All quotes, unless otherwise identified in this chapter, are from the author's interview with John Saul.)

Saul describes his childhood as normal and says the kinds of bizarre experiences his young characters go through had no parallels in his life. "I didn't even get locked in closets and beaten," he told *People* magazine (Chambers and Blackman 1989). He found elementary school congenial and did well academically, although his attitude was businesslike even then. As he told interviewer Joni Blackman, "If you had to write 300 words on a subject, 300 words was exactly what they got. I sat there and counted them." Even before his teenage years Saul began to secretly toy with the idea of becoming a writer. "I had a seventh grade teacher who said I should seriously think about it." The teacher gave the students a list of twenty words, with the assignment to use them in a sentence. Displaying his characteristic sense of humor, the young Saul used all twenty of the them in a single sentence just for fun. The next day the teacher asked to speak to him.

The teacher told him, "John, you're fairly intelligent, and I think you knew *exactly* what I meant by the instructions for the assignment. On the other hand, I find it interesting that you were actually able to use all twenty words in a sentence that makes sense. Before the end of the year I'll try to come up with a list of words that you cannot use in one sentence." But by the time summer vacation arrived, Saul had won the bet, so his teacher confessed, "I have never advised a seventh grader to seriously consider becoming a professional writer, but I think in your case you'd better do it." That idea stayed with Saul and eventually germinated into a writing career.

After graduating from Whittier High School in 1959, Saul had difficulty settling on a college and a course of studies that suited him. He attended Antioch College in Ohio and Cerritos in Norwalk, California, then Montana State University and San Francisco State College, variously majoring in anthropology, liberal arts, and theater, but never obtaining

a degree. In the summers he worked on the University of Chicago ar-
chaelogical dig in New Mexico and Arizona, where he picked up a fair
amount of Native American lore. He became disillusioned with his initial
major, anthropology, after he chanced to meet legendary anthropologist
Margaret Mead, famous for her study of culture and sexuality in Samoa
and New Guinea. She commented that she had spent more of her career
"locked up" in museums than out doing actual field work—a fate that
Saul did not wish for himself. Since he had aspirations of becoming a
playwright, he eventually decided to be a theater major at San Francisco
State College. "But I discovered I had very little talent as an actor," he
says. "Then I wrote a play and gave it to one of the professors to look
over, and he asked for a reader's fee. I got my dander up, and that was
pretty much the end of my career in the theater department."

Although never completing his academic training in theater, John Saul
has continued to dabble in it, even after becoming a novelist. He served
on the board of directors for Seattle Theater Arts and has had some one-
act plays produced in Los Angeles and Seattle. He wrote a musical, *Em-
press*, which he tried to get produced in New York. "We got the big
people from all the production companies to come to hear the songs.
They all liked it, but they thought the music was too old-fashioned for
today's audiences."

After forsaking college life, John Saul held a string of odd jobs, like
the typical budding novelist of romantic folklore. He has been a technical
writer, pulp magazine editor, and car rental agent and has worked as a
temporary typist through a secretarial agency. At one point he knocked
off a few formulaic sex novels, under a pseudonym, to pay the rent.
Always a quick writer, he was able to complete these slender books in
a week. However, his real interest was in writing comic mysteries. Unfortunately, there was not much of a market for these, and he accumu-
lated several unsold manuscripts and a sheaf of rejection slips.

In 1973 he got a job on the administrative staff of the Stonewall drug
and alcohol rehabilitation program, which primarily serviced the gay
community in Seattle. It was in the course of this job that he met clinical
psychologist Michael Sack, who became his closest friend and literary
collaborator. "Michael was essentially the drug and alcohol treatment
czar of Wisconsin at the time. He'd been involved in setting up Tellurian
Communities in Wisconsin and was working with the Joint Commission
on Hospital Accreditation to get therapeutic communities—TCs—li-
censed. There was a pilot project to set up credentialing in which a lot

of TCs agreed to be inspected. Stonewall was one of the groups that volunteered. Michael came out to do the on-site evaluation. That's when I first met him.''

Subsequently, John Saul moved to Oshkosh, Wisconsin, and with Michael's encouragement renewed his efforts to get one of his novels published. His agent at the time was Jane Rotrosen, whose former name was Jane Saul. ''She's my agent because she thought Jane Saul representing John Saul was too cute to pass up. We're not related at all. It was pure coincidence that when I sent a manuscript to the Kurt Helmer agency years ago, Jane was working there and was handed my manuscript. I was her very first client. I think my manuscript arrived the day after she started.

''She felt that John Saul was a terrific name to put on the cover of a book because there were few enough letters in each name so that it could be put into large type. And she said, 'You also speak reasonably well and are fairly attractive and you'll publicize well.' '' But she was having very little luck selling his comic murder mysteries to publishers and advised him to ''write to the market.'' At that time CB radios were a national craze, so Saul began a CB trucker thriller. ''And I wrote half a manuscript—without an outline, of course, because I didn't know what an outline was. I hadn't a clue where the plot was going. It was just getting bigger and bigger and further and further out of hand.''

He sent the half-completed manuscript to his agent, who showed it to her best friend in publishing Linda Grey, who was a senior editor at Dell. ''Linda liked the writing, but she already had her CB trucker book. And by the time I could finish the manuscript and Dell could publish it, the whole market for this type of book was going to be dead. What she really wanted was someone to write psychological thrillers to compete with Stephen King. And, did I think I could do that?

''I'd never heard of Stephen King at that point. *Carrie* had not come out as a movie yet. So I hot-footed it down to the local supermarket in Oshkosh, and *Salem's Lot* was on the stands. There were about a half-dozen books, all involving children and the occult in some way—children in jeopardy. And I thought, 'Surely I can do this.' So Michael and I came up with three basic one-line ideas. Jane said, 'Linda Grey really liked the one about the two little girls in a cave where everyone thinks one's crazy but actually it's the other one who's killing all their friends. Can you do an outline?'

''I thought, 'Oh sure, an outline! What's an outline?' But I said, 'Of course I can do an outline.' Starving writers will say anything. Michael and I decided an outline was probably a brief description of the action in each chapter. And I said, 'But I always do that when I write the book.' He said, 'Well, maybe I can sort of sketch out the action and you can work on it and let's see what happens.' So we worked for a couple of days and came up with an outline. Didn't have a clue whether it was the right thing to do or not."

Three days after receiving the outline Dell bought it for $50,000, which was a very large advance at the time. But they needed a completed 400-page manuscript within five weeks. "And did I think I could do it? Well, of course, I could do it. I was a starving writer. Starving writers can do anything. I looked at the outline, which was around twenty-eight chapters, and I realized each chapter should be about fifteen pages. When I was in college, I was always a great procrastinator and did my term papers the night before they were due, so I knew I could write fifteen pages in a day. So I pulled that trick off, too, at the rate of a chapter a day. At the end of each week I'd send in what I'd done to Linda Grey and be absolutely certain they'd call up and cancel the contract and demand the money back."

Of course, she did not do that. And John Saul has remained loyal to his agent and his editor ever since. He describes Linda Grey as "a fabulous editor who actually edits rather than acquires." In the 1980s he followed her from Dell to Bantam and then followed her again to Ballantine-Fawcett-Columbine-Del Rey, of which Linda Grey is currently president. "I think I'm the only person she still edits. I know I'm the only one she brought over from Ballantine."

It was a rare stroke of good fortune that John Saul broke into the horror genre just as it was taking off as a mass-market phenomenon, and that his publisher was prepared to launch his career with an unprecedented publicity campaign, including network television advertising—which had never been attempted for a book before—as well as a major promotional tour. Helen Meyer, who controlled the publishing company, was on the verge of retirement and had decided she had one more great publishing experiment left in her. "It was amazing. Helen Meyer really stuck her neck out, but in those days one person could do that. She was in total control of everything. The first run of covers had been done and they'd printed a million. She looked at the cover and said, 'I don't like it. I've changed my mind about the colors.' And they said, 'Mrs. Meyer, the entire run is printed.' And she said, 'So? Throw them away! I changed my mind.' "

Mrs. Meyer's goal was to take an unknown author, release his first novel as a paperback original, and put it on the *New York Times* best-seller list. "It had never been done. And it was her great slap at all the people who thought paperback publishing was third-rate. So she proceeded to do it. Afterward the paperback original market just blossomed. She really changed a lot in publishing. I was the guinea pig. I've been the guinea pig in a lot of publishing experiments. And the nice thing is, whenever the experiments flop, I don't take the rap because they always say, 'Well, we were experimenting anyway.' But if the experiment's successful, they give me part of the credit."

Among the other experiments *Punish the Sinners* was the first book published with a bar code. And *The God Project* was Bantam's first attempt at hardcover fiction. This was one of their less successful experiments. It did not sell as many copies in hardbound as the publisher had expected, although it did well when released as a paperback the following year. Following that experience Saul's next four novels went back to being released as paperback originals, and it was not until *Creature* in 1988 that Bantam once again tried a first release in hardcover.

John Saul's family's reaction to his success has been mixed. Initially, his mother's response was lukewarm. "When I called her up to tell her the good news about *Suffer the Children* selling for all this money, there was a long silence, and then she said, 'Well . . . pity you couldn't have sold a *good* book for that kind of money.' " But eventually she came to enjoy what he was doing. "She and my father were the type that would go into the bookstores and mother would make dad go stand in the back of the store. Then she'd stand in the front, pick up my book and yell, 'Look Jack, they have the new John Saul book!' "

His sister, however, forbade his niece to read his books. In a 1981 interview in *Twilight Zone* (Kramer 1981) Saul recounted an amusing anecdote that occurred after his niece turned thirteen and was attending summer camp. "The camp director was reading *Comes the Blind Fury*, and Allison said, 'My Uncle John wrote that book,' and the director said, 'Oh, really? I suppose you read this one already.' Allison said, 'No. I'm not allowed to read Uncle John's books,' and the director said, 'Well, that's ridiculous. . . . Read.' So my niece read *Comes the Blind Fury*, and when she came home, she told her mother she wanted to read the rest of them. She's a big fan of mine now."

Breaking into the ranks of bestsellerdom has had its rewards. Each of his books has sold over a million copies, and they have been translated into fourteen languages. And all of them are still in print. Quite a few bookstores stock all his titles, rather than just the most recent. As a result,

Saul has become a millionaire, with a 50-foot harbor cruiser christened "Opus" and three expensive cars that bear the license plates BOOK 6, BOOK 8, and BOOK 10. But other than allowing him to indulge in these consumer luxuries, he feels success has not basically changed him. As he once told James Kisner of *Mystery Scene*, "[Success] was so long in coming that I'm still waiting for it all to disappear" (1987, 4)

Not all the book earnings go to personal consumption. John Saul has a strong social conscience, shaped in part by the values he grew up with as a youth. While he has not been an active Swedenborgian for several years and has conflicted feelings about the church, he says, "I think my basic philosophy of life is still very Swedenborgian, if only in the overall terms of Swedenborgian thinking that salvation does not come through faith, it comes from the way you live your life, and that organized religion doesn't really mean much. Being a major contributor to the American Civil Liberties Union is much more important than going to church these days."

One of the ways that John Saul acts upon these principles is through the Chester Woodruff Foundation, which he and Michael Sack endowed. The name of the foundation is a composite of both of their middle names. "It's a little private foundation we set up. We used to do a lot of arts funding. Most of the money is going to AIDS now."

Besides financial rewards, John Saul has developed a loyal coterie of fans. Many teenagers write and tell him their mothers gave them the books that they used to read when they were teenagers. "That makes me feel very old indeed." Saul answers all his fan mail. He used to get a number of letters from adolescent female fans who wanted to know when *Suffer the Children* was going to be made into a movie because they wanted to play the part of Elizabeth, the killer.

Although the majority of those who write to him are teenagers, he has learned that his fans represent a great cross-section of society. "I was doing a book signing and a nun came up and wanted me to sign a copy of my newest book for her mother superior. I said, 'Your mother superior reads my stuff?' and she said, 'Yes. *Punish the Sinners* is her favorite of your books.'" At the other end of the spectrum he got a fan letter from killer cult leader Charles Manson: "He joined my fan club. Apparently Sirhan Sirhan put him up to joining because they're both in the same prison. It's rather creepy. Charlie's a little confused though. He mentioned that he really liked my work, especially *A Tale of Two Cities*; he really liked the guillotine part."

For relaxation he enjoys international spy thrillers. "Nazis make the best villains," he says. Saul enjoys the psychological tension of the chase and the narrow brushes with disaster. His favorite in this genre is Robert Ludlum, who continues to be with Saul's former publisher Bantam. But the writers whom John Saul admires most are of a prior generation: Noel Coward, P. G. Wodehouse, John O'Hara.

"With Noel Coward it was partly the disgusting fact that the man could do *everything*. When you can write, compose, do lyrics, sing, dance, and act, and play the piano, and also be a decent human being—the man was astonishing! One thing that I always admired about his plays was that they always appeared to be nothing but light pieces of comic fluff and days later you were still thinking about them. There was always some very serious message going on, but he believed you must entertain the audience. If you have something to say, you do not hit them in the face. You'll accomplish more by entertaining them.

"P. G. Wodehouse I just find a comic genius. I giggle hysterically when I read him. And I always thought John O'Hara's short stories and his early novels are simply terrific. *Appointment In Samarra* is a fabulous piece of work. The later novels got a tad ponderous. But in his prime he was so concise and could accomplish so much with so little. The economy of style that he was so brilliant at was what I really liked."

Saul's talent for humor is a trait he shares with other big-name horror writers, such as Robert Bloch, who early in his career was a professional gag writer and stand-up comic, and William P. Blatty, who produced screenplays for several successful comedies before authoring *The Exorcist* (Winter 1985). But despite his interest in comic murder mysteries, his love of P. G. Wodehouse, and his humorous style in conversation, John Saul generally squelches the comic impulse when he is writing his novels. Unlike Stephen King, who sometimes mixes the two, Saul does not believe in playing horror for laughs. "Sometimes I have a good time with minor characters and walk-ons. I get some chuckles out of them. But for the most part the kind of fiction that I'm known for does not lend itself to laughs. There's nothing that breaks terror as quickly as a good laugh.

"Take *Arachnophobia*, for example. I cannot do horror movies. I'm way too suggestible; they give me endless nightmares. All my friends wanted to go see *Arachnophobia*. I can handle anything with two legs, four legs, or six legs; I don't do no legs and eight legs. So I thought, 'All right, I can do what I did with the *Exorcist*,' which was go stand in the lobby. It turns out that the people who made *Arachnophobia* understood just how horrifying the whole concept of it was. They kept breaking the terror with laughs, and it worked well. The movie would've been utterly unwatchable without the laughs. And they weren't so often that they utterly destroyed it. It still worked as a thriller. But every now and then they'd just throw up some tomfoolery and crack everybody up, and it made for a terrific movie.

"But in a book you're spending so much time and energy building up that terror that you don't want to break it with laughter. If it gets *too* bad in a book, people can always set it down for a few moments and go do something else, then pick it up, which they can't do with a movie. So I really don't see trying to mix comedy in with thrillers in a book."

As if having second thoughts, Saul adds, "Actually I thought the character in *The Unloved*, Marguerite Devereaux, was pretty hysterically funny all the way through. And I have to confess that by the time I got to the final scene up in the ballroom where she's gimping around dancing for all the children she's killed, I was laughing hysterically. I just couldn't hold it together while I was writing that, and it got completely out of hand. 'Throw everything in! What the hell, go for it! Sure—pin the kid to the back of the chair with a butcher knife. Why not?' I suppose that became sort of the camp take-off on the Gothic novel."

Asked how he squares his generally sunny disposition with the pessimistic and downbeat endings of most of his novels, he says, "That's always been a bone of contention between me and my editor. I usually start off with something of a happy ending, and then she wants me to put in that one final twist where all of a sudden evil is going to rear its ugly head again. I've finally, in the last few books, gotten a little bit away from that, and actually in *Black Lightning* I think it's a very happy ending. It's the only possible happy ending that could come out of it."

Saul feels the setting of his novels is very important and will travel to the location in order to get the firsthand impressions that will ensure authenticity. "In *Hellfire* there's a lot of real places. The mill I used as a model is near Easton, Massachusetts. The mansion is George Plimpton's family place. The masoleum is at Roche Harbor up in Puget Sound. In fact, for a long time they always kept *Hellfire* in stock in the store at Roche Harbor, and people would do dramatic readings of the masoleum section in the bar at night."

At times finding the right setting is the key to making the plot work. A case in point was *The Unloved*. The story lacked credibility. "It was ludicrous. I didn't believe a word of it. The problem was we'd set it in Carmel, California, and I said, 'Wait a minute. These aren't Californians. This is some decadent old Southerner. And the minute we stuffed it down on that miserable Spanish-moss clad island in that crumbling plantation house off the coast of the Carolinas, it worked instantly. The problem with the story wasn't the characters, it was the location."

A frequent device in Saul's plots is an attempt at explanation by a psychologist. This is a device that was used by Alfred Hitchcock in the movie version of *Psycho* (which scared the wits out of John Saul when he saw it in his teens). Hitchcock used the psychologist to explain the killer's motivation to the audience. But in Saul's novels the psychologist always has the *wrong* explanation for the protagonist's actions, which is pretty humorous considering that Saul's chief collaborator, Michael Sack, is a clinical psychologist. "The psychologist always has a legitimate explanation," Saul remarked, "but that doesn't necessarily mean it was what was really going on. Actually in a lot of the earlier novels I was never totally convinced *what* really was going on. The idea was that there were three levels: the real level, the psychological level, and the occult level. Either someone's crazy, really angry, or possessed, and I always tried to write them so the readers could draw their own conclusion. So if you believe in ghosts—fine, they're possessed. If you don't believe in ghosts—fine, they're crazy. Or if you really like nasty people, they're just mean. So we would throw the psychologist in to give the good psychological foundation for it all. Granted they were wrong. They weren't necessarily wrong. It's just that in this case their expertise was not called for.

"With the techno-thriller it's a whole different thing because when the horror's coming right out of modern technology, you don't need three levels. Part of the thing that makes a psychological thriller scary is that you don't really know what's going on. You don't know whether this person's crazy or possessed or just making the whole thing up. Part of the fun of it is to try to figure out what's actually happening here."

John Saul is actively involved in the development of other writers. He is a frequent lecturer at the Pacific Northwest Writers Conference. He is not associated with Horror Writers of America, and his work does not get included in the many anthologies of supernatural literature edited by members of that network. "Basically, I don't consider myself a horror writer in the first place," Saul replies. "I've been sort of lumped in as a horror writer because it's the easiest place for book stores and publishers to categorize me. I've never felt comfortable with the label. And I'm not a horror fan; I don't read it at all. As for the anthologies, they're always asking me to contribute, but I don't write short stories, so that pretty much leaves me out of it."

His advice to aspiring writers is "Don't pay too much attention to writing teachers. God, that's fatal! I never took a writing course in my life. I've sat in on some though and oh my God! Every time I hear a writing teacher talk what I hear them saying is 180 degrees off from what they should be saying. It's truly frightening. I have a friend who's an academician and wants to write desperately, and he has so completely bound himself up with the rules of the structure of novels that he's incapable of writing anything. Basically you think up a good story and you sit down and tell it as best you can. There aren't any rules! It's much simpler than what people imagine it to be.

"If a high school kid thinks he should write, then he or she should write. Sit down and write! And some of them are awfully good. There was some girl who started writing to me when she was twelve, and she had problems with one of my books. She was very careful to tell me that she really liked the books a lot. But she had found some structural weaknesses, and as it turned out, she was right. She also had some suggestions on how they could've been fixed and she was right on those, too. I sent a copy to my editor, who said, 'How old is this kid?' So I wrote back encouraging her and thanking her for the letter and telling her that I thought her criticisms and solutions were right on the money and said, 'I really think you should very seriously consider becoming an editor. You truly have a gift for it.'"

When conceiving his novels, Saul does not start out by imagining a compelling central character. Instead, he begins with a catchy main concept and develops the characters and setting out of that. Saul got the concept for *Creature* while watching a news report on human growth hormones, in which the reporter speculated about being able to design your ideal body type. Saul's first association to this news item was the possibility of a coach using these hormones to make the hometown football team invincible. The idea for *Comes the Blind Fury* came directly out of a line from the poet Milton. "I was browsing through *Bartlett's Quotations* one day, and I ran across the line, 'Comes the blind Fury with th' abhorred shears/And slits the thin-spun life.' And I thought, 'That's a great title for a John Saul novel! Now all we need is a plot.' And in *Guardian* the one-line idea was: Everybody makes promises to their best friend that 'If you die, I'll take care of your kid.' But what if it really happens and the kid turns out to be a monster?"

Saul does not generally read in the horror genre and particularly avoids reading the work of prominent writers like Dean Koontz and Stephen King, as he does not want to subconsciously pick up one of their themes and copy it in his next book.

Saul is unabashed about admitting he prefers cruising on his boat to the hard work of sitting down at a keyboard and writing. But even when he is not at his desk, his mind is churning out story ideas. "There's always a plot cooking, a story being kicked around and 'what if' being discussed. The actual writing takes the least amount of time. What takes all the time is the thinking it up and the structuring of it in your mind." Once he has done the outline, he completes a first draft at the rate of a chapter a day, with no breaks, just as he did with *Suffer the Children*. He generally spends mornings thinking through what he will write and then sits down at the keyboard in the afternoon. He tries to put the book out of his mind in the evening and relax, but as he told Stanley Wiater, that can be hard to do. "When I'm in the middle of a book . . . I find then that I'm living in the town that it's set in, not Seattle" (1990, 179).

Saul calls himself a "card-carrying coward" because of his active imagination. He admits to sleeping with a nightlight so if he wakes up in the middle of the night, he will know he is not dead. When he is writing tense scenes, his imagination takes over to the point that once, while putting such a scene on paper, a squirrel jumped up against the window, and the unexpected noise sent him flying out of his chair. However, he appreciates it when his subconscious starts to take over.

"I always know that something's going really well when things get totally out of hand and the characters simply take over and go do what they want to do and the book writes itself. When I'm having to sit there and have to make everybody say anything or do anything interesting, then it's not working at all.

"I often wind up with strange surprises. In *The God Project* Dr. Malone was the hero of the piece, I thought. Right through the outline, he was the hero, and as I was writing it, all of a sudden he's pulling open the bottom drawer of his desk, taking out a bottle of brandy, and toasting the success of *his* project. And I thought, 'Wait a minute! This is the good guy, this isn't the bad guy!' And so I went back through everything I'd written, and up to that point there was nothing where he was absolutely branded the good guy, but in every single instance could simply have been pretending to be the good guy while really being the architect of the whole thing. And I thought, 'Well, that's interesting! I'll leave it that way and see what happens.' And it worked out fine."

Another such instance occurred in *Shadows*. "I was a little surprised when Amy cropped up on Josh's computer and didn't seem to be a very nice person." These moments when the plot asserts a life of its own usually occur in the heat of the actual writing, rather than coming to him in a flash as he is brushing his teeth or forming in his mind as he is having breakfast. "It pretty much happens at the typewriter. I know the scene that I intend to write. But sometimes it's unwritable, because it turns out it was an interesting idea but I can't really speak it. If scene after scene turns out to be non-expandable from the outline, I'm in deep trouble, and it's probably not going to work. In fact, I've abandoned books halfway through."

Saul would be happy to have one of his books made into a feature film for theatrical release. "A really terrific movie can sell a whole lot of books, and the nice thing is it can only do wonderful things for your career as a novelist. A really bad movie cannot hurt you. Basically, it disappears so fast that no one notices it was there. People don't go see bad movies in droves and then stop buying the author's books. So it's really a no-downside deal." Once a book is optioned for possible film production, Saul essentially has no control over what happens to it. And he would be unlikely to be consulted about the screenplay. "Hollywood doesn't like novelists. They want to do it themselves."

He was somewhat disappointed with the results when David Gerber made *Cry for the Strangers* into a television movie in 1982. "It was beautifully photographed, beautifully produced, but in order to keep the action line intact, they had taken out all the motivation for the actions." At present he has two books that have been optioned and might at some point be made into films. "*Creature* is in development again at Fox. It's been in development several times. *The God Project* is optioned. Someone's poking at it. Those two seem to have the best shot at making it. But if they make a mediocre television movie, then the one that had a really good shot at being a terrific movie will be wasted."

In addition to films, a new type of book spin-off is computer games. "There's a group in Los Angeles working on a CD-ROM game based on *Shadows* called *Beyond the Shadows* where Amy has gotten possibly completely out of hand and it's up to you, as Josh, to find out what Amy's up to, and it turns out her personality's fragmented among computers all over the place. The Internet is now involved, of course."

As for future projects, Saul is waiting to see how his newest novel, *Black Lightning*, fares. It is a departure for him, since it is set in a big city and deals with a serial killer. He is a little nervous about it because "Everybody likes this book way too much." His next novel will be another "urban thriller" set in San Francisco and will have more occult elements.

2

The Horror Genre

Take almost any deviation from customary experience, stretch it far
enough, and you produce horror.

Kirk J. Schneider, *Horror and the Holy* (1993)

Horror is an emotion. It is also a genre of writing. Many authors are not
happy with the name "horror." In fact, the speciality association Horror
Writers of America almost changed its name in 1992. Various alternate
labels for the genre include tales of terror, supernatural fiction, macabre
tales, dark fantasy, fright fiction, the chiller (as a variant of the thriller),
and weird tales—the name associated with the genre in the 1930s. The
objection of some authors is that "horror" suggests a purely visceral
reaction, whereas their writing aims at something higher than this. Stephen King, however, sums it up this way in *Danse Macabre*:

[T]he genre exists on three more or less separate levels, each
one a little less fine than the one before it. . . . My own philosophy . . . is to recognize these distinctions because they are
sometimes useful, but to avoid any preference for one over
the other on the grounds that one effect is somehow better.
. . . I recognize terror as the finest emotion . . . and so I will try
to terrorize the reader. But if I find I cannot . . . I will try to

horrify; and if I find I cannot horrify, I'll go for the gross-out.
I'm not proud. (1979, 36–37)

Regardless of what we call it, though, it is clear that there is a recognizable body of work that appeals to a segment of the public. Despite a dip in the fortunes of the horror genre in the past decade, the abiding popularity of Gothicism and the supernatural is demonstrated by the fact that half of the twelve mass-market paperbacks that sold over two million copies in 1994 were by authors associated with the horror field: Anne Rice, Stephen King, V. C. Andrews, and Dean Koontz. And this popularity shows no signs of fading soon.

THE MEANING OF GENRE

Genrefication in the modern sense became solidified around the 1930s with the rise of pulp magazines such as *Black Mask* (mystery), *Weird Tales* (horror), and *Amazing Stories* (science fiction). They were called "pulps" because they were printed on cheap paper that deteriorates quickly. And there was an incredible number of such magazines. At one time there were thirty-six specializing in the science fiction genre and over fifty in the detective genre, according to Lee Server (1993). But under competition from the comic books, and with the collapse of a national distribution system for magazines in 1954, the pulp magazines were largely replaced by a type of cheap, expendable book, mass-marketed in drugstores and on newsstands. Known as the "paperback original," it was a distant descendant of the nineteenth-century Gothic blue books and shilling shockers.

The publisher most involved in pioneering the paperback original was Ian Ballantine, founder of Bantam and Ballantine Books. The paperback original, unlike the paperback reprint, never comes out in hardcover. Therefore, until recently it was an item not subject to acquisition by libraries or discussion in book reviews. In a society that divides books into high-brow (elite) art and low-brow (vulgar) entertainment, the paperback original was definitely considered to be in the latter category. The paperback originals were commonly written in one of the popular genres.

Many of the modern genres have common roots in the Gothic. Prior to the last few decades it was common for an author to write in several genres without becoming typecast. As late as the 1950s authors such as Frederic Brown wrote simultaneously in the mystery, science fiction, and horror genres without having to masquerade behind different pen names. Anthony Boucher's name is primarily associated with mystery now because of the annual Bouchercon convention. But Boucher, like Brown, also penned both science fiction and horror stories, some of which are collected in *The Complete Werewolf* (1969).

Scholar and mystery novelist Dorothy Sayers's *Omnibus of Crime* (1929) was a broad collection of stories grouped into three inclusive categories: detection-and-mystery, supernatural, and blood-and-cruelty (i.e., non-supernatural horror). *Ellery Queen's Mystery Magazine* published stories by Stanley Elkins that fell in the horror category: "The Specialty of the House" (1948), about a gourmet club for cannibals, and "The Blessington Method" (1956), about the sinister Society for Gerontology. And the 1970 edition of the classic reference work by Jacques Barzun and Wendell Hertig Taylor, *A Catalogue of Crime*, contained a section on supernatural stories.

The rigid categorizing of authors by genre is largely a marketing device employed by publishers and booksellers to facilitate the marketing of books to definable segments of the reading public. Some of these genres can become very specific, to the point where books are labeled by subgenre, as is the case with recently published romance novels, which will plainly state on their covers whether they are historical, contemporary, Regency, romantic suspense, and so on. As Eric Rabkin (1994) has pointed out, this strategy appeals to some readers because it guarantees them a predictable reading experience in which they revisit a particular literary formula that they find comfortable and familiar. It fits in with the contemporary love of fast-food chains, which guarantees an experience of sameness in an otherwise changing and unpredictable world. A similar impulse is behind the popularity of series novels. For instance, in the mystery genre if you like private investigator V. I. Warshawski, you can revisit the same character over the course of several more books.

There are a couple of problems with this system, however—one for authors and the other for readers. Authors can become "typecast," or become "brand names," as Stephen King (1982) put it in his essay about how he became one. Thus labeled, they become trapped in a particular generic "ghetto," from which they can escape only by publishing under pseudonyms, or pen names. Some authors even adopt pen names to address different audiences (or market segments) within the same basic genre. For example, mystery writer Ruth Rendell also penned detective fiction under the pseudonym Barbara Vine, and Stephen King's alias was Richard Bachman.

At the other end readers may eventually tire of the formulas and conventions of a particular genre, which get worn-out and boring. So genres have to develop over time and introduce some novelty. The trick is to keep them familiar enough while introducing a bit of variation to prevent predictability. There are several possible strategies. One is to expand the conventions of the genre. Anne Rice did this with *Interview with the Vampire* (1976), in which she introduces the character of Louis, the reluctant vampire.

Another strategy is to create something unique by combining genres. Dean Koontz mixes genres so regularly that he coined the term "cross-genre" to refer to the type of novel he writes. Possibly the most brilliant example of a generically hybrid novel is William Hjorstberg's *Falling Angel* (1978), which combines the hard-boiled detective atmosphere of Raymond Chandler with Louisiana voodoo and the Dr. Faustus theme of bartering with the devil. Hjorstberg's novel has the distinction of being the first mystery in which the detective, the victim, and the murderer are all the same person.

A final method of coping with genre burnout is to make fun of the standard conventions, as Roman Polanski did in his movie *The Fearless Vampire Killers, or, Pardon Me, but Your Teeth Are in My Neck* (1967).

GOTHIC FICTION

As Stephen King has pointed out in *Danse Macabre* (1979), the classic mad scientist figure can be traced back from Frankenstein to Faust to the Greek mythological figures Daedalus, Prometheus, and Pandora. In a sense horror writing has very ancient roots. Tales of monsters, the supernatural, and the unknown predate recorded literature. The most ancient tale recorded in the English language, *Beowulf*, concerns the slaying of the troll Grendel and contains horrific elements. In the Elizabethan period Shakespeare wrote *The Tempest*, in which Prospero commands the spirits and the forces of nature through magic, and playwright Christopher Marlowe wrote *Dr. Faustus* about a man who sells his soul to the devil—a theme that the German poet Goethe also interpreted in his nineteenth-century play *Faust*.

But to understand most of the conventions of modern horror fiction, we need only go back to the Gothic novels of England at the beginning of the nineteenth century. Horace Walpole's *Castle of Otranto* (1764), subtitled *A Gothic Tale*, is considered the precursor of the genre and was the book that gave it a name.

Elsa Radcliffe defines the archetypal Gothic story as comprising the following elements:

> 1) the supernatural; 2) a quest or a wrong to be righted; 3) a setting that includes an old dwelling, traditionally a castle; 4) a fantasy of wealth suddenly acquired, or inheritance; 5) mystery, suspense, and intrigue; 6) a fantasy of romantic love in some form, often including a love-hate, trust-fear ambivalence between men and women; 7) romanticism of the past and an historical setting—no longer necessarily medieval, but of a generation past or more; and 8) confrontations between the Forces of Good and Evil. (1979, xii–xiii)

The more of these elements the plot includes, the more derivative it is of the Gothic influence.

The Gothic novel did not catch on as a popular phenomenon until thirty years after the appearance of Walpole's book. The heyday of the middle-class craze for Gothic novels was from 1790 to 1820. The Minerva Press, founded during this period, became a specialty publisher for Gothic literature, similar to the role of Arkham House in the twentieth century.

The mass readership to support the Gothic novel craze was made possible by the development of the circulating library, whose role was similar to our modern video rental stores. For a modest fee middle-class women on a limited budget could consume several otherwise costly novels a year. Servants, students, and others who could not even afford that contented themselves with the shilling shockers, or blue books, so named because they had a cheap blue paper cover and sold for a shilling. These were either severely condensed versions of Gothic novels (the precursor of *Reader's Digest* versions) or original works by imitators. During his schoolboy days the Romantic poet Percy Bysshe Shelley, future husband of the author of *Frankenstein*, was very fond of these sensationalistic little blue books, according to Peter Haining (1978).

Gothic as a popular genre really began with author Ann Radcliffe, whose *The Mysteries of Udolpho* (1794) and *The Italian* (1797) are the best known of her five novels. Suspense, an important element in her plots, was built through the postponement of anticipated horrors. That is, if there is a door that "must not be opened," the reader plods on in the hopes of eventually finding out what horrible sight lies beyond that door. As Walter Kendrick (1991) and others have indicated, Radcliffe's main innovation was to include apparently supernatural happenings in the plot and then provide a rational explanation for these at the end. This device is sometimes referred to as Gothic *expliqué*, from the French word for "explained." The Gothic thus is the ancestor not only of the modern tale of terror, but also of the modern mystery, which requires the detective to wrap up the puzzling events with a satisfactory explanation by the concluding chapter.

The label "Gothic" derives from the awe-inspiring style of architecture employed in Britain during the period when it was Catholic. To Protestant England, Catholicism was both superstition-ridden and sinister—bent on taking over the world for the Papacy. Images associated with Catholicism inspired in these readers creepy feelings similar to those that voodoo imagery inspires in the Southerner. Hence, the Gothics made liberal use of such gimmicks as gloomy ruined abbeys, decadent monks, and manors attended by superstition-ridden Catholic servants, as documented by Sister Mary Muriel Tarr (1946). But at the same time that the middle-class Protestant readers could enjoy the vicarious chills of the "Catholic superstition," in the end they could enjoy a sense of superiority to the novel's gullible servants by being given a rationalistic explanation for the apparent spooks.

Ann Radcliffe's plot devices were copied, with only minor modifications, by a host of less talented imitators. The notable exception to this uniformity was Matthew Lewis's *The Monk* (1795), which created a scandal due to its explicit sex and violence and left him with the lifelong nickname "Monk" Lewis. The plot included a monk who rapes and murders his sister and also murders his mother. The novel is also notable for its unembarrassed use of the supernatural—a female demon—as opposed to the general run of Gothics, which suggested supernatural events, but then explained them away by the end of the novel. In this respect Matthew Lewis's writing is more closely related to the modern tale of terror than is Ann Radcliffe's.

British novelist Jane Austen satirizes the predictable Gothic clichés, props, and gimmicks in her novel *Northanger Abbey*, published in 1817: an uncannily fascinating portrait, a secret passage, strange hints from the housekeeper, and a lamp whose flame dies out at the worst moment, leaving the heroine in total darkness. Although Radcliffe's works are rarely read except by scholars, the familiar classics *Jane Eyre* (1847) and *Wuthering Heights* (1847) by the Brontë sisters, published forty years after the height of the Gothic craze, are still within the broad sweep of that tradition.

Mary Shelley's *Frankenstein* (1818), by abandoning any trappings of the supernatural, became the first major departure from the Gothic formula and pointed the direction that a branch of modern horror and science fiction would take. Other milestones on the way to modern horror include *The Devil's Elixirs* (1815) by German painter and conductor E. T. A. Hoffman, author of "The Nutcracker," and the dark fantasy "The Sandman" (1816), which, according to John Sladek (1988), was part of the inspiration for Fritz Lang's classic movie *Metropolis* (1926); Eugene Sue's *The Wandering Jew* (1845), which plays a role in the 1960 novel by Walter M. Miller, Jr., *Canticle for Leibowitz*; Wilkie Collins's *The Woman in White* (1860); Villiers de l'Isle Adam's *Contes Cruels* (1883); Robert Louis Stevenson's *The Strange Case of Dr. Jekyll and Mr. Hyde* (1886), which in some ways is an antecedent of *Psycho*; Rudyard Kipling's *The Phantom Rickshaw and Other Tales* (1888); Oscar Wilde's *The Picture of Dorian Gray* (1891); and Bram Stoker's *Dracula* (1897).

Stoker, an Irishman, deliberately stood one of the British Gothic clichés on its head in *Dracula*. He opens the novel with a Transylvanian woman urging British traveler Jonathan Harker to put her rosary and crucifix around his neck as a protection, and the peasants constantly perform the sign of the cross in Harker's presence. Harker, with his English Protestant sensibility, is quite uncomfortable with all this "superstition," but it turns out the peasants are right, and by the end of the novel Harker is willing to use a fragment of the consecrated eucharistic wafer as a spiritual weapon against Dracula.

Robert Louis Stevenson's story "The Body Snatchers" (1881) could be considered the first "medical thriller," predating Robin Cook's *Coma* (1977) by almost a century. In it some unscrupulous doctors regularly resort to murder to supply the medical college with bodies for anatomy class.

Although the Gothic in its classic form does not exist anymore, the label is still sometimes applied to a diverse assembly of fiction. Victoria Holt's novels are called Gothic romances, Stephen King's stories are inaccurately termed Gothic horror, and Tennessee Williams's plays are called Southern Gothic.

GHOST STORIES

Sir Walter Scott, author of *Ivanhoe* (1819), is often credited with inaugurating the English ghost story as a short fiction form in 1818 with the publication of "The Tapestried Chamber" in *Blackwood's*, a sensationalistic magazine that Edgar Allen Poe parodied in his satirical story "How to Write a Blackwood Article" (1838).

In the nineteenth century the British developed a curious custom, discussed by Kendrick (1991), of reading ghostly tales to a circle of friends around the fire on Christmas Eve. Charles Dickens's *A Christmas Carol* (1843), with its ghosts of Christmas past, present, and future, is the most familiar remnant of this fad. But magazines of that era abounded with ghost stories in their Christmas issues. Fiction was reflecting trends and events in society. As Peter Washington entertainingly discusses in *Madam Blavatsky's Baboon* (1995), spiritualism had begun to develop a middle-class following around 1850, with the spirits of the departed materializing at seances and speaking to their relatives through the lips of a medium or through Ouija boards. Arthur Conan Doyle, author of the Sherlock Holmes stories, became an ardent spiritualist. Scientific study of the occult began in 1882 with the founding of the Society for Psychical Research. The scientific study of mystical experience was also an interest of William James, the Harvard psychologist, whose brother Henry James wrote the famous ghost tale *The Turn of the Screw* (1898).

This late Victorian period perfected a genteel and sentimental type of ghost story typified by Oscar Wilde's "The Canterville Ghost" (1891), in which a little girl develops a humorous relationship to a ghost, similar to the one between Lydia and Beetlejuice, which contemporary children are familiar with. In the end she frees the ghost's soul through the sincerity of her prayers, and is rewarded with a casket of jewels. But with the beginning of the twentieth century a more loathsome and horrific note began to introduce itself into the ghost story as practiced by M. R. James (1862–1936). F. Marion Crawford's "The Upper Berth" (1886) was an early example of this new type of ghost tale.

These short stories were an ephemeral art form. The magazines they appeared in have been lost, damaged, or discarded, and the stories have become inaccessible to later readers. An important development in the first half of the twentieth century was the publication of hardbound anthologies of reprinted ghost stories, which preserved these ephemeral classics in a more durable form. Some of the most influential anthologies were Vere H. Collins's *Ghosts and Marvels* (1924), Dorothy L. Sayers's *Omnibus of Crime* (1929), and Phyllis Fraser and Herbert Wise's *Great Teals of Terror and the Supernatural* (1944). This period also saw the first academic studies on the subject, Dorothy Scarborough's *The Supernatural in Modern English Fiction* (1917) and Edith Birkhead's *The Tale of Terror* (1921). Horror fiction, which had been considered a pleasant diversion at best and a low form of entertainment at worst, now had acquired a degree of recognition as a literary form worthy of study.

AMERICAN HORROR

As Les Daniels (1975) has suggested, during the earliest years of the American colonies the demonic was treated as a frightening reality, not a subject for fiction. Following on the heels of the Salem witch trials and the execution of those convicted, clergyman Cotton Mather published *The Wonders of the Invisible World* (1693), describing a Satanic conspiracy against the Christian colonists. Puritan clergyman Jonathan Edwards's published sermon *Sinners in the Hands of an Angry God* (1741) invited the reader to imaginatively contemplate the terrors of Hell, but its purpose was to convert, not divert or entertain.

Horror fiction in America is generally thought to have begun with Charles Brockden Brown, who wrote in the United States during the heyday of English Gothic novels. A. Robert Lee (1990) states that Brown's books were greatly admired by Mary Shelley, the author of *Frankenstein*, and her husband Percy, the Romantic poet. Brown had to adapt the classic Gothic style to the American continent, which lacked the crumbling castles and moldering monasteries favored by his British contemporaries, Ann Radcliffe and "Monk" Lewis. Two of his better known novels are *Wieland, or, The Transformation* (1798) and *Edgar Huntly, or, The Memoirs of a Sleep-Walker* (1799), which deals with themes of madness.

Washington Irving is best known for his short story "The Legend of Sleepy Hollow" (1819) about the schoolmaster Ichabod Crane and the Headless Horseman. A satirical aspect of the story is that the suggestible schoolmaster was easily spooked because he had a habit of reading the Rev. Cotton Mather's paranoid tracts. Other fantastic stories by Irving include "The Devil and Tom Walker" (1824) about a businessman who sells his soul to Satan, "The Spectre Bridegroom" (1819), and "Rip Van Winkle" (1819).

The next generation of writers includes Nathaniel Hawthorne, whose

House of the Seven Gables (1851) was a romance with Gothic elements, including a family curse by a falsely condemned witch. His most macabre short stories include "Young Goodman Brown" (1835) about a colonist who comes upon a group of his friends worshiping the devil in the woods and "Rappaccini's Daughter" (1844) about a beautiful girl raised by her scientist father among poisonous plants so that she would be deadly to any lover.

Edgar Allan Poe, well known for his grotesque fiction, was a contemporary of Hawthorne's and a great admirer of Charles Brockden Brown. His fiction includes detective stories such as "The Murders in the Rue Morgue" (1841), tales of terror such as "The Cask of Amontillado" (1846), supernatural stories such as "Ligeia" (1838), and even stories that could be loosely considered science fiction, such as "The Facts in the Case of M. Valdemar" (1845). He popularized the unsettling technique of telling the tale from the first-person perspective, using a deranged character as the unreliable narrator.

For decades after his death Poe enjoyed little esteem by the literary establishment in the United States. This was due partly to the fact that his work consisted almost entirely of short stories, which were not valued as an art form by nineteenth-century critics. Also, the radically subjective point of view in Poe's narration was several decades ahead of its time. It was the French who preserved Poe from oblivion for modern readers. Baudelaire, the French poet and author of *The Flowers of Evil* (1857), became the self-appointed translator and promoter of Poe and won for him literary admirers such as Guy de Maupassant and Stéphan Mallarmé.

Other important American writers who wrote fantastic and grotesque stories include Fitz-James O'Brien, who died in the Civil War, and Ambrose Bierce, who survived the Civil War and wrote *Can Such Things Be?* (1893) and *Fantastic Fables* (1899). His best-known short story is "An Occurrence at Owl Creek Bridge," which was hauntingly filmed by Robert Enrico in French in 1961 and was later broadcast on the "Twilight Zone" series.

It is impossible to discuss early-twentieth-century American writers without mentioning H. P. Lovecraft, who influenced a generation of writers, as Donald R. Burleson (1985) discusses. Lovecraft and his imitators were noted for the flowery extravagance of their prose style, which had an antique flavor more properly suited to Poe's day, or earlier. He was also known for the demonic monsters of his "Cthulhu Mythos," who are part supernatural, part science-fictional. *Supernatural Horror in Literature* (1945) was Lovecraft's critical testament. His literary legacy of magazine stories was preserved through the reprinting and anthologizing efforts of his friend August Derleth, founder of the Arkham Press, still in existence, which exclusively publishes horror fiction.

Weird Tales, the most prestigious pulp magazine of supernatural fiction, was launched in 1923 and became the prime vehicle for Lovecraft and his protégés, including Robert Bloch, best known for his novel *Psycho* (1959)—which became a hugely successful Alfred Hitchcock movie—and Richard C. Matheson, author of the classic *I Am Legend* (1954), the first successful attempt to deal with a traditional horror motif using science-fictional techniques. In his novel vampirism has become epidemic, and a lone scientist discovers the bacteriological basis for it. The book was the basis of two successful movies. Another important contributor to *Weird Tales* was the versatile and erudite Fritz Leiber, whose *Conjure Wife* (1943) was made into three different film versions.

THE 1970s HORROR BOOM

The 1970s saw a great upsurge in the production and consumption of horror fiction, the effects of which still continue. This horror revival borrowed heavily from Roman Catholic belief and ritual in order to breathe a new sense of conviction into timeworn plots. *Rosemary's Baby* (1967), *The Exorcist* (1971), *The Omen* (1975), and their sequels are the most notable examples, though there were scores of imitators. These books not only were best-sellers in their genre, but also sold so many copies that they competed successfully with mainstream, or non-generic, fiction. And their film versions became big-money hits with mainstream movie audiences. This procession of blockbuster books and movies generated a momentum that established horror as a hot commodity for publishers and created a favorable atmosphere for launching the careers of such commercially successful writers as Stephen King, Dean Koontz, Peter Straub, and John Saul.

This use of Catholicism to launch a new interest in horror literature was in one sense a return to roots of horror in the Gothic literature of the nineteenth century. Ann Radcliffe and her imitators used the props of a vanished medieval Catholicism to establish an uncanny atmosphere. But *The Exorcist* and its close relatives did not just use Catholic symbols to establish mood; they borrowed Catholic beliefs to create a sense of authenticity and believability.

Writing about William Blatty's *The Exorcist*, Dean Koontz stated,

> Blatty's weaknesses of style are more than balanced by his tremendous conviction. . . . Too many writers . . . do not themselves believe in the existence of Good as a living force in the universe. Their demons, therefore, don't ring true. (Koontz 1994, 208–212)

The production in 1823 of *Presumption*, a popular stage play based on Mary Shelley's *Frankenstein*, five years after the novel's publication, was a precursor of what, in the late twentieth century, was to become a lucrative, mutually reinforcing relationship between horror films and novels. Initially, this took the form of big-box-office horror films adapting the blockbuster novels being turned out by Blatty, King, Levin, and Straub. But by the mid-1980s this polarity was reversed as a segment of the younger generation of writers was drawing its inspiration from gory horror films and the anarchic images of rock video, exploring more explicit violence and sexuality. These writers sought to model their prose on the increasingly explicit special-effect images that played on the physical sensation of revulsion. An unofficial spokesman for this movement was author David J. Schow, who coined the term "splatterpunk" in 1984 to describe the trend. He describes his own writing style as follows: "Basically I like to keep one hand right over your heart, with the other one poised to rip your intestines out and strangle you with them, as a fallback" (quoted in Kies 1992, 143).

Many horror writers were not pleased with the trend of greater explicitness. Robert Bloch, for instance, considers the horror story to be a type of morality play, in which good should generally triumph. He is very critical of what he sees as the mindless violence of more recent horror films and their prose imitators, the splatterpunk writers. Bloch put it concisely: "There is a distinction to be made between that which inspires terror and that which inspires nausea" (quoted in Ross 1989, 64).

The opposite pole from the splatterpunk trend is what has been called "quiet horror," whose chief spokesman is writer, editor, publisher, and former Horror Writers of America president Charles L. Grant. This style relies on stimulating the reader's imagination rather than simply providing an explicit description. As Grant told Stanley Wiater, "Explicitness is lazy writing. . . . They don't know how to suggest it, so they spell it out" (quoted in Wiater 1993, 70).

CHILD IN PERIL

The child in peril is a relatively recent invention in the supernatural story. There is a section in Bram Stoker's *Dracula* (1897) where Lucy Westerling, now a vampire, menaces young children, but the primary purpose of this section is to underline her utter depravity, by Victorian standards, as evidenced by the corruption of her supposed "feminine maternal instinct."

Probably among the earliest child-in-peril stories are those by Guy de Maupassant. The first of these *contes cruels* (cruel stories) was "Moiron" (1887—English title: "Revenge"), in which an exemplary schoolmaster becomes distraught by the fatal illness of his three children and gets revenge on God by poisoning his pupils. He feeds them candies in which he has inserted ground glass and broken needles. (And we thought razor blades in the Halloween candy was a recent innovation!) The other de Maupassant tale, which has more of a supernatural element, is "Little Louise Roque" (1885), in which a government official rapes and murders a twelve-year-old girl. The dead victim keeps appearing to him—or is it only a hallucination?—until he finally writes out his confession and commits suicide.

In both these de Maupassant stories the children are purely victims, but in Henry James's novella *The Turn of the Screw* (1898) the children are seen by the narrator as both innocent victims and corrupt beings. The story is narrated by their governess, who believes the children are under the influence of the malevolent spirits of their former governess and her lover, who died accidentally. There is a strong element of sexual tension in the novel, and at the climax the narrator unintentionally kills the young boy in the course of struggling with him to rescue him from the spirits, or so she believes.

From James we must fast forward to William March's *The Bad Seed* (1954), which employs pseudo-scientific theories about a hereditary taint instead of ghostly influences. The story concerns a highly intelligent, but depraved, eight-year-old girl who commits murder and gets away with it because she is able to conceal the depth of her evil behind a convincing mask of innocence and virtue. The notion of a child being born purely evil apparently struck a chord with the public, as Sabine Büssing (1987) documents, for March's novel was produced as a play by Maxwell Anderson, and a Warner Brothers movie version was released in 1956. Shortly after this Henry James's novella *The Turn of the Screw* was dusted off and resurrected as *The Innocents* because it fit the mood of the times. It was made into a play and then a movie in 1961, with screen adaptation by Truman Capote.

Another novel about juvenile evil that became very successful during this period was William Golding's *Lord of the Flies* (1955), which was made into a movie in 1963. It is a tale of psychological horror, in which a group of English schoolboys, stranded on an island, get in touch with their innate barbarism and murder one of their classmates in a devilish ritual of their own invention.

The most influential novel of the 1970s was *The Exorcist*, featuring a young girl who had been possessed by the devil. Anne Rice's *Interview with the Vampire* (1976) was innovative in several respects, including its introduction of Claudia, a preadolescent girl who becomes the vampire Louis's victim and thereby is transformed into an immortal, perpetually frozen in physical immaturity. Though physically a child, she becomes more ruthless than Louis and attempts to poison and slaughter their master, the vampire Lestat.

Stephen King, too, had included children among the group of vampires in *Salem's Lot* (1975). In the short story "Children of the Corn," collected in *Night Shift* (1978), King has a group of children lead a murderous cult that kills anyone over the age of nineteen. And, of course, *Carrie* (1974) ends with massive destruction when the adolescent protagonist's telekinetic power is unleashed. Children in peril in Stephen King's stories include Danny in *The Shining* (1977) and the girl Charlie in *Firestarter* (1980), although in the latter case she is the one with supernatural powers, and the people that are threatening her are ruthless government agents. In both *The Shining* and *Firestarter* the children get away safely in the end.

Beginning with *Flowers in the Attic* (1979), V. C. Andrews produced a still popular series of non-supernatural suspense novels with strong Gothic elements, in which the horror comes from coldly calculated child abuse and a recurring theme of incest. The early John Saul novels, particularly *Punish the Sinners* and *When the Wind Blows*, displayed not only many of the same Gothic trademarks, but also a prominent ghostly element and at least three or four violent killings in each book.

Andrews believes child-in-peril stories are popular because they accentuate a fundamental element of terror, which is lack of control: "Unfortunately, the people most likely to be caught in circumstances beyond their control are children'' (quoted in Winter 1985, 173).

POSSESSION STORIES

The Exorcist (1971) is the preeminent novel of supernatural possession. The earliest forerunner is *The Strange Case of Dr. Jekyll and Mr. Hyde* (1886), which was retold from the servant's perspective in Valerie Martin's very clever novel *Mary Reilly* (1991). Dr. Jekyll experiences periodic possession by an alternate personality that assumes control of his actions, but the mechanism underlying this is science-fictional rather than supernatural. Robert Bloch's *Psycho* (1959)—a descendant of Poe's and de Maupassant's tales of madness—also deals with possession by an alien personality. In this instance it is the personality of the dead mother. But the mechanism in this case is psychological. After murdering his mother, Norman Bates unconsciously denies the reality of his crime by developing a dual personality, in which one side of himself incarnates attributes of his dead mother. Richard Condon's *The Manchurian Candidate* (1959), in a psychological context, explored how someone could be brainwashed and hypnotically programmed to enter an altered state of consciousness where he would go against all his normal values and commit an assassination.

Werewolf tales generally are stories of possession. The werewolf periodically becomes transformed and generally has no memory of his actions during this period. When possessed by the wolf nature, he may act contrary to his normal personality, attacking those whom he loves. In contrast, the vampire story, which is much more common, involves a gradual, but permanent, transformation that changes the core personality, so that it seems more accurate to say that Dracula's victims are corrupted rather than possessed.

Although outright supernatural possession is relatively rare in horror literature, tales of supernatural influence abound. Apparitions lure individuals into dangerous places, inspire tortuous nightmares, or suggest violent deeds to people. In Bram Stoker's *Dracula* (1897) the vampire exerts a supernatural influence on his charges from a distance.

John Saul's early supernatural stories deliberately inhabit a nebulous borderland between outright tales of supernatural possession and influence and psychologically oriented stories of split personalities. Elizabeth in *Punish the Sinners* and Melissa in *Second Child* appear to be possessed by a spirit, but there are also psychological dynamics at work.

VAMPIRE STORIES

At present the biggest trend in horror appears to be vampires. Many of the contemporary authors draw inspiration from the type of vampire motif developed by classic supernatural writer Joseph Sheridan Le Fanu. His elegant story "Carmilla" (1872) emphasizes the erotic, even tender element in the vampiric relationship between two women. One of his admirers is Anne Rice, who continues to write interesting novels that top the mainstream best-seller charts. Robert Aickman has also written elegant and unusual vampire tales, including the short stories "Pages from a Young Girl's Journal" (1973), collected in *Cold Hand in Mine*, and "Into the Wood" (1971), collected in *The Wine Dark Sea*. Chelsea Quinn Yarbro has authored a series of historical novels featuring the Count Saint-Germain, who only engages in consensual vampirism.

More women writers seem to be found in the vampire subgenre than in other areas of horror. Besides Anne Rice and Chelsea Quinn Yarbro, Suzy McKee Charnas, Poppy Z. Brite, and Nancy Collins have achieved recognition from fans and critics.

The vampire trend got a boost recently from the film versions of *Bram Stoker's Dracula* (1992), directed by Francis Ford Coppola, and *Interview with the Vampire* (1994), based on the Anne Rice novel. The popularity of the trend is also indicated by a continued outpouring of non-fiction handbooks, such as Rosemary Ellen Guiley's *The Complete Vampire Companion* (1994). Among the outstanding recent vampire novels are Dan Simmons's *Carrion Comfort* (1989) and *Children of the Night* (1992), Kim Newman's *Bad Dreams* (1990) and *Anno Dracula* (1992), and F. Paul Wilson's *Midnight Mass* (1990).

JOHN SAUL'S PLACE IN THE HORROR GENRE

As mentioned at the beginning of this chapter, many of the best-selling popular novels fit into the horror genre. Among the best-selling horror writers two are female, Anne Rice and V. C. Andrews, and the rest male, of whom Stephen King is the undisputed king. It is impossible to know what, if anything, future generations will think of their work. It seems likely that Stephen King's name will survive the decades due to the critical mass of novels and story collections he has authored, the numerous movie adaptations, and the proliferation of books about him by academics and fans. King was a horror fan from childhood, and he cut his eye teeth on the EC horror comics, whose gruesome excesses led to a censorship crusade against the comic book industry in the 1950s. He told Douglas Winter, in *Faces of Fear* (1985), that he has never wanted to write anything but horror.

Dean Koontz, the other heavy-hitting male horror writer, is a prolific, craftsmanlike writer, who at the start of his career authored romance novels, science fiction, and horror under various pseudonyms. He is a founder and past president of Horror Writers of America and actively promotes the genre.

Peter Straub, who became a household name with *Ghost Story* (1979) and who coauthored *The Talisman* (1984) with his friend Stephen King, has the most literary aspirations. His intent is to write serious novels within the horror format. In recent years he moved into more of a mainstream, cross-genre niche with the publication of a series of horrific crime-mystery novels, *Koko* (1988), *Mystery* (1990), and *The Throat* (1994). He has promoted newer horror writers through editing short story collections.

In contrast to these authors, John Saul was never a horror fan, did not have a burning desire to write horror, and is not a booster of the genre. By temperament and by choice he is not a member of the informal club to which the others belong. And in turn he seems to be treated pretty much as an outsider by the "establishment" of horror critics and editors. He garners no Bram Stoker awards or World Fantasy Convention trophies. He is not sought after to pen introductions to reissues of classic works of fantasy. There are no limited-printing collector's editions of Saul's works. Rare book dealers sell first editions of his novels for a fraction of what those of Stephen King, or of less widely known genre luminaries like Charles Grant and Robert Aickman, command. Consulting contemporary overviews of the horror genre, such as the checklists of landmark novels at the back of Douglas Winter's *Faces of Fear* (1984) or Stephen Jones and Kim Newman's *Horror: 100 Best Books* (1988), one would get the impression that John Saul does not exist. Nor does Stefan Dziemianowicz mention Saul in his reviews of the year in horror fiction in the annual *What Do I Read Next?* (Barron et al. 1994).

Saul does not define himself in terms of the genre and does not pay homage to the past authors who are enshrined as its icons. Because his work is not derivative of theirs in any but the most general way, it is difficult to categorize his place in relation to the genre. Robert Aickman, for example, can be easily identified as one of the last masters of the classic British ghost tale. Anne Rice has become the most widely known innovator on the classic vampire story and consciously strives for the polished stylishness of Le Fanu. Saul is much less easy to place. His earliest books used a combination of the child-in-peril and supernatural possession formulas. (The pedigree of these two formulas was discussed in separate sections earlier in this chapter.) Saul laced the early novels with plenty of murdered corpses and some classical Gothic trappings such as the ancestral curse, the haunted house, and the mysterious portrait. With the exception of his second novel, *Punish the Sinners*, Saul's protagonists were mostly adolescent females, and so were his most ardent readers. In the beginning he was writing to the market, and until he was well established, he did not deviate too much from his basic formula. Sometimes he made the possessed girl into a grown woman, as in *When the Wind Blows,* or into a boy, as in *Cry for the Strangers*, and gradually, the killings extended from the peers of the possessed child, as in *Comes the Blind Fury*, to adults and even parents, as in *Nathaniel*. But this was only minor tinkering with the established formula.

In recent years Saul has branched out increasingly into male protagonists and male-female duos such as Josh and Amy in *Shadows*. He has dropped most of the stereotypical Gothic props and uses more science-fictional devices to drive the horror, as did Mary Shelley in *Frankenstein* and Robert Louis Stevenson in *The Strange Case of Dr. Jekyll and Mr. Hyde*. With the financial security of having several million-copy best-sellers under his belt, Saul presumably feels freer to write that which interests him. His latest venture, with *Black Lightning*, is into the serial-killer horror territory staked out by Robert Bloch and more recently developed by Thomas Harris and Peter Straub.

SELECTION CRITERIA

There was not enough space in a single volume to do a detailed analysis of all nineteen of John Saul's published novels. Therefore, certain selection criteria had to be employed. Although any selection criteria are ultimately arbitrary, I endeavored to establish selection guidelines that were logical and objective, and not merely based on personal taste.

As a matter of practicality, the John Saul novels published after 1988 are the most easily accessible, since all but one were published in hard-back and therefore are more likely to have been purchased by public libraries. Furthermore, the paperback reprints of the later novels are more likely to be in stock at bookstores. I decided to analyze propor-tionately more novels from this post-1988 group because copies of the books will be much more easily found by the student and general reader, and because there is a much greater variety of plot formulas among this group of books.

There appear to be three basic subgenres within Saul's body of work: (1) *Gothic horror*, consisting of ghost stories with Gothic elements; (2) *science-fictional horror*, sometimes termed techno-thrillers; and (3) *"hard-boiled" horror*, employing elements of the detection-mystery-crime story genre.

Of the John Saul novels published before 1988 only two fell into the science-fictional horror category; after 1988 he wrote six more. In short, science-fiction-based horror comprises the bulk of his more recent work. Among Saul's science-fictional horror novels I discerned three further subdivisions: stories devoid of the supernatural, others with supernatu-ral trappings or atmosphere, and a few with some frankly supernatural phenomena mixed into the plot.

For straight science-fictional horror with no supernatural elements, the books chosen were Saul's earliest science-fictional novel, *The God Project* (1982), and his most recent one, *The Homing* (1994). These are novels in which the horror comes from physical transformation, particularly trans-formation into monstrous animals. In *The Homing* it is transformation into an insect-like creature. Other novels in this category are *Creature* (1989) and *Guardian* (1993).

Science fiction with supernatural trappings includes *Brain Child* (1985) and *Shadows* (1992). Whereas the former group of novels concerned being transformed into an animal, these are about being transformed into a machine. *Shadows* also has the distinction of being the only novel by Saul with a distinctly cyberpunk flavor. (See Chapter 10 for a discussion of cyberpunk.) The supernatural flavor of *Brainchild* comes from sequences that appear to be due to reincarnation or spirit possession, but that are really caused by brain surgery and technological alteration of memory. In *Shadows* the existence of two children's personalities in computer cy-berspace enables them to wreak effects that appear supernatural.

The novels that blend science fiction with unabashedly supernatural phenomena include *Sleepwalk* (1990), in which technological mind control through the implantation of micromachines is combatted by Native

American nature mysticism, and *Darkness* (1991), where a form of science-inspired vampirism, using medical technology, is blended with telepathy, dolls that magically cry, and a weird religious cult.

To illustrate the Gothic horror strain within Saul's body of work, I chose his debut novel, *Suffer the Children* (1977), which established the basic thematic pattern, and his final Gothic supernatural novel to date, *Second Child* (1990). Between them these two novels illustrate most of the Gothic themes and patterns repeated throughout the pre-1989 paperback-original novels. At this time there is only one John Saul novel that illustrates what I have termed the "hard-boiled" horror genre. This is *Black Lightning* (1995), his most recent book, which blends in elements of the detective or crime novel.

While some readers will undoubtedly feel disappointed that their favorite novel is not included in the analyses, this selection does provide examples of Saul's writing during the earliest, middle, and most recent stages of his career and examines all the major subtypes of his plot formulas, with the additional advantage of concentrating on the novels that are most contemporary and readily obtainable.

3

Suffer the Children
(1977)

"But do you think all children are like Elizabeth? . . . Do you think
they'd all play with her the way Elizabeth does?"
John Saul, *Suffer the Children*, 1977

Suffer the Children was John Saul's first novel and an instant best-seller.
Published in 1977 as a paperback original by Dell Publishing, it was
dedicated to his confidant and literary collaborator, "For Michael Sack,
without whom this book would not have been written." This novel established the basic John Saul formula which, if it were a cocktail, could
be described as follows: add one part *Psycho*, one part *The Exorcist*, and
a dash of *Turn of the Screw*; blend well and serve thoroughly chillingly.
From Robert Bloch's *Psycho* comes the notion of an insane split-
personality killer, from William Blatty's *The Exorcist* comes the idea of a
spirit-possessed individual who is unaware of her actions, and from
Henry James's *Turn of the Screw* comes the plot device of a fundamental
uncertainty about whether supernatural or psychological forces are responsible for the odd things that happen. In addition, the novels are
typically set in a small town, and there are several killings scattered
throughout the plot.

The next four novels, all of which were published by Dell, followed
this basic recipe. *Punish the Sinners* (1978) is about a priest, Monsignor

Peter Vernon, who appears to be possessed by the spirit of one of the Grand Inquisitors and who provokes teenage girls to commit suicide. However, in the end it is not he who is blamed, but his friend Peter Balsam, whom he has driven half-mad. In *Cry for the Strangers* (1979) Robby likes wandering on the beach with his little sister during the storms. He comes under the influence of the spirits of an Indian tribe who want vengeance against the "strangers." *Comes the Blind Fury* (1980) is about an adopted child, Michelle, who feels neglected when her parents give birth to a younger sister. She then comes under the influence of the ghost of a blind child, who directs her to push her peers off cliffs into the ocean. In *When the Wind Blows* (1981)—the only John Saul novel featuring psychological child abuse reminiscent of V. C. Andrews—the aristocratic Diana Amber hears the spirits of the dead babies calling to her from a cave and becomes homicidal when the wind blows.

PLOT

The primary plot line in *Suffer the Children* concerns the two girls Elizabeth and Sarah Conger and their progressive descent into a maelstrom of occultism and murder. A secondary and related plot line concerns the deterioration of the relationship between the girls' parents, Jack and Rose Conger, and Jack's search for comfort outside the marriage in the embrace of his secretary, Sylvia. A third narrative line concerns the reactions of the townspeople to the disappearance of the murdered children and Police Chief Ray Norton's attempt to balance his investigatory duties and his personal friendship with Jack.

Several of the basic plot elements are cleverly set out in the second chapter. Jack and Rose are musing about whether anything sinister happened to a local girl who was missing for several hours and was found coming out of the woods bruised and suffering from amnesia. Rose relates this to the traumatic incident a year before when Sarah was attacked in the woods, after which she stopped speaking and began to behave bizarrely. Jack recoils from the mention of this, since, as the reader will later learn, he was the attacker. The mention of Sarah leads into a discussion of whether she will eventually be well enough to attend public school again. She has been attending the White Oaks School for disturbed children since she stopped speaking. Rose is opposed to placing Sarah with "normal children" because, with the exception of Elizabeth, who is so patient and kind to her little sister, children "can be cruel"

(36). Jack is about to pour his third cocktail, and Rose is expressing her disapproval of his drinking when suddenly they hear Sarah's piercing scream issue from the upstairs playroom. The parents rush in to find Sarah huddled in fear in the corner and her sister, Elizabeth, oblivious, fully concentrating on a Ouija board. The Ouija board is an old-fashioned device that can supposedly be used by spirits for communication by guiding the person's hand to spell out messages. Elizabeth tells her parents that Cecil, the pet cat, startled Sarah by brushing up against her as they were concentrating on the Ouija board. Jack asks Elizabeth where the board came from, and she says she got it out of the attic near where they found the old portrait. Elizabeth is referring to the oil painting of an unknown girl, apparently an ancestor, to whom she bears an uncanny resemblance.

This scene brings into conjunction all of the essential elements of the plot in embryonic form: the disturbed marital dynamics, the Ouija board messages emanating from the restless spirit of the girl in the portrait, Elizabeth's growing abstraction, Sarah's increasing distress, the children from the town who will be victimized, and the cat who is about to disappear.

However, it only becomes clear in retrospect how rich this scene is in half-revealed potentialities. The warning signs are initially presented in such an oblique or understated way that the reader is likely to be just as unaware of what is happening to the children as are Rose and Jack. In this sense the author initially has the reader apprehend events through the parents' mentality and perspective. The narrative at first focuses on their marriage problems, reflecting the couple's own preoccupation with themselves, and the reader only subliminally notices the clues about the amount of time Elizabeth spends abandoned by the benign neglect of her parents and how she increasingly fills that time in an obsessive preoccupation with the Ouija board.

The next piece of information the author thrusts into the foreground of the reader's consciousness is the increasing deterioration of Sarah's behavior. Sarah has a tantrum at dinner, shatters a glass bowl of pudding against the wall, and throws a heavy piece of silverware through the glass panel of the French door. She bites Mrs. Goodrich, the housekeeper. At school she eats a box of chalk and overturns the classroom furniture. Sarah seems the problem child, Elizabeth the perfect child. Again, this is a piece of misdirection, and the reader's preoccupation with Sarah mimics the parents' excessive focus on their younger child—a one-sidedness that exacerbates Elizabeth's problems. We do not become aware of how disturbed Elizabeth has become until things have gone too far to avert disaster.

Gradually, the reader's attention begins to shift from Sarah to Elizabeth. At first it is a question of minor discrepancies. The reader is privy to a scene that no one else observes: Elizabeth walking into the woods—which she is forbidden to enter—carrying Cecil, the cat. Later it is noticed that Cecil is missing, and despite searching, there is no sign of him. Mrs. Goodrich, the housekeeper, spots Elizabeth coming out of the woods and reports it to the parents. Jack questions his daughter, and she denies it. He emphasizes the importance of staying in the yard, and yet the next day Rose observes the girls coming out of the woods together. Jack decides to confront Elizabeth and goes up to the playroom, where he once again interrupts a scene of the two girls around the Ouija board with Elizabeth concentrating on the board and Sarah intently observing Elizabeth. When he demands an explanation for her disobedience, she replies that she cannot remember going into the woods or what happened there. She only remembers coming out of the woods.

This gap of memory parallels Jack's experience a year previously. Sarah was following a rabbit into the woods, and Jack was coming up behind her. The next thing he remembers is carrying Sarah out of the woods, and she was badly bruised and in a state of shock. Elizabeth was a witness to that scene and knows what her father cannot remember: that it was he who bruised and battered Sarah, frightening the child into mute autism. That was a year ago, shortly after they discovered the portrait of the unknown girl in the attic. It was after witnessing this scene that Elizabeth herself disappeared unobserved into the woods for the first time. A month ago the parents had the old portrait cleaned and hung it above the fireplace in the back study. Is it coincidental that in the past month or so Sarah's condition has taken a turn for the worse? Another odd detail: As Elizabeth snuck into the woods carrying Cecil, she pulled the rubber band out of her hair so that it hung freely over her shoulders, the "old-fashioned" way. This is another subliminal clue: Untying the hair signals a shift of consciousness in Elizabeth; she is identifying with the mysterious girl in the portrait, whose hair also hangs loosely.

So far the author has presented events to the reader primarily from the parents' limited viewpoint. But approximately a third of the way into the book there is a shift. The reader is taken into the woods with Elizabeth and Sarah and allowed to see directly what has so far been hinted at. Elizabeth, in a sort of trance, rises from her bed in the middle of the night and goes into the woods wearing an antique dress with her hair flowing long like the girl in the portrait. Sarah follows her through the woods, to the embankment overlooking the ocean, and down the face of it to a cave leading to a shaft. At the bottom of the shaft is a skeleton wearing a gold bracelet set with an opal—the same gold bracelet is worn by the girl in the portrait. The skeleton is that of Beth, who was abandoned to starve at the bottom of the shaft by her father, the present-day Elizabeth's great-great-uncle, whose name was also, coincidentally, Jack Conger.

Elizabeth descends into the shaft on a rope ladder, carrying a bag in which is the dead body of Cecil and a set of doll clothing, in which she dresses the dead cat. She then enacts a macabre version of Alice in Wonderland's mad tea party and the Cheshire cat. She pretends to be eating cake and drinking tea. Smiling brightly she asks the cat, "Isn't this nice?" (132). When the dead cat naturally does not respond, Elizabeth becomes petulantly annoyed at his silence. "I spend my life with you and what do I get from you? Nothing. Nothing! . . . Don't do that. Talk to me" (133–134). She spanks the dead cat and then, like Lewis Carroll's Red Queen, cuts its head off in a fit of rage. It is clear that the anger she is venting on Cecil reflects the resentment she feels toward her equally mute sister and also toward her self-absorbed parents, who are too busy to talk with her. To underline this, the author has Elizabeth immediately look up to see Sarah watching her over the edge of the shaft and utter a reassuring falsehood, "Sarah. . . . Did you see that naughty baby? She isn't like you" (134). Elizabeth climbs back up the ladder and transfers the bracelet from the skeleton's wrist to Sarah's. Is she making it up to Sarah with a present, or does this represent an unconscious wish that her little sister would end up as a skeleton, too? As it later develops, the bracelet—which the Congers will recognize from the portrait—will incriminate Sarah and contribute to transferring the blame for the murders from Elizabeth to her.

The gruesome tea party is repeated three more times, but with new characters added each time, as Elizabeth, in her "Beth" persona, sequentially lures three playmates to the cave. Using the abusive tone that adults sometimes adopt with children, Elizabeth directs her terrorized playmates in sadistic psychodramas. In these she enacts her love-hate relationships with significant adults, using the child victims as stand-ins. The first two children, Kathy Burton and Jimmy Tyler, are substitutes for her mother and father. The last boy, Jeff Stevens, represents Beth's father, who lived four generations previously.

In the most repulsive of these episodes Elizabeth bullies her frightened playmate Jimmy into enacting her father's pedophilic attraction to Sarah by forcing him to make copulatory movements against the putrefying corpse of the dead cat. In effect, then, he is committing symbolic incestuous pedophilia while engaging in actual zoophilic necrophilia. This particular perverse piece of drama brought protests from the critics. Certainly, if taken literally, it is a scene of horror that inspires physical revulsion more than psychological terror, like the green liquid that Linda Blair vomited up in the film *The Exorcist* four years earlier. But the author does not play the scene in great detail. It is presented sketchily, more as an idea than a fully articulated image. And as an idea it is so excessive and over-the-top that it has the potential to edge into unconscious or deliberate satire—the literary equivalent of a gory movie with transparently obvious special effects or of a camp cult movie like *The Rocky Horror Picture Show*.

The plot strand dealing with the relationship between the parents shows us a couple in crisis. A year ago Jack Conger came out of the woods carrying a badly injured Sarah. He cannot recall what happened, but the event has cast a pall over the marriage. Jack is now impotent, and his wife Rose is sexually and narcissistically frustrated. She begins to wonder if Jack feels threatened by her financial success as a real estate agent. But despite herself, she cannot help but personalize his seeming disinterest, taking it as an indication that she is no longer attractive. Consequently, she frequently lashes out at him verbally, which does not help the situation, and on at least one occasion he hits her, after which she retorts, "At least I'm fairly close to your size" (45). Jack withdraws and begins drinking more, which Rose then nags him about. Eventually, he has a sexual encounter with his secretary, Sylvia Bannister, and discovers that he is still capable of normal sexual responsiveness, just not with Rose.

On the one occasion when Jack shows some affection to his daughter Elizabeth, letting her sit on his lap in response to her request to be treated as though she were "small again," Rose becomes quite tense. In an icy tone and with "accusing eyes" directed at Jack she snaps, "Take your chair, Elizabeth" (144). Eventually, Jack recovers his memory of what happened in the woods a year before. He had felt a sudden sexual attraction to eleven-year-old Sarah and then a surge of irrational fury at her, as though she were to blame for arousing him. Instead of sexually violating Sarah, he had savagely pummeled her until his fury was spent.

When Jack confesses this recovered memory to Rose, she is naturally aghast, although she had suspected it. They have a quarrel, and he tries to force sex upon her, but finds to his chagrin that he is still impotent with her. She mocks him, "You can't do it, can you? . . . Only little girls? Well, I'm not a little girl, Jack. I'm a woman, a real woman. Now get off me" (285).

As Jack and Rose's relationship unravels and the rawer levels of emotion are expressed, there is a parallelism in what is going on in the cave, as Elizabeth becomes more and more frenzied, culminating in her completely losing control and badly mutilating the bodies. In the end Jack does not leave his wife for his secretary. They remain together, bound by mutual guilt after Sarah is institutionalized for supposedly murdering the three missing children. Eventually, the couple dies in a boating accident, or was it a mutual suicide, or even murder-suicide? The life preservers had all been taken out of the boat before it sank. Taken out by whom? Jack or Rose? We are told that Jack was usually careful about "things like that" (347), so the implication is that it was he who engineered the apparent accident, without Rose's foreknowledge.

The third plot strand takes us outside the closed circle of the family to the surrounding community. The parents whose children are missing, stirred up by Marty Forager, the town drunk, are on the verge of forming a vigilante committee. Since all the disappearances have taken place on Conger Point, suspicion is directed at Jack Conger, and there is murmuring among the townspeople that Police Chief Ray Norton is protecting the Congers because of his personal friendship with Jack. They have always had some resentment of the high and mighty role that the Conger dynasty used to play in the town, and now they want something done, or they will take matters into their own hands. Dr. Belter, Sarah's psychiatrist, is also suspicious of Jack. He knows Sarah would be too small to overpower the missing children. Jack has a history of blackouts, and there is the incident of his attacking Sarah. Dr. Belter confides his suspicions to the police chief. Ray Norton's immediate reaction is to chastise him for revealing confidential information and to reaffirm not only that he believes Sarah to be guilty, but also that this is the outcome that will be best for everyone; the town will "calm down" when word gets around that Sarah has been taken to an institution (329), and as long as there are no more disappearances, Chief Norton does not intend to poke any further into it.

CHARACTERS

In her study of children in horror fiction, *Aliens in the Home* (1987), Sabine Büssing delineates two basic types of child protagonists: the blond-haired, blue-eyed ones and the brunettes. According to her model, each physical type symbolizes a quality of soul. Blondes with their golden hair and china-blue eyes signify the "angelic" type. But this outward appearance of innocence and beauty renders them that much more dangerous and corrupt should they fall under the sway of the evil powers. In contrast, the brown-eyed child represents the "animal" type. When playing the role of victim, this type's eyes "are compared to those of does or rabbits—harmless and defenceless creatures," whose eyes are "big and round and moist and shimmer like velvet" (3). The two central protagonists, Elizabeth and Sarah Conger, are the exemplars of these two types.

Elizabeth is a blonde angelic child. At one point she is even pictured with the moonlight seeming to "form a halo around her head" (128). Her mother thanks God that Elizabeth is there to do that which she cannot: effectively care for Sarah. And Elizabeth does exhibit a remarkable patience with her sister. Early in the novel we are shown a scene where Elizabeth is content to amuse her sister by repeatedly building a tower of blocks, which Sarah keeps knocking down. But in a John Saul novel if any character looks perfect or too good to be true, you can be sure that he or she has a shadow side. And it is an old Gothic convention that of the heroine's two potential husbands, the one who looks guilty is really innocent. So Elizabeth, of course, has that hidden dark side to her where she goes down into a black hole and acts out all of the family's pathology for it.

Elizabeth is more strong-minded than any of John Saul's other possessed-child murderers, however. She succeeds for several years in doing something none of the rest of them ever do—freeing herself of the influence of the curse. Even while in a blackout and under the influence of the ancestral ghost, she develops insight into what is happening. She realizes that the children she has killed are not the actual people whom she or Beth, the spirit, hates. She suddenly sees she has killed innocent victims, becomes furious at the ghost of Beth, and vents her fury by kicking the bones of Beth's ancient skeleton apart. However, her rebellion does not permanently save her. Fifteen years later, when the corpses are unearthed and her sister Sarah is plunged back into madness, Elizabeth heeds Beth's last destructive summons and plunges herself and her pet into the sea.

Granted that from the point of view of actual psychiatry, Elizabeth's becoming an insane killer seems a rather exaggerated reaction to sibling rivalry and parental neglect. It is not scientifically credible or realistic and perhaps for that reason has to be propped up by the supplementary mechanism of a sinister ghostly influence. But this type of fantastic fiction is not supposed to be judged by the standards of ordinary realism. The psychological explanation for Elizabeth's homicidal blackouts is not meant to be any more convincing than the science-fictional explanation of how time travel works and merits the same willing suspension of disbelief. In both of these examples it is enough that they have become well-established conventions of their respective genres. Robert Bloch established that psychological conflicts can create homicidal split personalities, just as Bram Stoker established that garlic protects against vampires. The reader either accepts this as part of the genre or finds some other type of fiction to read.

The character of Sarah is left relatively undefined. Sarah cannot speak, nor do the readers have any special privilege of access to her inner thoughts. We are in the position of her parents and psychiatrist, of having to make sense of her rather confusing behavior. It does seem clear, however, that she is upset about what Elizabeth is doing to the children and is trying her best to warn her mother. There is an interesting scene of role reversal that occurs when Elizabeth leaves the cave after her last frenzied hacking up of the children's bodies, and Sarah slowly wanders about trying her best to fit the dismembered pieces of the corpses back together. This is a mirror image of the scene, much earlier in the book, when Sarah had thrown a wild tantrum at dinner, smashing a glass bowl and throwing silverware about. In that scene after everyone leaves the table Elizabeth absently cleans up the mess and picks up the silverware, trying to set everything back in order.

Rose, the mother, does not come across as a terribly sympathetic character, even though she is as much a victim as anyone else in the novel. Two factors contribute to the negative way in which she is presented: her tendency to lash out verbally and her withdrawal from mothering either of her two daughters. She is presented as a perfectionist, someone who would never have a hair out of place or the tiniest spot on her clothing. At the office she double- and triple-checks her paperwork to make sure her co-workers cannot catch her making a mistake. At home she comes across as controlling, critical, and a bit self-righteous. And yet she feels completely inadequate in the face of Sarah's chaotic behavior and thankfully abandons her care to Elizabeth and the housekeeper. As for her elder daughter, Rose does not even perceive that she has needs.

At one point she complains to Jack: "Not only do I have to be Mrs. Conger, but I have to be a loving mother to a traumatized child, a loving wife to an impotent husband, and push real estate on the side" (141). She mentions her career, Jack, and Sarah. But there is no mention in this statement of Elizabeth. It is as though her older daughter does not exist for her, except to the extent that she fulfills part of Rose's role for her. This is one of the things that makes her a less than sympathetic character.

However, to be fair to Rose, she remains in a frustrating marriage and makes an effort to be civil to a husband who drinks too much, has un-conscious pedophilic urges, hits her and has severely beaten his younger daughter, and sleeps with his secretary while Rose remains sexually frus-trated. If we take her at her word, the reason she puts up with this is not for financial security—since she is doing well in real estate—but because she feels she has to protect her daughters from Jack.

Another way the author has stacked the deck against Rose is by intro-ducing the character of Sylvia Bannister, the secretary. If Rose is pre-sented as a domineering shrew, Sylvia is a prefeminist "Good Woman" with a heart of gold who is self-effacing and whose primary interest is to nurture her boss, Jack. Like the perfect male-fantasy woman, there are no strings attached. She has sex with Jack and shows him he is still capable of performing like a man, but does not try to entangle him into any commitments. Her love for him is so pure and selfless that she is ready to step aside from being a competitor with Rose because she knows that in his heart Jack does not want to give up his marriage. Naturally, in contrast to this idealized character, Rose comes off a poor second.

Jack, unlike Rose, has nothing to be self-righteous about. He is a weak character, full of self-doubts, who is guilty on every front. He seems to be always reacting to situations rather than acting upon them. Yet some-how he seems more sympathetic than Rose. Part of it is that the author gives us more access to Jack's thoughts than to Rose's, so that we are more likely to identify with him. Perhaps, too, we feel sorry for him because he is the underdog. He seems more a victim than a villain, be-tween the hundred-year-old curse that he broods about and his inability to remember what happened in the woods. He, too, fails to give Eliza-beth the attention she needs, but he seems to try harder. He does talk to her about not going in the woods. And on one occasion he innocently accedes to her request to sit in his lap, but then Rose intervenes, presumably viewing this scene as fraught with sexual innuendos. As for his behavior in the woods with Sarah, it seems that it may be an enchanted wood, and that he fell under some kind of spell. What he did was bad enough, but at least he did not rape his daughter and leave her to die like the earlier John Conger did.

These two sets of characters—Elizabeth and Sarah, Rose and Jack—are like complementary mirror images of each other. Physically Sarah most resembles her mother, but on the surface Elizabeth seems to have her mother's temperament. Elizabeth appears controlled and perfectionistic, like Rose, yet she is the one susceptible to blackouts and fits of murderous rage. Sarah is overtly identified as the troubled one of the pair, just as Jack is in relation to Rose, yet she is innocent of any real wrongdoing. The effect of all these role reversals, mirror images, and surface/depth contrasts is to highlight the notion of shared responsibility in a family. There is no single culprit; there is no single victim. The family is an interlocking system, and each member is a piece of the puzzle. Even the actions of long-dead members of the extended family contribute to the present situation.

It seems important to mention the role of the psychiatrists: Dr. Belter, who treated Sarah at White Oaks School, and Dr. Felding, who is her therapist at Ocean Crest Institute. Although Saul dedicates his book to Michael Sack, a clinical psychologist, it is ironic that in this novel and many of his later ones psychologists and psychiatrists come off as ineffective and misguided. True, Sarah's therapists are portrayed as sincere, kindly, and genuinely concerned, but her first psychiatrist, Dr. Belter, apparently misinterprets the evidence and suggests to Jack that he is the killer and then repeats the same claim to the police chief. Worse still, after Sarah has recovered and has become able to function in a fairly normal manner, Dr. Felding causes Sarah to relapse into a complete mental breakdown by urging her to confront memories she is unable to handle.

THEMES

Suffer the Children is essentially a family drama, and the characters in the community are almost superfluous. As a commentary on the perils of family life, the novel paints a grim portrait. Eventually, all of the central characters look outside the family to meet their needs. The mother looks to her career, the father to alcohol and his secretary's bed, Elizabeth to the bloody rituals in her cave, and Sarah to the insane asylum. Eventually, they all return to water. Elizabeth, Rose, and Jack drown literally. Sarah drowns in the chaos of her own mind.

Communication, or rather the failure thereof, is one of the most obvious themes of the novel. The extreme case is Sarah. She does not engage in normal communication through speech. The parents demonstrate a subtler form of the same disorder. Although they are physically capable of speech, they are usually too busy for all but the most cursory communication. At one point Elizabeth eagerly invites her father to play with her, and he is on the point of accepting when suddenly he "remembered Sarah" and shakes his head, saying he had better see if he can "help your mother with Sarah" (39). And her mother constantly signals that she does not want to know about Elizabeth's problems by telling her what a "great help" she is (57) as she abandons the task of caring for Sarah to the older child. Having no one to communicate to, Elizabeth turns to the Ouija board and the ghost of Beth. The usual question about Ouija boards is, Who is it that is spelling out the messages—are you in touch with a spirit or just your subconscious?

There are three instances in the book when the difficulty of communicating to a parent figure is underlined. In the first instance Sarah is trying to alert her mother to what happened to the cat. As Rose leafs through a magazine, Sarah touches her hand to every page that has a photograph of a cat. Then she ties the blood-flecked cat's collar to her mother's ankle, but is not understood. Eventually, in order to get through to her parents she brings home the severed arm of one of the children whom Elizabeth has dismembered. But their reaction is to blame her, and she is committed to an institution for the insane.

In the second instance Elizabeth has begun telling Jeff Stevens about the "secret place" as a prelude to luring him to the cave. Sarah, who has already seen one child be murdered, knows where this is headed and starts screaming. In the car on the way home Jeff comments to his parents, "She's crazy," meaning Elizabeth. The parents assume he means Sarah, and they chastise him for talking that way. He in turn does not realize that they misunderstood him.

The third instance occurs at the end of the book, fifteen years later, when Jack and Rose are dead, possibly victims of suicide by drowning. Sarah is still at the asylum, but has regained normality and is able to converse animatedly. Elizabeth has inherited the ancestral home and continues to live there. She has no memory for the murders she committed. She has sold the woods, and excavation for the foundation for an apartment complex is under way. The construction crew unearths the secret cavern. With the bodies found the district attorney wants to prosecute Sarah, who had made enough progress to be considered for release from the asylum. Sarah's psychiatrist presses her to try to remember how the children were murdered. At first Sarah recovers only fragments of memory; then suddenly she is flooded with the realization that it was Elizabeth who hacked them to pieces. As Sarah recovers this memory, she screams, "Elizabeth . . . Beth," identifying her sister as the murderer, just before she collapses back into her previous state of blank, autistic muteness. But the psychiatrist misinterprets that Sarah, overcome by the flood of memories, was calling to Elizabeth asking for help. And Sarah, reimprisoned in her mutism, is unable to correct him or communicate the identity of the true killer. Elizabeth, who is present when this occurs, is shaken by the severity of her sister's relapse and later returns home and jumps off the cliff into the sea.

These are three examples of incomplete or misapprehended communication. But there are also examples in the novel of correctly received communication that produces tragic results. Jack's and Elizabeth's blackouts could be called failures of internal communication. Some deep level of Jack's memory is unable to communicate to a more conscious level of his mind, analogous to the way Sarah is incapable of speaking in the sunlit world of her parents of what is going on down in the twilight world of the cave.

When this internal lack of communication, or failure of memory, is repaired, the results are negative. Jack remembers what happened in the woods and why he beat Sarah. But when he shares his recovered memory with his wife, she turns on him, and later they both die under circumstances that suggest suicide. When Sarah remembers what Elizabeth did, she goes mad again. And when Elizabeth recalls the sinister spirit of Beth, she takes her own life. The message of this novel is clear: Remembering does no good. And yet one is compelled to remember. The only escape from the memories is death. And even then they may come back to haunt the next generation. Except in the Congers' case the family line would appear to have died out with Elizabeth's death and Sarah's madness.

One other aspect of memory and forgetting is very important. The parents forget about Elizabeth's needs. Her mother in particular forgets to name her among the list of duties she recites to Jack. This is analogous to the earlier generations' forgetting of Beth. Beth's picture was left in the attic, neglected, with no name plate attached to the frame, unlike the other ancestral portraits. In this respect her restless spirit is like that of the forgotten children in *Comes the Blind Fury, When the Wind Blows, Hellfire,* and *Nathaniel,* each of whom was buried in an unmarked or inadequately marked grave. She was deliberately "forgotten" in a cave by her father so that she would starve to death. Elizabeth is starving, too, but emotionally, not physically.

A DECONSTRUCTIONIST READING OF *SUFFER THE CHILDREN*

Deconstructionism is a relatively recent method of analyzing texts whose main exponents are European, particularly French. Deconstructionist criticism can be quite difficult to read and understand. A primary premise of this method is that there is no privileged reading of a text. That is, there is no one, single, correct understanding. The extreme opposite of deconstructionism would be a literalist point of view, such as that of some religious sects that believe there is only one correct meaning for a biblical passage.

According to deconstructionists, each person reads a text differently. The author's intention or opinion as to the meaning of the text is not privileged and is not to be automatically valued over any other reading of the text. Also, the meaning does not inhere in the text itself because the reading of a text can be modified by its relation to other texts. Once one knows of Freud's interpretation of the play *Oedipus Rex*, one can no longer read or experience the play in some "pristine" form, as if in isolation from Freud's text or the other texts that have preceded and followed it.

Finally, deconstructionists like to subvert the text and break down the illusion of a coherent and self-contained narrative that the author constructs. They look for loose ends that can be used to unravel the text or for ways in which the text refers back to itself, underscoring its artificial and illusory nature.

We shall begin our analysis by considering the connection between our text, *Suffer the Children,* and *Alice in Wonderland,* which like the Conger curse predates Saul's novel by about a hundred years. We cannot know for sure whether John Saul deliberately intended the allusions to Alice that we find in his novel, but that is unimportant from the deconstructionist point of view. That we can find them is sufficient reason for commenting on them. There are certainly a number of parallel elements. In addition to the Tea Party, the Cat (reminiscent of the Cheshire Cat), and Off with His Head (the cat's head), in the prologue we see the original Beth pursuing a Rabbit into the forbidden forest, where her father rapes her and leaves her to die. The original title for Lewis Carroll's book was *Alice's Adventures Underground*, which certainly sounds like a reference to Elizabeth's cave. Another coincidence: There is evidence that Lewis Carroll—like Elizabeth's ancestors—had pedophilic interests concerning little girls.

When we follow the Rabbit, in the first pages of the novel, into the maze of the plot, we become Alice. The act of imaginative reading casts us into a kind of sleep, or trance, until at the end, we, too, like Lewis Carroll's Alice, awaken, and return to our mundane activities, where our adventure is revealed to have been a fantastic dream. Thus we can be reassured that the grotesque occurrences in the cave, in which we were temporarily submerged, need not be taken at face value.

Like horror filmmaker David Cronenberg, Saul is concerned with boundaries between self and others and how they break down. In the later novels *Nathaniel* and *Darkness* this concern is symbolized by the theme of cannibalism, in which one person is literally incorporated into another person on a purely physical level. *Suffer the Children* and the novels that follow its pattern explore the more abstract way in which boundaries between minds break down, as one consciousness invades another.

These novels of supernatural possession also break down the boundaries between reader and protagonist and blur the edges between the reader's life—sitting in the chair, book in hand—and the protagonist's life. Although few, if any, readers of Saul's fiction will have personally undergone being possessed by a spirit, we can resonate imaginatively with the concept. When we speak of being lost in a book—of being entranced by a story to the point that we lose track of time—we are referring to the story taking *possession* of us in that moment.

True, it merely posesses our imagination and does not impel us to physical action—except for the action of turning the page (often well into the wee hours of the night). Nevertheless, it is an outside force— one that is immaterial as well—taking a hold of us. We allow it to do so willingly because it fills empty time and because something in the main character, setting, or plot attracts us and holds our attention. Similarly, Saul's haunted heroines also invite the possessing entity, unwittingly, because it fills a void in their lives and resonates, as they eventually discover, with their darker impulses.

The reader who gets hooked by a well-crafted horror novel experiences, upon coming to critical junctures in the plot, a mixture of dread and fascination that compels the reader inexorably on to the next sequence of action despite a rising sense of fearful apprehension. On this level the reader is not only interested in what happens to the main character—in this case, Elizabeth. The reader is not only feeling her feelings. The reader has in some sense *become* Elizabeth by virtue of being analogously drawn down into the dark depths of the cave by a consciousness that is both exterior and interior: the consciousness of the author, who is weaving the spell of the story.

Just as Elizabeth confuses the significant people in her life with the characters being directed in the dramatic space of the cave, we as readers are, with greater or lesser degrees of awareness, appropriating the characters and events of the story by relating them to the emotionally significant people and happenings in our own lives. And after we have vicariously vented our anger at these significant people, through the medium of the characters in the novel, we can mentally turn to the author and say—as Elizabeth does to the skeleton of the ghost Beth—"Why did you do that? . . . I don't hate them. . . . It's you who hate them" (310–311).

The parallelism between the act of reading and the condition of being possessed by an alien consciousness is most completely and consciously articulated by John Saul in his most recent book, *Black Lightning*. As will be discussed in Chapter 12, in *Black Lightning* Saul has perfected and unveiled new literary techniques to produce a more intensive level of parallelism between the objective situation of the reader and the imaginative situation of the character.

A final subversive aspect of the text that should be mentioned is the psychologist's commentary near the end of the novel. The nineteenth-century Gothic *expliqué*, as discussed in Chapter 2, allowed the rationalistic Protestant reader to feel the vicarious thrills of indulging in "Popish" (or Catholic) superstition, confident that at the end the author would reaffirm the middle-class Protestant worldview by providing a contrived, rational explanation for the goings-on that had appeared supernatural. *Psycho* popularized the device of the psychiatrist coming on at the end of the story to give the rational, scientific-sounding explanation of the uncanny events that have just transpired. Saul plays with this convention and satirizes it in a subversive way by having the psychologist come on stage near the end of the novel to give the *wrong* explanation of events.

4

Punish the Sinners
(1978)

There was an aura about Neilsville, an aura that Peter Balsam had
felt the minute he had arrived but had not been able to define. A
word had flashed into his mind . . . *Evil.* It covered the town like the
stink of death, and Peter Balsam's first impulse had been to run.

John Saul, *Punish the Sinners*, 1978

Punish the Sinners, John Saul's second novel, was published as a paperback original by Dell in 1978. He felt fortunate that he completed the
manuscript before *Suffer the Children* first appeared at the bookstores, else
he might have been intimidated during the writing by his first novel's
commercial success. The novel returns to the origins of Gothic fiction, as
represented in *The Monk,* which utilized gloomy Roman Catholic trappings and featured what the nineteenth-century authors called "the sinister machinations of priestcraft." (See Chapter 2 for a discussion of
Gothic fiction.)

PLOT

Punish the Sinners begins with a brief prologue: A four-year-old boy
witnesses his sister murdering his parents while the parents are in the

midst of sexual intercourse. Next the sister hangs herself with an extension cord. The severely traumatized boy is sent to a Catholic orphanage.

Following this, the story opens with Peter Balsam arriving in the suffocatingly small desert town of Neilsville, located in John Saul's home state of Washington. He remarks that he thought towns like Neilsville only existed in New England—a playful reference by Saul to the Maine settings favored by rival horror novelist Stephen King.

Peter has been engaged to teach Latin and psychology at St. Xavier's Catholic High School. Peter will be the first lay teacher in the history of the school, which is run by his old friend Monsignor Peter Vernon. Peter Balsam and Monsignor grew up together in a Catholic orphanage and then were in seminary together until Peter Balsam forsook a priestly vocation for a marriage that also failed to last. Upon encountering Monsignor Vernon, whom he has not seen in thirteen years, he is surprised by how much his friend has changed, from the easygoing individual of their youth to the rigid and fanatical priest who will now be his superior.

Monsignor shows Peter his classroom, which is decorated with a statue of St. Peter Martyr, a thirteenth-century Inquisitor, in place of the usual statue of the Blessed Virgin Mary. He questions Peter about a thesis he wrote suggesting that suicide may not be sinful because the person who commits it may be too irrational to be at fault. He raises concerns that Peter's views may be heretical. Yet despite his disapproval and contempt for Peter's views, he is anxious that the newly arrived teacher stay because—in some way as yet unrevealed to the reader—Peter is the linchpin to a devious plan that Monsignor Vernon has worked out for the purpose of suppressing a clique of four teenage girls who pose a personal challenge to him and his authority.

Peter is encouraged to remain in Neilsville by a romantic liaison he develops with Margo, a divorcée and therefore an "outsider," like himself. He also develops a kinship with Sister Marie, a kindly, progressive nun. Shortly after the school year begins Peter's female students begin attempting suicide. Two of them slash their wrists, one slashes her legs, and another hangs herself with an extension cord. There is a growing community suspicion that Peter's psychology class is somehow responsible for the deaths.

Peter, however, is conducting his own investigation into the suicides and the Society of Saint Peter Martyr, a prayer group composed of Monsignor Vernon and five elderly priests, who drug him and sexually use him. He becomes convinced the Society is producing these girls' deaths using psychic mind control. His theories are dismissed by the Bishop and by Dr. Shields, the hospital psychiatrist, who attributes the multiple deaths to a psychiatric syndrome called "suicide contagion." Dr. Shields suspects that Peter is psychologically unbalanced. Margo and Sister Marie also begin to doubt him. Peter struggles with an impulse to flee Neilsville, but decides he must stay because only he understands what is happening well enough to be able to stop it. He sneaks into the priest's study and finds a file of newspaper clippings revealing that Monsignor was the traumatized little boy whose sister, the "Modern Lizzie Borden," slew herself and their parents. This represents a major plot twist because up to this point the reader has been allowed to believe Peter Balsam was that boy in the prologue. Monsignor Vernon then surprises Peter, hypnotically saps his will to resist, and kills him with a thrust of a blade.

In an epilogue the reader learns that Peter is buried in an unmarked grave, which is repeatedly desecrated by the angry townspeople. Judy Nelson, the last member of the clique, kills herself on Peter's grave. Each year some girl from the town will repeat a similar suicide at the supernatural behest of the Society of Saint Peter Martyr.

CONTEXT

Popular fiction often reflects the same social concerns that can be gleaned from the newspaper headlines of the period. Along these lines there are three topical elements to *Punish the Sinners*: the polarization of conservative religious factions during the modernization of the Roman Catholic Church in the wake of the reforms instituted by Vatican Council II, the fear of "suicide contagion" that swept various small towns in the seventies, and the scandal of sexual abuse of children by clerics, which has only recently inundated the national consciousness.

Saul's portrait of Neilsville, published in 1978, surely has its inspiration in the conservative reaction to the sweeping church reforms that took effect after the end of Vatican II in 1965. One of the most important symbolic changes was the elimination of the Latin Tridentine Mass, which had been the official Roman Catholic worship service since the Protestant Reformation. In place of ancient Latin, the liturgy was now conducted in modern English. Other changes accompanied this: Altars were rearranged so that the priest faced the congregation, the guitar frequently replaced the organ, women no longer covered their heads in church, lay people administered communion, and many religious orders of nuns shed their severe medieval-style garb.

More significantly, there was an atmosphere of liberalization of moral strictures and a declaration in favor of individual conscience and religious freedom for other denominations. French Archbishop Marcel Lefebvre was a leading figure in the right-wing "traditionalist" backlash against Vatican II. His clerical followers established the Society of Saint Pius X and set up headquarters in the tiny Swiss hamlet of Econe and a seminary in Ridgefield, Connecticut, where they continued to celebrate the Mass in Latin in defiance of the council. The Society of Saint Pius X opposed the council's declaration that other religious denominations had a right to religious liberty. This reassertion of religious intolerance and dogmatic purity maintains continuity with the assumptions that legitimized the Inquisition, the legal proceedings for detecting and punishing heresy in the Middle Ages. Although the Inquisition is recalled now primarily for its use of torture and brutal execution, the harsh practices that characterized the excesses of the Inquisition were typical of that period of history and not peculiar to Roman Catholicism. The Protestant Reformers and their successors engaged in a fair share of brutal repression toward the Papists, heretics, and witches, wherever they acquired the secular power to do so. The most well known use of the Inquisition in the horror genre is Edgar Allan Poe's short story "The Pit and the Pendulum" (1842). Other period pieces have similarly gone back in time to exploit the terrors of the Inquisition. But Saul's accomplishment in this novel is to bring the Inquisition forward into a modern setting by the device of reincarnating a dreaded Inquisitor and his companions. Although there is no factual resemblance between Archbishop Lefebvre and the evil Monsignor Vernon, it is likely that the existence of the ultra-orthodox Society of Saint Pius X gave Saul the germ of the idea for the inquisitorial Society of Saint Peter Martyr.

This in itself could have provided enough material for one novel, but Saul also added the post-sixties panic over a teen suicide epidemic, eccentrically melding it with the notion of an ultra-orthodox religious conspiracy. The first public awareness of the phenomenon of a "suicide cluster" was in Berkeley, California, in 1966. In the succeeding decades, highly publicized examples of "serial suicide," or "suicide contagion," among teenagers occurred in Plano, Texas (seven teenagers in one year); Omaha, Nebraska (three in five days); Westchester County, New York (five in one month); and Leominster, Massachusetts (eight in two years). Media coverage of this "copycat" suicide phenomenon peaked in the mid- to late 1980s, with various official theories proposed by experts including the depressing effects of heavy metal song lyrics and the influence of popular satanic cult folklore.

The other newsworthy topic reflected in the novel is the sexual exploitation of parishioners by clerics. The novel is prophetic in highlighting an issue that was still relatively obscure at the time of publication, but that would soon explode into an inundation of court cases, newspaper stories, and talk show topics. Although Saul's novel does not portray sexual molestation of a child by a priest, it dramatizes a related situation involving an adult victim who is manipulated by the religious trappings of the abuser and finds it difficult to admit what is actually happening. Moreover, it portrays the witch's brew of lasciviousness, hypocrisy, repression, self-alienation, misogyny, and sadism that characterizes the psychological state of the most malign abusers.

CHARACTERS

Many critics have felt that characterization is not Saul's strongest suit. He develops his stories starting from a plot concept, not from a vividly imagined character. The development of the characters' personalities is generally subordinate to the action, and the reader rarely learns much about the prior history of the characters. As is generally true of popular genre fiction, secondary characters, and even sometimes primary characters, tend to be easily recognizable types rather than unique personalities.

Peter Balsam, the protagonist, is an individual who is lonely and looking for meaning in life. He has difficulty making decisions, and his resolve often crumbles in direct confrontation, particularly with Monsignor Vernon. Even after his eyes are opened to priestly corruption, he finds it hard to shake the conditioning that prompts him to automatically respect the clergy. He seems unable to leave Neilsville without explaining and justifying himself to Monsignor and in effect getting permission from the very man who is out to destroy him. The origin of this Hamlet-like ambivalence is never explained. The few fragments of Peter's past that the reader learns about do not explain the inner workings of his personality. The only development that emerges with clearly drawn motivation is Peter's determination to make Neilsville his personal "last stand." We are told that in the past he has experienced crises of identity and failures of commitment—in his pursuit of a priestly vocation, in his subsequent marriage, and in his teaching profession. Over the course of the book Peter decides he can no longer run from his failures, and now is his last chance to reverse the pattern. This is what leads him to stay on against his better judgment, and despite his increasing isolation and imperilment. Unfortunately, his resolve fails him at the critical moment, and not only is he killed, but also his identity is annihilated.

Peter establishes a romance with divorcée Margo Henderson, but their relationship is not enough to anchor his life with meaning and identity. He continues to be propelled by a crisis of faith, and although he is repelled by Monsignor's fanaticism, he has a longing, despite himself, for the aura of certainty and security that is dogmatism's lure. The author contrives it so only three choices seem possible for Peter: (1) embrace a fanatical religious zealotry that is at bottom life-hating and evil, (2) reject religion for a barren scientific materialism that is incapable of sustaining his life, or (3) continue in an indefinite state in which beliefs coexist peacefully with doubts. The first alternative is embodied in Monsignor Vernon and the Society of Saint Peter Martyr. The second is symbolized by the Skinner box: the dilemma of the rat caught in the maze. The uneasy middle ground between these opposite poles is articulated by the Bishop: "The Church is in a constant state of paradox . . . there is no absolute truth. Truth changes along with the times. The trick to being comfortable with the Church is to balance tradition with change" (224). Unfortunately for Peter, the middle ground is shaken by the spiritual equivalent of an earthquake and is rendered uninhabitable. Faced with an insoluble choice between equally unattractive alternatives, he decides his destiny must be to free the town from its spell by killing Monsignor Vernon.

Margo Henderson, Peter's love interest, is not presented as much of a character in her own right and exists primarily for her contribution to the plot. Margo's relationship to Peter is useful to the development of the action in that it gives Peter a motive to stay in Neilsville, even after he begins to have impulses to leave. More importantly, the relationship with Margo establishes that Peter is heterosexually well-adjusted, and therefore his seduction by the sybaritic priests becomes a more repellant violation of Peter's person, particularly as reflected in the eyes of Margo, who tries to suppress feeling betrayed by this homosexual infidelity. Also, Margo is a sounding board for Peter to discuss his fears, doubts, and theories concerning Monsignor Vernon and the Society of Saint Peter Martyr, thus creating an opportunity for the reader to eavesdrop on his thoughts. Ultimately, Margo draws back from Peter because she accepts the opinion that he is mentally ill, voiced by Dr. Shields, who represents the materialistic conceptions of psychiatry.

Monsignor Vernon's character is the most mysterious, even though we are given a great deal of information about him. He is the only character whose childhood history we have any details about. The reader learns about his parents, his sister, his early proclivities, and his trauma. Yet much remains a puzzle. As Peter Vernon watches him, the Monsignor's face reveals abrupt alterations in mood and moments of absent-mindedness and confusion. The author allows us only the minutest direct glimpse into the inner thoughts of Monsignor Vernon, so that it is hard to know for sure whether he slips in and out of alternate personalities as does the protagonist in *Second Child*.

In addition to these individual protagonists, there is a group of minor characters that are almost indistinguishable from each other: Judy Nelson, Karen Morton, Penny Anderson, and Janet Connally, who form a clique, and Marilyn Crane, the outsider. These teenagers represent Saul's stock characters—his literary repertory company that keeps starring repeatedly in his books, thinly disguised with costume and makeup changes. Many of his early novels feature a constellation composed of the shy victim, the needlessly cruel bully, and the ambivalent accomplices. In this particular incarnation Marilyn Crane is the shy, socially awkward girl who is teased unmercifully by her peers. Judy is the leader of the peer group and Marilyn's prime tormentor. She has a talent for devising complicated, cruel pranks, such as hanging a crucified toad in Marilyn's locker. Karen and Penny and the boy Jeff Bremmer are the characters who feel some pity for Marilyn, but lack the courage to resist group pressure. Karen's sympathy for Marilyn stems in part from feeling on the margin of the peer group herself. The child of a low-income single-parent, she cannot keep up with the other girls' stylish clothes, and her figure has developed earlier than her peers'. Karen has nagging fears that she may lose favor with the group and allows Judy to enlist her help in luring Marilyn to a phony "come as you are" party. Despite these few details of individuality, the teenagers are there as fodder for the plot, and their personalities are of no greater importance than those of most murder victims in a detective story or a "teenie-kill" film like *Friday the 13th*. In the end what is significant about them is that they keep the plot moving by killing themselves in bloody ways—all slashing themselves with razors, with the exception of Janet Connally, who achieves the less gory distinction of hanging herself with an extension cord, like Monsignor's sister did years before.

The parental figures are deficient in ways familiar from Saul's other novels, such as *When the Wind Blows, Comes the Blind Fury, Hellfire,* and *Second Child*. Judy's father is indulgent and a refuge from a strict mother.

Karen's father is dead, and she feels the absence of fatherly attention; she seeks a disappointing substitute in sexual relations. Leona Anderson and Inez Nelson are non-nurturing mothers who are too fixated on adhering to social conventions and on pleasing Monsignor. The ludicrousness of Inez Nelson's anxiety about maintaining appearances at the cost of substance is highlighted when her daughter Judy is hospitalized for a suicide attempt. Although Judy furiously rejects her mother's visits, Inez contrives to be seen on the hospital grounds every day so that she can pretend to the town that her relationship with her daughter is fine. Geraldine Crane, Marilyn's mother, is too concerned with her idea of success to understand her daughter's needs. She does not take her daughter's problems with the peer group seriously. In order to fulfill her own ambitions, she naively pushes her ugly duckling into social situations that are beyond her capabilities, causing her to be emotionally wounded on several occasions.

THEMES

Punish the Sinners stands out among Saul's literary output on three counts: its historically factual underpinnings, the extremely downbeat ending, and some frank sexual interludes. In Saul's subsequent novels—up until *The Homing* and *Black Lightning,* sex for the most part is either absent altogether or peripherally alluded to, but not described. However, in *Punish the Sinners* sexuality is central and described with at least a minimum degree of detail, mostly concerning what many continue to refer to as "perverse" sexuality: sadomasochism, homosexuality, and orgiastic behavior. Saul is not being particularly modern in this respect. The classic text of the Victorian era, Bram Stoker's *Dracula,* identifies the horrific with that which was socially defined as sexually perverse, such as the thinly veiled seduction of Jonathan by a pair of female vampires: "The girl went on her knees, and bent over me, simply gloating. There was a deliberate voluptuousness which was both thrilling and repulsive" (Stoker [1897] 1965, 44).

Our attitudes toward sexuality have changed since then, but combining sexuality with coercion or violence still produces feelings of anxiety, discomfort, or even revulsion in many readers. The sexuality in *Punish the Sinners* is not used as a break from the gloominess of the plot, but instead contributes to keeping the reader in a state of anxiety and tension. The homosexual rape of Peter by the group of elderly priests, who do not appear to be aware of what they are doing, and Monsignor's whipping of himself seem designed to elicit some revulsion from the average reader. The author then rekindles these negative emotions by referring subsequent sex scenes back to these disturbing ones. For instance, Jim Mulvey's seduction of Penny Anderson and Karen Morton has elements designed to remind the reader of Peter's emotionally disturbing experience. There is a similarity among the characters. Karen, Penny, and Peter, in three separate scenarios of seduction, are emotionally vulnerable and seek primarily to be comforted. Instead, their physical passions are manipulated. Karen and Peter are both vulnerable because they have been orphaned. Penny is manipulated in the same way Peter was, by secretly drugging her. After losing their "virginity" (in Peter's case, this represents an initiation into homosexual acts), they each feel disgusted, exploited, and alone. For each of them sexual initiation becomes a prelude to death.

Peter's relationship to Margo is quite different from these exploitative ones. It is egalitarian and mutually respectful. In fact, Margo initially pursues him. In contrast to the somewhat explicit sexual descriptions of the bad relationships, the author does not dwell much on the physical side of the good relationship. Although Peter and Margo have a sexual relationship that is apparently satisfying, their lovemaking is never described, nor are their intimate feelings developed and expanded upon, so that the romance comes off as rather bland and passionless, particularly in contrast to the overwrought descriptions of the contrasting "bad" relationships, which are described in explicit sexual and emotional detail. In terms of the text the most emotionally profound episodes in the relationship between Peter and Margo occur not when they are in bed together, but when she is being a voyeur, spying on him at the Society of Saint Peter Martyr, smelling his stained underwear for evidence of ejaculation, and feeling revulsion.

Monsignor Vernon's behavior in the confessional is voyeuristic and an extension of his fateful premature witnessing of sexual intercourse. In the old-fashioned North American Catholic confessional the priest sat in a dark closet-like booth, the priest wearing a robe-like cassock, and heard the penitent's sins through a screen. As Monsignor Vernon's female adolescent parishioners confess their first heterosexual experimentations, he intrusively presses for the most intimate details, which is humiliating for them and pruriently fascinating for him. He is both excited and repulsed by these young girls' sexual experiences. As they reluctantly relate the intimate details, Monsignor becomes aroused by the images, which he pictures from the physical perspective of the female.

These episodes form a seamless whole with his traumatic childhood experience of discovering his parents in sexual congress, a scene that was at once exciting, repulsive, and confusing, and that he viewed from inside a dark closet while wearing a piece of his mother's apparel. Wearing mother's things, as a literary device, symbolizes that he was psychologically identified with her, at least at that moment. It could be inferred that as the little boy witnessed what went on in the bedroom, he experienced the forbidden and dangerous excitement from an imagined female-identified perspective.

SUSPENSE

Suspense is that state of psychological tension, anticipation, and expectation, which the author tries to induce in the reader, that makes the reader want to press on to find out what happens to a sympathetic character, or to see how the villain is defeated, or to learn the solution of some mysterious happenings. It plays an important part in the typical horror novel. A common feature of John Saul's novels is uncertainty about whether psychological or supernatural forces are at work. This becomes a central mystery, and a variety of clues keep the reader interested in the ultimate solution.

In the final chapter Monsignor reveals he had a personality change five years before when he received an anonymously mailed scrapbook that opened the repressed memories of his early childhood trauma. "It made me see what I had to do" (407). He created the Society of St. Peter Martyr as a vehicle for his personal vengeance and duped the members into believing the society's work was the will of God.

But other passages belie this explanation. Several chapters earlier Monsignor implied that as a child he knew himself to be the reincarnation of St. Peter Martyr: "I tried to tell you so long ago, when we were in school together. But the time wasn't right. . . . It's in the names" (284). And the prologue indicates that he did not repress his childhood memories: "The little boy did not forget. Not while he was small, and not while he grew up. Always, he was aware that something had happened. . . . And his sister had caused it to happen. His sister was evil" (11).

Uncertainty remains about whether Monsignor really is a reincarnation of St. Peter Martyr. On the positive side there is the fact that the members of the Society of St. Peter Martyr chant in an archaic Italian. How would they know this language, and why would they want to use it, unless this is a manifestation of either reincarnation or possession by the spirit of St. Peter Martyr? Similarly, there is the invitation written in the same handwriting as found on the antique letter authored by Peter Martyr. Did Monsignor deliberately forge the handwriting, has he become so obsessed that he has unconsciously adopted the handwriting, or is it a manifestation of possession or reincarnation? Also there is the coincidence of the names—Peter Vernon, Pietro de Verona. And the psychic ability—perhaps Monsignor just stumbled upon it as Peter Balsam theorizes. But what about the orgiastic sexual behavior? Neither Monsignor nor the other priests seem aware they are engaging in it. Could repressed sexual impulses be spontaneously expressing themselves without their conscious awareness, or are they under the possession of some demonic power whose instruments they have become? At the end of the novel the reader is still left with these questions unanswered. The failure to resolve these questions is typical of Saul, who likes to leave it up to the reader to decide if the happenings are due to supernatural forces, abnormal psychology, or deliberate criminal behavior.

A JUNGIAN READING OF *PUNISH THE SINNERS*

Jungian psychology is a major school of what was formerly called "depth psychology," since it focuses on the deep undercurrents of the mind more than surface thoughts and behaviors. The two major schools of depth psychology are the psychoanalytic theories of Sigmund Freud, who is discussed in Chapter 7, and the archetypal psychology of Carl Jung. A central concept in Jung is the *archetypes*, which are pre-existing categories in the human psyche, or mind, somewhat like ideal "forms" of the Greek philosopher Plato. Jung considered religious deities of different cultures to be manifestations of a single archetype. For example, Eve of the Bible and Pandora of Greek mythology represent similar archetypal explanations of how suffering was loosed upon the world. Jung was particularly interested in the analysis of religious myth, and therefore his concepts are well suited to an examination of the religious themes in *Punish the Sinners*.

Jung theorizes that there is a masculine principle of the soul, the *animus*, and a feminine principle, the *anima*. These masculine and feminine principles exist within both genders and must be honored. Jung advocates the restoration of a balance between these two principles, both internally in the personality and externally in myth, religious belief, and ceremony. Many of the religions that preceded the Christian era included goddesses among their pantheons and at least to that extent acknowledged that women could embody the divine. Jung pointed out that Judaism and Christianity present an image of God that emphasizes the masculine principle. This is a point that has also been made by contemporary feminist theologians such as Rosemary Reuther. Jung saw the popular veneration of the Virgin Mary in Catholicism as representing an intuitive recognition of the importance of the anima principle. Although the Virgin Mary is clearly differentiated from God in Catholic theology, in popular devotion she is often treated as a feminine avenue to approaching God, similar to the Shekinah in Jewish mysticism. Jung believed that the popular devotion to Mary in Catholicism balanced the otherwise one-sided patriarchal character of Christianity. Some Protestant theologians criticize the tolerance of devotion to Mary as the Catholic Church's concession to ancient matriarchal religious practices revering fertility and earth, which were suppressed by Christianity, particularly around the time of the Protestant Reformation.

The author has three characters whom he has named with variants of "Mary." Is it only coincidence that the three most sympathetic women in the book have names that are related to the Virgin Mary? These three are the progressive and humanistic Sister Marie, the teenage girl Marilyn who remains good-hearted despite vicious teasing, and Peter Balsam's supportive and maternal lover Margo. Linguistically, Marie and Marilyn are variants or direct derivations of Mary. And although Margo is actually derived from Margaret, phonetically it is quite similar to Marie. These names do not appear to have been accidentally chosen. One can see that the name he chose for the town was deliberate: the satirical appellation "Neilsville," a word-play on "kneel" (with echoes of the old beatnik putdown "Squares-ville").

The symbolism of the Virgin Mary plays an important function thematically. The first indication of this is when Monsignor Vernon is giving Peter Vernon a tour of the school. Peter notes that each classroom except his own has a statue of the Blessed Virgin Mary in a niche in the wall. In his room, which is a focal point for Monsignor Vernon's deadly machinations, the Virgin has been replaced by Peter Martyr, the Inquisitor.

This replacement of a female religious symbol by an image of an authoritarian male saint signifies a larger spiritual imbalance in the way religion is viewed in "Kneelsville": The feminine aspect of The Godhead has been eclipsed by the patriarchal concept of a wrathful Old Testament divinity and by a Manichean asceticism that negates sexuality.

Throughout the plot the Virgin subtly attempts to reassert her influence through the helpful ministrations of Marie, Margo, and Marilyn and through a vision that Marilyn communicates to Peter. In Marilyn's vision the six priests of the Society of Saint Peter Martyr are unmasked as false priests, equivalent with those who condemned Jesus to death. The Virgin is sorrowful, and the palms of her hands are bleeding in identification with Christ and with Karen Morton, who has just mutilated herself under the mind control of the priestly coven. But Peter devalues Marilyn's intuition, does not accept the vision as genuine, and fails to see the warning.

Monsignor Vernon is clearly an opponent of anything female, earthy, or related to fertility. His vision is grim and ascetic, based on denial of the body. He inflicts pain on his body—lashing himself while seated in front of a hot fire—in order to induce the numbness of a trance state, in which he is able to negate earthy sensuality and deny any longing for the feminine. Of course, this ambition contains the seeds of its own failure because psychologically any extreme imbalance is a distortion and leads to an unconscious compensation. For example, Monsignor's self-inflicted whipping actually focuses attention on his body, in a distorted form of sensuality. Rather than becoming detached from the feminine, he becomes obsessed with it, but in the form of murderous rather than sensual passions. And his Society of Saint Peter Martyr becomes a coven, in which sexual licentiousness prevails, but unconsciously.

This result is predicted by Jung's theory of the *shadow*, which is formed from the rejected and disowned parts of the personality. Any type of fanaticism, or one-sided personality development, causes the shadow to grow. But the shadow, rather than being recognized as a part of oneself, is often "projected" onto others. That is, one's perceptions of others become clouded and distorted because they are invested with the disowned qualities of self by the shadow-bedeviled individual. For example, Monsignor projects his own sexual corruption onto his female students. When they recount their adolescent sexual experiences, he attributes to them his own twisted passions and feels a loathing toward them that he should properly direct at himself.

Peter Balsam becomes the repository of Monsignor's shadow in a very concrete fashion. Monsignor manipulates the file of newspaper clippings so that it appears to relate to Peter, thereby transferring the horror of his early childhood to Peter, and then kills him.

In the Catholic formula Mary's opposite is Eve, who brought death into the world by heeding the serpent and pursuing knowledge (sexual knowledge, according to some), causing her to be cast out of the mythical

Garden. To the degree that traditionalists focus on Eve as being to blame for the evils of the human condition, feminists rightly label this a misogynist idea. In Monsignor Vernon's personal mythology it is his sister Elaine who is blamed as the bearer of death that caused him to be cast out of his home. Yet Saul hints that Elaine, like Eve, bears only partial responsibility. The reader learns that Elaine was pregnant at the time she killed her parents and herself. A plausible explanation for her act is that Elaine was sexually abused and impregnated by her father, a coarse and violent individual who wishes his wife had "more of the whore" in her. In desperation over the legacy of abuse, and brought to crisis by the pregnancy, she slays her father with a cleaver, and carried away by her fury, she also slaughters her mother.

As the story line comes full circle, Peter now takes the place of Elaine/Eve. He seeks the forbidden knowledge, which takes the form of Monsignor's secret newspaper clippings file. Having tasted of this knowledge, he now must die. Like Elaine he is sexually abused, and is coerced into participation in homosexual acts, which assimilate him to the female sexual role considered so debased by Monsignor Vernon. He feels a shame akin to that which Elaine probably felt, and even Margo finds it difficult to maintain her empathy with him, much as Elaine must have feared her mother would react. He feels totally abandoned and ready to kill his abuser, Monsignor Vernon.

Although this is one possible interpretation of the text, a surface reading of the story could easily reduce it to homophobic stereotypes. The unrelenting evil of Monsignor Vernon and his acolytes, and the indecisiveness and final passivity and failure of Peter Balsam, could be clichés for popular views of homosexuality as, at best, a form of moral weakness and, at worst, a predatory social ill. To the extent that "homosexuality" remains socially equated with "feminized male," Peter's failure becomes a fault of femaleness, which is equated to "weakness."

5

The God Project
(1982)

The superstition of science scoffs at the superstition of faith.
Richard Hurrell Froude (1803–1836), English Churchman,
Leader of The Oxford Movement

The God Project was John Saul's first book published by Bantam and also his first hardcover book. It was released in September 1982 in hardcover and June 1983 in paperback. It represents a radical change from Saul's original best-seller formula. Saul's first five books are about revenge and the supernatural. In these stories the body and mind of the central character, or protagonist, are taken over by supernatural entities. In contrast, *The God Project* is a blend of science fiction and detection, similar in many ways to the self-styled "techno-medical thrillers" of popular author Robin Cook. One signal of the change in formula is the omission of Saul's usual prologue about events that occurred a century before the main action begins.

GENRE

Like the early science-fictional horror classics *Frankenstein* and *The Strange Case of Dr. Jekyll and Mr. Hyde,* or the modern Robin Cook best-

seller *Mutation*, the engine of Saul's novel is the egotistical presumptu-
ousness, or hubris, of the chief scientist, Dr. Hamlin, who is unrestrained
by moral limits in his experiments. He seeks to plunder nature's deepest
secrets in the pursuit of power. In classic science-fictional horror the forbidden experiments produce a dangerous, part-human creature, like
Frankenstein's monster or Mr. Hyde. In this genre the scientist is a figure
of power like the Gothic witch, but without the supernatural trappings.
The scientist's dreadful powers derive from the mastery of natural laws.

Many modern readers have lost belief in a spirit world. For them it is
logical to shift to scientific achievement the emotions of awe and dread
that were formerly associated with the supernatural. Perhaps this is why
many now find the existence of aliens and flying saucers more congenial
than that of ghosts and goblins. For this type of reader science-fictional
horror is more emotionally convincing than supernatural horror.

Unfortunately, upon first release *The God Project* was not as commercially successful as Saul's earlier novels. Whether consciously or not, Saul
seemed to retreat to familiar ground in his next novel, *Nathaniel*, which
returned to his old standby, the supernatural-revenge motif. *The God
Project* was not a total commercial disaster, however. It did well the following summer as a paperback, and many fans wrote expressing interest in a sequel showing what happens to the boys, Jason and Randy,
when they grow up. However, John Saul has no plans at this time for a
sequel.

HISTORICAL CONTEXT

John Saul's plots are typically based on a succinct "what if?" concept,
and he likes to use anxieties that are current in the popular imagination.
For this novel he chooses the fear created by a mysterious disease, like
sudden infant death syndrome (SIDS), and the public's sense of vulnerability in relation to its dependence on giant pharmaceutical corporations.

Saul's heroine, Sally, spends a lot of time trying to come to terms with
SIDS, including blaming herself, looking for an alternate explanation,
and attending a support group. SIDS was very much in the public mind
in 1982, when this novel was published. An indication of this is that in
1981 the *Reader's Guide to Periodical Literature* first established a separate
listing for articles about SIDS. Prior to that they had just been lumped
under "Infant Mortality."

In the novel the genetic alterations are produced by deliberately tainted salve unwittingly injected by a gynecologist. Saul makes the point that patients and even physicians have to essentially trust the pharmaceutical corporations, and this trust can be betrayed. He makes analogies to the thalidomide and DES scandals. Thalidomide was a sleeping pill that caused birth defects such as "seal limbs" and other gross deformities when given to pregnant women. DES was a hormone given to prevent miscarriage, but daughters of women receiving DES later showed a much higher than normal rate of a rare cervical cancer. Although both of these drugs affected fetal development, neither of them caused changes in the genetic code, such as Saul postulates in the novel.

Another highly popular author who has fantasized about the horrific potential of genetic engineering is Robin Cook, whose novel *Mutation* (1989), published several years after *The God Project,* deals with scientist Victor Frank (his name is a variation on Mary Shelley's character Victor Frankenstein) and his mutant son VJ. It is instructive to compare Cook's treatment of this topic with Saul's.

PLOT

The plot of *The God Project* develops from two narrative strands that interweave and eventually intersect. The first strand concerns a family tragedy, the death of the Montgomerys' daughter, Julie, apparently from SIDS. Rather than being pulled together by this catastrophe, the family members are driven apart by their diverse reactions to the apparent senselessness of the death. SIDS was a condition that had an unknown cause. Rather than accepting this ambiguity, several family members fill in the blank by imagining a cause that fits their own psychological predisposition.

Julie's grandmother, Phyllis, silently blames her daughter Sally. She believes "Babies don't just die. . . . There's always a reason" (16). She criticizes Sally for having a career instead of being a full-time housewife and feels Sally somehow failed to properly care for Julie. Sally picks up on her mother's feelings, and it triggers her own sense of guilt. It seems she and Steve had considered aborting Julie, and Sally wonders if unconsciously she had not loved her child enough, and therefore the child had given up living. In her guilt she draws back from her husband, and in her grief she is unable to be fully present for her surviving child, Jason. Jason feels he might be responsible for Julie's death and interprets his mother's withdrawal as signifying she is angry at him for hurting Julie. And in truth his mother is vexed with him; she does not see his self-centered reaction to the death as childish, but judges it as emotional callousness.

While Sally and her son Jason are privately wrestling with guilt, her husband, Steve, wants to just forget it all and put it behind them. But Sally will not forget; she wants to probe deeper and find the "real reason" that Julie died. This process leads Sally to a SIDS support group, where she is befriended by Jan Ransom, another mourning parent. In the course of conversation she learns by chance that she and Jan have the same gynecologist, Dr. Wiseman, and that both conceived despite having had contraceptive devices (IUDs) implanted in their uteruses. This strikes Sally as an unlikely coincidence, and she stops looking inside herself for the cause of Julie's death and begins directing her gaze outward. At this point the detailed psychological examination of the family's grief process falls away as the novel is revealed to be not about SIDS, but about a secret genetic research project gone awry.

The second plot strand is the story of the Corliss family. The Corlisses are a counterpoint to the Montgomerys. They, too, grapple with a tragedy—the disappearance of their son Randy on the day after Julie Montgomery's death. But whereas the Montgomerys are pitted against each other by the senselessness of their tragedy, the Corliss family's response is to pull together. Lucy and Jim Corliss have been divorced for several years, but when he learns of his son's disappearance, he immediately comes to the support of his ex-wife, and she sees that he has grown into a responsible and caring man during their long separation.

Lucy goes to the police, convinced Randy has been kidnapped, but the police treat it as a probable runaway. Lucy is no more willing to accept the police's assessment than Sally Montgomery was willing to accept the doctors' diagnosis of SIDS, so she begins her own investigation, which crosses paths with Sally's, when both of them happen to go to the school nurse to obtain their children's medical records. The nurse points out to them that both their sons were part of a research study conducted by the mysterious Children's Health Institute for Latent Diseases (CHILD). This arouses Lucy's suspicions because she had discovered at the hospital that her dead infant had also been part of the CHILD study.

After comparing notes, Sally discovers that, like herself, Lucy was a patient of Dr. Wiseman's and conceived despite an IUD. At this point the two plot strands become fused as Lucy and Sally join forces to fight a conspiracy that ultimately proves too large for them. They discover that Randy was kidnapped by experimenters from the God Project, a top-secret research project sponsored by CHILD with funding from the military and from a major drug company, Pharmax. Randy, Jason, and his deceased sister, Julie, were part of a group of children whose genetic structure was secretly manipulated at conception. The purpose of the project is to breed a mutated human who will be relatively impervious to physical injury, hence the military's interest.

The experiment was conducted without the knowledge or consent of the children's parents. When women went to Dr. Wiseman for an IUD, he would also insert BCG salve, which was supposed to prevent an allergic reaction to the IUD coil. He was not aware that the salve was designed to secretly affect the DNA of the woman's unfertilized egg. All the female children produced by this experiment died from unknown causes and were diagnosed as SIDS.

After disappearing, Randy has been held prisoner at the Academy, an isolated research institute run by the God Project. Using her computer skills, Sally hacks her way into medical data banks and comes up with a list of all the children targeted by the CHILD research project and is able to convince police Sergeant Bronski of the existence of the conspiracy.

In this course of their battle with the God Project conspiracy Sally has to fend off attempts by Steve to have her committed to a mental hospital. In contrast, Lucy enjoys the unconditional support of her ex-husband, Jim. Randy escapes from the Academy and is reunited with Lucy and Jim. Through his testimony they have proof of the existence of the conspiracy. But family togetherness is doomed to not last long in this novel. In order to engineer a cover-up, military special agents murder Lucy and Jim Corliss just as they and Randy have become a family once again. And though Steve and Sally Montgomery become reconciled, their son, Jason, begins to seem so alien to them that in the epilogue they unsuccessfully try to kill him with nerve poison.

CHARACTERS

Although *The God Project* cast aside the supernatural-revenge formula, Saul did retain two of his trademark devices: children as protagonists and the murder of blood relatives. Randy and Jason are the protagonists, or central characters. Like the protagonists in Saul's previous novels, they are simultaneously victims and monsters. They are victims of a scientific experiment, rather than the psychic forces that bedevil the protagonists of *Suffer the Children* and *Punish the Sinners*. While Saul's spirit-possessed characters often seem on the verge of coming apart emotionally, Randy and Jason are always unemotional and self-possessed (to make a bad pun). Rather than going into insane rages, they are relatively calm, even after Jason's mother tries to kill them. They are not quite as cold and emotionless as the child prodigy VJ in Robin Cook's *Mutation*, but they definitely exhibit fairly weak emotional attachments. For example, Jason does not mourn his sister's death. And although there is a possibility that he may have contributed to her demise, he does not feel particularly guilty over it; his main concern is that he will be blamed. Likewise Randy, when his parents are killed, is only concerned about what will happen to him now that they are gone; otherwise, he does not seem particularly affected by their deaths.

These children are the creations of a purely intellectual and pitiless "Science" and are therefore branded by the same lack of normal human feelings. They are portrayed as not really human because they lack emotional and physical vulnerability. Physically, they are able to overcome and repair injuries to their bodies almost instantly, bringing them several degrees closer to immortality than the rest of humanity.

Unlike Saul's earlier child protagonists, who are isolated figures, Jason and Randy have each other. They are set apart from other humans by unique physical abilities, which create a bond between them. This bonding between similar-age children, who must defend themselves against adult violence and evil, is a motif, or pattern, that emerges again in *Nathaniel, Darkness, Shadows*, and *The Homing*. The boys' victimization and fears, their ability to bond with each other, and their generally nonviolent behavior make them more sympathetic figures than many of Saul's earlier child protagonists.

The primary antagonist in the novel is Dr. Hamlin, by virtue of his attempts to control and manipulate the boys for selfish ends. Dr. Hamlin is a typically modern evil scientist. He is not like the ultimately decent Dr. Jekyll or Dr. Frankenstein (or Victor Frank of Robin Cook's *Mutation*), who eventually recognize the evil consequences of their arrogance and seek to put the dangerous genie back in the bottle, at the cost of their own lives and the monster's. Hamlin is unambiguously without morality. Yet he is not a totally isolated evil genius. Dr. Hamlin belongs to a network of malign social forces. His experiments are made possible by the financial support and political protection of business and military leaders who themselves have left moral considerations behind in their search for profits and power. The focus on this multi-leveled conspiracy of social forces creates a typically modern tone of cynicism and distrust that can be traced from the hard-boiled detective novels of the 1930s through to the contemporary paranoia of novelists Kurt Vonnegut and Thomas Pynchon.

A minor character who deserves mention is Dr. Hamlin's assistant, Louise Bowen, who uses her sweet-talking ways to lure Randy to the Academy. Unlike Hamlin, who considers the inmates of the Academy to be no more than lab animals, she sees them as little boys and feels some attachment to them. Her hesitation about reporting Randy's escape gives him the head start that he needs. Ultimately, however, her loyalty to Hamlin wins out. She is a true believer in his perverted vision of science. Although playing only a minor role in this novel, she foreshadows Saul's full-blown development of a female villain, Hildie Kramer, in *Shadows*.

Another notable minor character is Sally's mother, Phyllis. She represents the principle of the "family curse" that is found in many of Saul's novels and is central to *Suffer the Children, Comes the Blind Fury, When the Wind Blows*, and several others. In some of Saul's novels the curse is of a supernatural nature and is transmitted by a spirit who causes past tragedies to be reenacted. In others, like *The God Project*, it is a purely psychological phenomenon in which one generation instills its neurosis in the next, as is the case with Phyllis. When Sally was still a child, Phyllis lost an infant, felt guilty about it, and felt she got no support from those around her; she simply carried on mechanically out of a sense of duty, but with an emotional withdrawal that was perceptible to Sally. Now that Sally has lost a child, Phyllis instills the seeds of guilt in Sally and then returns home immediately after the funeral, deliberately leaving her without emotional support or assistance. Her parting counsel to Sally is to forget about her dead daughter and just fulfill her daily duties to her surviving family.

A surprise character is Dr. Malone, the pediatrician. He appears to be a sympathetic character who helps Sally gain access to the medical data banks and foils her husband's attempts to commit her to a mental hospital. However, in a final twist he is revealed to be insincerely playing this part while secretly being an agent of CHILD and a key player in the God Project. According to Saul (see Chapter 1), this twist of character was not planned, but emerged spontaneously as he was completing the final chapters of the book.

SUSPENSE

Suspense in Saul's books often begins with a discordant note, a small ripple on the otherwise calm surface of the narrative. It is the first signal that all is not as it seems. There is the vague sense of a threat, but no clear indication of the direction in which it lies or when it will strike. The reader begins scanning the text for clues that will bring the threat into focus.

In *The God Project* the first false note is the impassive behavior of Jason Montgomery as observed through his father's eyes after his sister's death. Next Sally becomes obsessed with the feeling that something other than SIDS caused her daughter's death. The typical reader may wonder whether Sally is going mad. The suspicion develops that Jason was somehow responsible for the death.

Meanwhile Jason's friend Randy has always wanted to go live with his father, so when the strange woman tells him his father sent her for him, he gets in the car. At first this seems like a good idea, but soon he feels uneasy about it, and as a result, so does the reader: "They were heading out of Eastbury on the road toward Langston. That was where his father lived so everything was all right. Except that it didn't quite *feel* all right. Deep inside Randy had a strange sense of something being very wrong" (29). Eventually, it becomes clear that Randy has been abducted.

These two plot lines, one centering on the Montgomery family's reaction to Julie's death and the other on Randy Corliss's kidnapping, will eventually come together. Meanwhile the author is dropping hints concerning the boys' physical invulnerability. He starts early on by mentioning how Randy jumped off the roof at his friend Billy's house without hurting himself and then dared Billy to do the same. But when Billy landed, he fractured his leg. Later the school nurse tells Randy's mother that he bragged about being able to play with poisonous spiders without getting hurt. At first these hints do not register with the reader, but they accumulate subliminally, so that when the truth finally becomes apparent, this whole pattern of little episodes is illuminated and falls into place.

Once the outline of the threat becomes clarified, the focus of suspense becomes the conflict between the opposing sides and how it will be resolved. In the first place will Randy escape from the Academy before he is killed in the experiments? Two-thirds of the way through the novel, he devises a plan, but Louise Bowen, Dr. Hamlin's assistant, guesses his intention. When she hears a noise at night, she checks Randy's room. Finding it empty, after a moment of indecision she alerts the staff. Her early discovery of his absence reduces the amount of time Randy had counted on having for his escape, and this raises the level of tension for the reader. As Randy is nearing the electrified fence that surrounds the Academy, he hears the barking of the dogs coming toward him through the woods. His plan is to swim through the culvert for the stream that goes underneath the fence. It appears he will succeed, but as he reaches the end of the culvert, he finds it blocked by a metal grate. He is trapped, and the reader's tension level is ratcheted up yet another degree. But then he finds a means of escape using the same unusual physical powers for which Dr. Hamlin imprisoned him at the Academy to study.

Meanwhile Sally and Lucy have used the computer to gather incriminating information about the CHILD experiments, including a list of all the children who either mysteriously disappeared or died of unexplained causes. They have convinced Dr. Malone and Sergeant Bronski of the conspiracy. The CHILD people are trying to cover their tracks. The Academy is closed down, and the remaining children are executed. The tide appears to be with Sally and Lucy. The reader is anticipating the chastisement of the villains.

But then, two chapters before the end of the novel, after Sergeant Bronski has searched the Academy and found physical evidence to support Randy's testimony, Dr. Hamlin's allies in the military high command send operatives to blow up the car containing Bronski, Randy, and his parents. Ten seconds before the bomb is about to be detonated, Bronski has an intuition of impending disaster and orders everyone out of the car, but he is a hair's breadth too late. Only Randy survives. The cover-up succeeds in hiding all the evidence of the genetic experiments. And in a last-minute plot twist the reader learns that it was really Dr. Malone who was Dr. Hamlin's on-the-scene ally in the experiments. Dr. Wiseman was just a harmless dupe. Malone only pretended to befriend Sally in order to find out how much she knew about CHILD and the God Project. Sally and Steve accept defeat, knowing they, too, will be killed otherwise. They are powerless against the superior forces of the military-industrial complex and must agree henceforth to act as though they believe its lies. In the epilogue Sally goes to Dr. Malone, unaware that he betrayed her, and asks him to give her something that can kill the boys. Even this one attempt at revolt, when Sally and her husband try to poison the boys, plays into the hands of the God Project scientists, who use it as yet another experiment to test the limits of the boys' invulnerability.

THEMES

The novel is carried along mostly by plot and suspense. It does raise a thematic issue, but never fully explores it. The issue is the humanity of the mutants. Dr. Hamlin argues that though they appear human, the boys are not because of a genetic deviation. Since they are not human, it is therefore permissible to kill them. Since he writes for entertainment, rather than to convey a "message," Saul does not pursue this argument as far as he could. For instance, if one genetic difference is enough to place someone in a different species, wouldn't that make Down's syndrome babies, who have a defect in one chromosome, members of a non-human species? On the other hand, even if we were to accept that mutants are not human, does that automatically deprive them of any rights? This is an issue that has been raised by the animal rights movement with regard to species less intelligent than ours. Animal rights activists argue that humans are not justified in capturing, exploiting, and killing creatures just because they belong to a different species. Certainly this argument should hold just as true for a species of equal intelligence to humans.

The boys, once have they become conscious of their relative immortality, will of necessity develop a different attitude toward life than ordinary humans. As a result, they may inspire fear or loathing. But does that mean it is morally right to kill them? If it is justified to kill them because they are potentially more powerful than the rest of us, then aren't animals justified in attacking and killing humans for the same reason?

Nowhere in the book are Jason and Randy depicted as actually evil. If anything, they represent an amoral force, or a different order of morality, that is outside of conventional human categories of good or evil. In this aspect they have something in common with Amy Carlson of *Shadows* after she has been turned into a disembodied intelligence. Although they are monsters, Jason and Randy are not particularly violent. Unlike the children in Saul's earlier novels, they do not commit a series of gruesome murders. Jason may have accidentally smothered his sister, but it was more likely that the genetic defect killed her. Randy kicks at his mother, but only because she is holding onto him as he is trying to escape from a burning car. A young boy accidentally kills himself trying to imitate them, but that is not directly their fault. At the end of the novel Jason threatens to kill his parents, but only after they try to kill him with a nerve poison. Even then he only warns them that if they attempt it a second time, he will kill them.

The fact is that all the fatal violence in the novel comes from the "normal" humans. Dr. Hamlin has the experimental children put to death in the decompression chamber when the cover is blown from the secret project. Dr. Hamlin's military supporters order their agents to blow up the car containing the Corliss family. Dr. Malone drives Dr. Wiseman to suicide by threatening him with disgrace. And Sally and Steve Montgomery try, but do not succeed, in poisoning the two boys.

While Hamlin argues for the morality of killing the boys using a narrow, self-serving "logic," Sally eventually arrives at a similar conclusion from an emotional and interpersonally oriented viewpoint. Sally is repulsed by the boys for five major reasons: They do not associate with other children, they lack normal emotions, they are insensitive to suffering because of their own inability to feel pain, they do not respect parental authority, and worst of all, they have a sense of superiority due to their inability to be physically harmed. She concludes from this that they are inhuman and dangerous.

When a child is fatally injured trying to imitate one of their dangerous stunts, the boys shrug and say to Sally: "People who can get hurt shouldn't play our games. They should just do what we tell them to do. . . . We're special and that makes us better than other people" (333–334). Sally argues that because of their special abilities they should experience a greater than normal sense of responsibility to avoid even accidentally harming other people. But the boys shrug this off, too.

Sally's reasons for feeling they should die seem more sincere than Hamlin's, but is she fundamentally any different from him when she decides to try to kill them? In one sense her motives and his are opposite. Hamlin and his collaborators stand outside the ordinary human community and are on an egotistical quest for power. Hamlin is trying to develop invulnerable mutants for military purposes. He wants them to be inhuman in order to serve his power-hungry goals. If they are too "human" (too mortal), he has no scruples about disposing of them. Sally, on the other hand, is part of the human community and is concerned about threats to that community. Her decision to destroy the mutants is intended not to serve egotistical purposes, but to protect the community.

When she does make the decision to kill, she finds it emotionally very painful, as opposed to Hamlin's matter-of-fact attitude. From this point of view, Hamlin and Sally represent radically different perspectives. His is elitist and emphasizes the naked will of the sovereign individual, whereas hers is communitarian. Hamlin's way-of-being in the world tends toward what feminists call patriarchal. In the next section we will explore some of the feminist themes found in the novel.

A FEMINIST READING OF *THE GOD PROJECT*

Feminist literary criticism grew out of the turbulence of the women's liberation movement, which developed in the politicized 1960s and whose seminal text, Simone de Beauvoir's *The Second Sex* (1949), was published almost two decades earlier. The women's movement embraced vigorous differences of opinion, along the spectrum of political radicalism, cultural separatism, and attitudes toward lesbianism and normative heterosexuality. An important concept in most feminist theorizing is the notion of "patriarchy" as a complex of legal, social, and cultural practices characteristic of many different types of societies, economies, and political systems throughout history. The effect of patriarchal practices is to limit and suppress the potential of women, maintaining the majority of women in a subordinate status in relation to men as a class. As a result of the consciousness-raising by the women's movement during the last thirty years, there is broad acknowledgment of the historical oppression of women. But many would disagree with the more radical feminists who believe such basic social institutions as the family, and even the concept of gender, are instruments of patriarchal enslavement.

At a minimum, feminist literary studies have critiqued negative or limiting stereotypes of women in fiction and have attempted to unearth historical and contemporary examples of women's writing that has been neglected by the literary establishment. Feminist critics have been open to the study of popular literature, to which many women authors were consigned by the critical establishment. In view of the social barriers that existed toward female authorship, some feminist critics have been willing to examine diaries, letters, or oral narratives as sources of women's literary creativity. On a broader level feminist critics seek to expose vestiges of patriarchal ideology in all types of texts and at all stages of literary and artistic production and consumption. Although some male critics consider themselves to be feminists, there are those who feel feminist criticism should be grounded in the "women's community." To the extent that feminist criticism is a method, it should be capable of being learned by anyone, just as women have been able to master the presumably male-oriented methods of criticism that have been traditionally taught in academia. On the other hand, to the extent that feminist criticism represents a sensitivity whose wellspring is the unique experience of being female in this society, a male critic could never aspire to full status. Nevertheless, even if the reader were to grant that cutting-edge feminist criticism is an enterprise best undertaken by an individual who is both theoretically trained and female, it certainly is possible for a male to have become informed by feminist criticism and thus much more sensitized to fictional representations of gender than the prior generation.

As a result of the new awareness, there have been some concessions to an alternative presentation of woman protagonists. One thinks of such films as *The Jagged Edge; Fatal Attraction*; Mike Nichols's recent movie *Wolf*, where the woman saves the hero by killing the monster; and Al Pacino in *Sea of Love*, which is a role reversal of the heroine-in-peril theme. That these films still remain largely the exception is evidenced by the fact that they continue to stand out in one's mind. And despite some advances in the public sensibility, an action film primarily centered on a tough, independent woman is a box-office risk, as demonstrated by the poor showing of *V. I. Warshawski*, in which Kathleen Turner played a hard-boiled private eye.

Feminist criticism, in short, is primarily concerned with the relation between gender and power and with an accurate reflection of the full range of women's experiences, regardless of whether these fit stereotypical notions of feminine psychology. A feminist analysis of *The God Project* can proceed on two levels: the surface content of the story or the deeper underlying symbolism. Starting with the obvious surface, a central issue for the feminist political movement has been the degree to which women are in control of or alienated from their bodies and reproductive capacities. In *The God Project* the average reader feels morally outraged by the way in which Dr. Hamlin and the military-industrial complex that supports him consider themselves privileged to use women's bodies for their own ends. Sally, Lucy, and the other women who are unwittingly part of the secret experiment lost control of their own bodies without even knowing it. They were used as the involuntary breeders of genetically altered human guinea pigs, who were later kidnapped from them.

Although almost everyone will react to this exaggerated fictional scenario as a clear violation of the human rights of the kidnapped children and an infringement on the reproductive and human rights of the mothers, feminists maintain that there have been and continue to be many subtle ways in which society attempts to alienate women from control over their own bodies. In many societies women are under pressure from the extended family to produce children, particularly a male heir. Some political leaders have viewed the fertility of the female population as a necessary resource for the production of future soldiers to fuel their military aspirations and have denied women control over their bodies by legal restrictions on the dissemination of birth control information (as was the case in the United States in the early part of this century).

Some feminists such as Phyllis Chesler have suggested that the psychiatric profession has had a bias against women, being prone to interpret a woman's attunement to emotional issues as a sign of psychological weakness. In *The God Project* Dr. Wiseman is all too ready to label Sally's reaction to her baby's death as hysteria and tries to persuade her husband Steve to have her involuntarily committed to a psychiatric hospital. Steve is ready to accept the opinion of the socially credentialled male "expert" over the felt experience and convictions of his intimate partner. This is not due to malevolence on Steve's part, or even Dr. Wiseman's. It is a result of their social bias that makes them prone to interpret an emotionally upset woman as hysterical.

Dr. Malone appears to represent an exception. He seems to really listen to Sally, instead of being just another paternalistic, condescending member of the medical establishment. But beneath the mask of liberality he represents the most deliberate and calculating example of elitist, hierarchical paternalism.

Mary Belenky in *Women's Ways of Knowing* (1986) has sought to gain recognition for the type of subjective and personal learning style that appeals to many women more than the abstract method of analysis favored by many men, particularly scientists. The plot of *The God Project* seems structured to show that women's ways of knowing often prove to be the most accurate. Although the police in their institutional authority deem her son to be a runaway, Lucy "knows" this is not true.

Similarly, Sally is convinced that *something* happened to her daughter, Julie, despite official medical explanations to the contrary. Intuitive ways of knowing are not only the prerogative of women in the novel. Sergeant Bronski has a feeling of something being amiss when he sees the same van twice. But in the seconds it takes him to reason out his intuition, he misses his chance to escape from the impending explosion of his vehicle.

Likewise, Randy senses that something is not right when he gets into the stranger's car, but he ignores this intuitive voice because the stranger's explanation appeals to his logical mode of analysis.

Just as men may have intuitions that they unfortunately ignore, some women suppress their personal reactions and ally themselves with the inhuman ideals of the power structure, as in the case of Louise Bowen, who continues to serve the "cause of science" and "military preparedness" despite the fact that they are killing children.

Although women are presented as being at a disadvantage due to men's tendency to dismiss their opinions, the female protagonists are not passive or weak. Sally in particular is both determined and resourceful, as demonstrated in her networking with other women and her computer sleuthing. And men are presented as being capable of change for the better. Lucy's husband transforms himself from a selfish, immature person to a caring and supportive partner. And Steve eventually vows to trust Sally's intuitive judgments. It is the men entrenched in the upper echelons of social power who are recalcitrant to change.

On a deeper, less overtly articulated level, *The God Project* is about men's envy of women's ability to give birth. To clarify this, go back to one of the earliest science-fictional horror classics, *Frankenstein*. *Frankenstein* is often read as man affronting God by stealing divine-like powers of creation. In this reading of the story the scientist becomes an awe-inspiring figure, like a modern Prometheus or Lucifer.

But *Frankenstein* can also be seen as a critique of the misogynists' ambition for solitary procreation in isolation from womanly participation. As Professor Eric Rabkin (1994) has pointed out, this novel and its successors flirt with the male fantasy of appropriating the woman's power of procreation. The scientist declares his independence of any female principle. By the power of cold intellect alone he is able to create life. But what kind of life?

There is something lacking in the product of such a one-sided act. The creatures thus produced always suffer from an overdevelopment in the logical sphere and a gaping hole in the emotional side of their natures. Doctor Frankenstein's creature feels acutely unloved and turns vicious because of this. Robin Cook's child prodigy VJ feels little need for love because his coldly rational intellect is so hyperdeveloped. And Saul's boy mutants are also emotionally frigid. In each of these cases the fact that the scientist-father's self-produced "children" are emotionally crippled reflects the emotional imbalance that the authors perceive in the scientific enterprise itself.

Some feminist critics such as Sandra Harding and Helen Longino view the values and methods of science as inherently oppressive and patriarchal. Although this viewpoint is controversial even among feminists (compare, for example, Koertge 1995), science certainly does seem at times to be a stereotypically masculine activity. Despite some great women scientists, the field has generally been dominated by men. And the culture of science favors a type of abstract, analytical thinking and solitary work style that many men find congenial. By dramatizing the tragic results of a certain type of scientific venture, the authors are critiquing the tendency of some men to isolate themselves from those qualities within themselves that are currently labeled "feminine." This alienation from their own inner "femininity" reinforces their tendency to depreciate women in society, since women are seen as the carriers of the "femininity" that these men reject within themselves.

6

Brainchild
(1985)

Reason is God's gift, but so are the passions.
John Henry Cardinal Newman (1801–1890),
English Churchman and Theologian

Brainchild, John Saul's second "techno-thriller," was issued as a paperback original by Bantam in 1985. It is unlike his earlier book *The God Project*, which was pure science fiction and suspense. In *Brainchild* Saul attempts to combine his favorite occult themes—a historical curse and a vengeful spirit that takes possession of one's mind—with science fiction elements—rebuilding a human brain with computerized microcircuitry.

GENRE

Brainchild is in the broad tradition of Mary Shelley's *Frankenstein*, but more specifically is a descendant of the science fiction subgenre of robot stories. Isaac Asimov in *I. Robot* (1950) was the first to codify the "laws of robotics": Robots shall not harm humans, shall obey all legitimate orders, and shall preserve themselves, except when this conflicts with the first two laws. Later science fiction writers challenged these conventions and ventured into new territory, exploring the boundary between human and robot. They stretched the boundary with the concept of androids, the next step in robot evolution. An android is a manufactured product designed so that it can almost pass for a human. Philip K. Dick's *Do Androids Dream of Electric Sheep?*—which was made into the visually brilliant movie *Blade Runner* (1982)—concerns the revolt of a group of androids against their human masters. It questions why a machine with highly sophisticated artificial intelligence could not be considered human in principle. Even more subversively, it implies that none of us can be sure we are not in some sense machines.

The question can be approached from another angle. If you begin to replace parts of a human's organism with artificial substitutes, at what point does the human become a machine? The bionic arm of the "Six Million Dollar Man" did not compromise his essential humanness. But the protagonist of the movie *Robocop* (1987), whose nervous system is wedded to electronic circuitry, appears to have become completely mechanized, though eventually it becomes apparent that a small element of individual human identity has survived.

Alex, two years before *Robocop*, experiences a similar predicament. He is a human who has been made into a robot. Fundamental parts of his brain are artificial. He is programmed to follow certain rules. Like Philip K. Dick's androids, he has even been programmed with artificial memories. Yet there is some small core of autonomy left in him that struggles to assert itself.

PLOT

There are three primary narrative threads in *Brainchild*. The first has to do with Alex's automobile accident and the consequences that follow—amnesia and a lack of emotion—and how he, his family, and his peers are affected by and deal with the these changes. The second thread has to do with the relationship between his parents and how it changes in the aftermath of the accident, particularly in their conflicting attitudes toward Dr. Raymond Torres, the brain specialist, and his method of treatment for Alex. The third narrative thread has to do with the process of detection. It concerns Alex's realization that Dr. Torres has done something to him and his attempt to discover what it is and how it links him to a series of murders of his mother's friends.

The structure of these narrative threads parallels the ones in Saul's first techno-thriller, *The God Project*. There, too, the story began by exploring a tragic medical problem, continued with the strains it put on the family, and ended with a detection plot trying to uncover what the doctors were really doing.

When the story opens, sixteen-year-old Alex Lonsdale is getting ready to take his girlfriend, Lisa Cochran, to the high school prom. He promises his parents he will not drink, but he gives in to peer pressure at a post-prom party in the old hacienda that Carolyn Evans's wealthy parents have just bought and renovated. Lisa gets disgusted when Alex chuga-lugs two beers and joins the revelry in the pool where the rest of the kids are swimming naked. She leaves the party on foot without saying a word to Alex. When he realizes she has gone, he gets in the car and goes after her, driving too fast. The car skids on a curve, and just beyond his headlights he sees the face of an old woman glaring at him with intense loathing. This sight causes him to lose control of the car and plunge over the cliff.

The stare that so affected him belongs to Maria Torres, an elderly Chicana cleaning woman, who was at the hacienda when the teenagers arrived and is now walking home. She is filled with loathing because they are desecrating the historic house of her ancestors with their decadent "*gringo* revelry" (39). Witnessing the accident, she is filled with joy, considering it an intervention by the saints in response to her prayers.

Alex suffers massive brain damage as a result of the accident. His only hope, and a slim one at that, is to be transferred to the Institute for the Human Brain in Palo Alto, California, which is run by the brilliant, but cold and dictatorial, Dr. Raymond Torres, successful son of the indigent cleaning woman Maria Torres. He has the family sign a lengthy document that gives him legal guardianship of their son and absolute control over all medical decisions concerning the boy's treatment. Using futuristic computerized surgical robots, Torres does massive prosthetic reconstruction of Alex's brain.

Alex survives and recovers normal functioning in most areas. In fact, compared to his lackadaisical academic performance before the accident, he is now quite brilliant, with a photographic memory and a drive to study and learn. But the accident does leave him with deficiencies in two important areas: first, he is unable to experience emotion, and second, he is without memories.

Not having emotions, he also lacks a sense of humor. His former friends, like Bob Carey and Kate Lewis, begin to become bored with his peculiar behavior. They say he is no fun anymore; he is too serious and always asking questions, due to his amnesia. For example, he is puzzled when he is invited to go to "the City," not knowing, as he would have before the accident, that his friends are referring to San Francisco. The only one who continues to stick with him is his girlfriend, Lisa, out of guilt. She feels if she had not walked out on him at the party, the accident would not have occurred.

Realizing that these abnormalities disturb people, Alex tries to figure out what is expected of him so that he can feign normal memory and emotion. Before the trip to "the City" he pathetically memorizes every reference to San Francisco in the *Encyclopaedia Britannica*, thinking, "if he watched carefully, and remembered everything he saw, sooner or later he would be able to act like everyone else" (130). With Lisa, he does not remember she was his girlfriend, although he accepts the fact after he is told. But he cannot grasp its emotional significance. He realizes she is looking for signs of affection from him, and he tries to feign these, although he has no idea what it feels like. An illustrative episode occurs in a pizza shop, where Lisa speaks sharply to Alex; then as they are leaving, she takes his hand and apologizes for getting mad. Alex tells her it is okay and drops her hand:

> "You mad at me?" Lisa asked.
> "No."
> "Then how come you don't want to hold hands?" Lisa ventured.
> Alex said nothing, but wondered silently why holding hands seemed so important to her. (145)

Eventually, Lisa begins to feel spooked by his behavior, particularly after Marty Lewis is murdered and Alex tells her he thinks there is going to be another murder. At that point she decides to break off the relationship.

The second line of plot development has to do with the shifts in the relationship between Ellen and Marsh Lonsdale, Alex's parents. At the beginning of the story we see them arguing. They argue about Alex; Marsh thinks he is an underachiever and accuses Ellen of coddling him. And they argue about money; Ellen wants more of it so she can remodel their house to "keep up with" Cynthia Evans. Marsh and Ellen still love each other, but there are tensions in their marriage.

After Alex is injured, they are forced to pin all their hopes on the success of Dr. Torres's treatment method. Marsh, who is himself a physician, feels slighted and humiliated by Dr. Torres's high-handed manner. When Marsh questions giving a sedative to Alex after he has just come out of a coma, Torres cuts him off instantly, saying he did not ask for Marsh's opinion and has no interest in hearing it. To compound the injury, his wife, Ellen, chimes in to support Raymond Torres. She has completely surrendered to his authority, and Marsh is a little jealous, noting Torres's expensive suit and chiseled features, "more suitable for a movie star than a scientist" (67).

Raymond Torres and Ellen Lonsdale had known each other in high school in La Paloma, when he was the son of a poor, uneducated Hispanic cleaning woman. And though he has put the town of his youth far behind him with his achievements, there is still unfinished business between himself and Ellen. She remembers him in high school as arrogant and almost scary, with frightening, smoldering eyes. She and her friends never liked him. But now she finds him quite handsome, possessed of inner strength and reassuring self-confidence. And he is the savior of her son. Torres, for his part, had thought he had put his memories of his high school years so far behind that they could no longer hurt him. To his surprise he finds himself suddenly stung once again by unwelcome feelings and memories that make him tremble. Ellen has no inkling of her effect on Torres or of how much hatred is bound up in his emotions—hatred that will soon turn upon her friends and her. Even when it becomes apparent to Marsh that Torres is hiding something—refusing to release Alex's medical records to them—Ellen defends him, accusing Marsh of becoming paranoid.

The third plot line concerns Alex's growing realization that things are not as they appear to be. He begins having strange flashbacks of memory, but these flashbacks are of things that could not possibly be his personal memories. For instance, the historic houses of La Paloma seem strange to him. He remembers them the way they were before they were renovated. He is able to confirm this by consulting old photographs and drawings of the town in the public library's collection. It is as if he were the reincarnation of some nineteenth-century Mexican settler and he is having flashbacks from his previous existence. In an effort to find out more about the earliest history of the town, he consults old Maria Torres, who tells him that the original Spanish-speaking landowners were slaughtered by United States cavalry after Mexico ceded the upper half of California in the Treaty of Guadalupe Hidalgo in 1850. Her great-grandfather, Don Roberto, was hung in the town square, and his wife and daughters were shot and buried in the courtyard of their hacienda. His son, Alejandro, escaped and swore revenge. Old Maria Torres believes Alejandro has returned from beyond the grave in the shape of Alex.

Alex has blackouts. He notices some lapses in his memory and becomes curious about them. Also at times strange thoughts in Spanish go through his mind: *asesinos, ladrones*—murderers, thieves. These are the thoughts that Maria Torres's grandfather, Alejandro, might have had concerning the Anglo-American settlers. There is a series of murders of women in La Paloma. The women were friends of his mother, and Alex has dreams in which he is the one killing them. Puzzled about all these strange occurrences, he begins his own investigation. He eventually realizes Dr. Torres has been manipulating him in some way. Taking his father's shotgun, he breaks into Torres's home and finds a notebook detailing how the damaged sections of Alex's brain were replaced with computerized microprocessors. He was then programmed with the appropriate memories that would make him kill and forget. But the real purpose of these murders was not to avenge what had been done to Torres's ancestors in 1850. That was just the cover story. The true reason he sent Alex/Alejandro on these killing missions was to avenge the insults Torres felt had been perpetrated against him in high school by Ellen Lonsdale, Carol Cochran, and their two murdered friends.

Alex kills Torres and then, unable to inhibit his programming, goes on to kill Carol Cochran, and finally attempts to kill his mother. But when his father wrestles the shotgun away from him, Alex begs Marsh to shoot him, telling his father he is no longer Alex, but "someone else . . . whoever I was programmed to be, and I'll do what I was programmed to do. Alex tried to stop me but he can't. Do it . . . Father. Please do it for me" (335).

And with that Marsh does. He kills his son.

CHARACTERS

Alex is the primary protagonist in this novel. As a character he is a cipher. He has no emotions and practically no memories. He tries to fit in because other people seem to get upset about his lack of emotions. He decides if he can act like everyone else, even if he still does not feel anything, that will be good enough because he has realized it does not matter what you really are. "The only thing that mattered was what people *thought* you were" (150).

Like most of Saul's youthful protagonists, Alex becomes a social isolate as the plot develops. Usually, they are shunned by their peers to start with because they are newcomers, and when they begin talking about their experiences with ghosts, the other kids begin actively teasing them or give them even wider berth. Alex is exceptional in that he was popular at the beginning of the book, and the things his peers reject him over are really quite petty.

It would be very difficult for the reader to have much empathy for Alex if Saul did not leave a spark of humanity in him. There is a tiny portion of Alex's personality that survives and tries to put a halt to the programmed killing machine that Alex has become. Our sympathy with that small fragment of humanity is what sustains some interest in the resolution of the plot.

Alex's parents, Marsh and Ellen, are normal people living an extraordinary situation. They do all that is in their power to save Alex's life, but eventually must come to terms with the realization that this is not their son.

Dr. Torres and his mother are the prime antagonists. Torres has established his own personal fiefdom in the Institute for the Human Brain housed in an old mansion, like the hacienda. He is pitiless and exacting with his employees. When Peter Bloch, the technician, fails to give Alex anesthesia before reprogramming the boy, Torres fires him instantly, even though the technician was duped by forged orders. There are no indications that Torres makes any effort to hire Hispanic employees. All the staff members mentioned are Anglos.

His mother, the elderly Maria Torres, is a woman as implacably vengeful as Heathcliff in Emily Brontë's *Wuthering Heights* (1847). She constantly nurtures her innate sense of injustice. A descendant of the landed elite, she works as a cleaning woman for the English-speaking Anglo-American families whose houses are on the land that should have still been in the possession of her family. She passes this sense of injustice to her son. She nurtures in him a sense of inherent hereditary superiority, while at the same time sensitizing him to every slight by the Anglos as a sign of their depreciation of him.

Meanwhile Torres's Anglo schoolmates have no clue as to the worldview shared by him and his mother. They correctly perceive him as angry and arrogant, without ever caring to penetrate that surface. Their ignoring of him is due partly to his personality and partly to the Anglos' unreflective prejudice against his ethnicity and social class. Even after he has attained wealth, status, and reputation, he still carries within him the wounds he casually received from his high school peers. Even when

Ellen has become totally deferential to his will out of abject gratitude for whatever he can do to save her son, his bitterness is still not assuaged, and he desires to see her and her girlfriends dead as revenge for scorning him.

While Raymond Torres misuses the modern technology of medicine to seek revenge, Maria Torres misuses the ancient technology of religion. Maria Torres's attitude to religion is similar to that of Monsignor Peter Vernon in *Punish the Sinners*. Under the rubric of Catholic imagery and belief Mrs. Torres subscribes to a vengeful God, not in accord with the gospel of love and forgiveness. She burns candles in church in thanks to the saints when tragedy strikes one of her "enemies"—individuals whom she barely knows and who have never personally wronged her. It may be too easy to dismiss this simply as her personal aberration. It must be admitted that in times of war military chaplains on both sides of a slaughter have each given their troops the impression that God would help them kill their enemies. And in peacetime religious rationalization is sometimes falsely used to foster complacency about social injustice.

THEMES

Although intelligent, John Saul was not the most disciplined student during his college years, attending four different schools and never graduating. Undoubtedly he received questioning looks from relatives and friends during those years. One can imagine him chuckling as he constructs the character of Alex because the cautionary tale of Alex's fate validates the choices the author made in his own life—to follow his instincts rather than slavishly conform to someone else's idea of discipline and achievement.

Before the accident Alex is a good-natured, appealing boy, but not the most devoted student. His father, a hard-working doctor with an ambitious wife, calls Alex an underachiever and wishes he could work harder. One must be careful what one wishes for, as W. W. Jacobs's classic horror story "The Monkey's Paw" (1902) warns us. In "The Monkey's Paw" the father wishes for a sum of money. The next day his son is mangled in the machinery at work and dies, and the insurance benefit equals the exact sum for which the father wished. Distraught, he wishes his son were alive again. But when he hears a loud knocking on the door, he imagines what condition his son's reanimated corpse will be in, so before his wife can open the door, he quickly makes his last wish, that his son be back in the grave again.

In *Brainchild* the father wishes that Alex could be a better student. Alex gets into an accident and suffers massive injuries. His father wishes he could survive. Alex does survive and becomes an excellent student. He has a photographic memory and never tires of studying. He is intellectually capable of skipping the rest of high school and going straight to Stanford University. Isn't this the answer to the father's wishes? The only problem is that Alex is now a monster. He is a robot who has been programmed to kill his mother. So in the end his father has to wish him dead. Worse than that—his father has to kill Alex himself. But like Lucy's fiancé, who has to stake her through the heart after she has been made a vampire by Dracula, Alex's father is able to perform the deed because he knows that the creature he is killing is not Alex, but a stranger.

The manner in which father and son become strangers to each other is through a form of psychological reprogramming, analogous to the way Dr. Marty Ames psychologically programs teenager Mark Tanner in *Creature*. Alex is given memories of the murder of the Mexican landowners in La Paloma in 1850. He is programmed to believe that the present-day inhabitants of La Paloma are murderers and thieves because their property belongs to the murdered Mexicans. In other words, Alex is politically radicalized by Dr. Torres. But this radicalization is not the product of a conscious, rational choice on Alex's part. He is brainwashed, without his knowledge or consent, and has now become a subversive secret assassin.

The idea of brainwashing is familiar to the Americans who lived during the Korean War, the Cold War, and the Vietnam War, as are the notions of secret enemies within our midst and multiple personalities. The 1950s television series "I Led Three Lives," based on the career of Herbert Philbrick, popularized the idea that anyone could have a secret identity, possibly even multiple levels of secret identities. Philbrick was ostensibly a patriotic American, but was secretly a subversive Communist agent. But even that was not his real identity because he was actually an FBI informant who was spying on the Communist Party. While Philbrick's hidden personalities were conscious choices, the Academy Award–winning movie *Three Faces of Eve* (1957), with Joanne Woodward, was a portrayal of a woman with multiple personality disorder who was not aware of her alternate personalities. She was subject to blackouts in which a different personality would take over. The novel *The Manchurian Candidate* (1959) was a fictional account of someone who is deliberately programmed to have a subversive dual personality of which he is not aware. The story concerns a Congressional Medal of Honor Winner who is programmed by the Communists to assassinate the President of the United States.

During the Vietnam War, when the nation was split along generational lines in its attitude toward continuing the war, many older Americans were shocked by what, to them, was the inexplicable behavior of some American youth—the protest marches, the disrespect for the President, the long hair, the burning of draft cards, and so forth. They were disposed toward accepting explanations that attributed the protests to the brainwashing of the young people by foreign Communist agents.

This type of explanation received some credit after the peculiar behavior of kidnapped heiress Patty Hearst, the daughter of a wealthy newspaper syndicate magnate. After physical intimidation and psychological manipulation by an armed radical group called the Symbionese Liberation Army (SLA) Patty Hearst donned a beret like Cuban revolutionary Che Guevara, called herself Tanya, and denounced capitalism and her parents. Armed with an assault weapon, she assisted her captors in robbing banks for the revolution. After she was caught, she stated that she had been subjected to isolation and torture by her captors to the point that she was no longer acting as herself when she was Tanya. Within a few years a group of people calling themselves deprogrammers began specializing in kidnapping people who had joined religious cults and trying to unbrainwash them, or rebrainwash them, depending upon your point of view, at the behest of their families.

The situation is analogous to that of the protagonist of *Brainchild*. He is no longer Alex; he has become Alejandro, just as Patty Hearst became Tanya. A new name goes with a revolutionary identity. When he carries a shotgun and kills the political enemies, he is Alejandro. So, too, the armed SLA bankrobber was Tanya, class enemy of the rich, *not* Patty Hearst, the heiress:

> Alejandro had killed them. And why not? To Alejandro, they were the wives of thieves and murderers, and as guilty of those crimes as their husbands. But in the darkness of night, in the visions generated by the remnants of Alex Lonsdale's subconscious, they were old friends, people he had known all his life, and he mourned them. (323)

Alex is the middle-class revolutionary, divided within himself. He feels solidarity with those who were the victims of injustice, but can he totally turn his back on the people he grew up with and advocate violence toward them? However, Alex is not free to reason his way out of this dilemma, since he is forced by his programming to execute the killings he was created to perform. The only free act left to him is to kill the person who put him in this dilemma, Dr. Torres.

The idea of the loss of one's internal freedom inspires a terror that is all the more eerie because it is purely of the imagination. In *Brainchild* the image that inspires terror is that of your body being generally intact, but with your brain changed mostly into machinery, with just enough of you left that you become aware of what has happened. In John Saul's later novel *Shadows* he explores the same fear of loss of autonomy, but there he leaves the brain intact and changes the body into a set of mechanized life support systems. In both novels the protagonist regains partial control of self and destroys the power of the mad scientist. Alex in *Brainchild* blows Dr. Torres's brains out with a shotgun in the spirit of "an eye for an eye, a tooth for a tooth." Alex has lost his brain; now so will Torres. Amy in *Shadows* kills one of her tormentors, Hildie Kramer, by taking electronic control of the elevator, and the main villain, Dr. Engersol, is killed by another enslaved brain that electronically seals off the ventilation system.

But though Alex in *Brainchild* and Amy in *Shadows* are both able to recapture enough freedom to revolt against their oppressors, they are powerless to undo the damage that has been done to them. Unable to defy the programming that drives him to kill his own mother, Alex opts for passive suicide and begs his father to shoot him. Amy, afraid of what she will become, asks to have her life support system disconnected, but at the last moment she changes her mind and becomes transformed into a completely non-organic creature with a personality unlike her former self.

Brainchild (and later *Shadows*) expresses a profound distrust of technology. The most common complaints against technology are pollution, depletion of natural resources, changes in the ozone, and the excessive vulnerability of dependent urban populations to catastrophe from massive technological failure. The ultimate fear concerning technology is of the danger of planetary destruction through nuclear war. But these fears all relate to the external influences of technology. In *Brainchild* and later John Saul novels it is not merely a question of being oppressed from the outside by technology. The new terror is that who, and what, we are within ourselves will be essentially, and irrevocably, altered through our increasingly intimate relationship with technology. This was the notion pioneered by communications theorist Marshall McLuhan in his book *Understanding Media* (1964), where he spoke of the electronic communications network as being an extension of the human nervous system.

There is an implicit thematic level where the story is self-referential, like Stephen King's *The Dark Half* (1989). Alex is a "brain child"—a creation of the mind. Whose mind? John Saul's. Alex is programmed to do certain things. Who programs him? The author. As V. C. Andrews said about writing fiction: "It's a very powerful feeling. It's like being a little god. . . . You are making the whole milieu and giving life to the characters. And you can wipe them out—and sometimes after they die, I bring them back to life" (Winter 1985, 172). And the master plan for the character is written in the author's notebook that contains the outline, like the book Alex discovers in Dr. Torres's desk drawer, "neatly penned in a precise hand" (311). But sometimes characters rebel against the author's plan and take on a life of their own. They draw their independence from the subconscious. Whose subconscious? The author's. For, after all, the author and the character share the same mind, or as Alex says to his creator, "I'm not your son . . . I'm you" (315). John Saul has described this experience of a character asserting his autonomy in his writing of *The God Project*: "and as I was writing it, all of a sudden he's pulling open the bottom drawer of his desk, taking out a bottle of brandy, and toasting the success of *his* project. And I thought, 'Wait a minute! This is the good guy' " (see Chapter 1).

A SOCIOPOLITICAL READING OF *BRAINCHILD*

A socio-political analysis looks at the role a piece of fiction plays in the larger context of the political, economic, and social forces of society. There is usually an assumption that there is a degree of conflict among different groups within society, and that this conflict is greater, or more open, at some times than at others, as when economic resources become scarce. Also, at any one time some groups have greater political and economic power and social influence than other groups. Traditionally, this analysis has been applied primarily to social classes, such as the wealthiest segment of the population versus the poorest segment. But it can be applied to any type of group. For instance, adults have much greater power and influence than children; hence, legislation protecting children always faces an uphill battle. Citizens have greater power than unauthorized immigrants. The white European mainstream has historically had more power than minority groups such as Native Americans and African Americans. Men traditionally have had more power than women, although that situation is gradually moving toward equity.

A sociopolitical analysis can look at a piece of fiction in terms of how accurately it reflects the conditions of the life of a group that is in power or out of power. How accurately does it portray the transactions of unequal power between the groups? A sociopolitical analysis can also concern itself with the underlying message of the novel. For example, critics have pointed out that until recently most Harlequin romance novels reinforced female passivity and an equation of male violence with passion. Finally a sociopolitical analysis can look beyond the specific content of the fiction to the role that its production and consumption play in society. Some critics believe that popular fiction is an empty mass diversion—like the Roman "bread and circuses"—that keeps the population quiescent and thus serves the purposes of the conservative groups within society. Of course, not all those who study popular culture agree with this view.

In *Brainchild* Saul portrays the human injustice that is at the heart of the settling of California and, by extension, of all the Western lands that were expropriated by conquest. Conquest always involves a devaluing of the conquered in order to justify the act and a sort of amnesia that settles over the descendants, for whom it is all too easy to forget how the land became theirs. In contrast, the generations of the conquered find it hard to forget their defeat or to swallow their resentment and suspicion.

Unfortunately, the novel only presents the simplest model of the events that overturned the Mexican rule of California and replaced the Spanish-speaking landowners with the Anglo-Saxons. The model is one of injustice and revenge. It applied then and continues to apply throughout the world. We see it played out between Palestine and Israel in the Middle East and between the Moslems and Serbs in the former Yugoslavia. And we see it in this country, where relations between ethnic groups are often strained.

But the formula "injustice breeds revenge" fails to provide a satisfactory understanding of conflict. Generally, each side has its atrocities that it must exact revenge for, and in this way the conflict is indefinitely perpetuated. To understand the forces that create and maintain the conflict, it is necessary to look beyond this simple formula. Is this expecting too much from a thriller, which, after all, is just meant to be read for entertainment? To ask this presumes that we can divide "entertainment" from "serious communication," as though the messages contained in the former are of no importance.

Saul presents only two models of how the children of the vanquished relate to the children of their enemies: remaining unassimilated, clinging to the old ways, and harboring ancient grudges like Maria Torres or superficially accommodating, but remaining fundamentally alienated, like Dr. Raymond Torres. One could argue that because of his assimilation, Dr. Torres poses a greater threat to the dominant social group, since he is prepared to take its advanced technology—in this case, medical technology—and bend it back into a weapon to be turned against that group.

It is unfortunate that Saul did not modify the plot to include another Hispanic character who could have demonstrated an alternative model of remaining faithful to one's ethnic identity without succumbing to hatred. There are individuals both of humble and of exceptional abilities who turn their efforts to goals such as seeking legal or political reforms, assisting other members of their group to advance through self-help, devoting themselves to the protection of the rights of a less fortunate group, or dedicating themselves to conflict resolution and reconciliation in the society. Others may pursue the arts and achieve self-expression through this means. But Saul does not present these alternatives for the reader to become aware of.

California has a history of unfair treatment of the minorities, including not only the Mexicans, but also the Chinese who, at the turn of the century, were denied basic legal protections and were not allowed to bring their wives to this country. And as recently as World War II citizens of Japanese descent were unjustly evacuated from the California seacoasts to detention centers fenced with barbed wire. Many of those detained had their property seized in their absence and were never able to reclaim it.

Despite these historical examples of the dominant Anglo-Saxons imposing their terms on these other groups, there nevertheless continues to be a siege mentality in which some members of the dominant Anglo group feel threatened by the minorities. This was evident in the recent passage of a state law in California banning services to undocumented immigrants, as well as in the continuing clamor to fortify the Mexican border and establish an English-only law that would proclaim English to be the only officially sanctioned language. These same undercurrents of fear and resentment of Hispanics and other immigrants can be seen in Florida and throughout the nation. Extremist political groups, whose mission is to fan the fires of fear and hatred, mail out propaganda promoting unrealistic worries that the Spanish-speaking population intends to take over the Southwest and secede from the United States.

While Saul intends the Torres family's quest for vengeance as an innocent plot device to supply the motive in his tale of terror, the unfortunate fact is that individuals who are susceptible to these extremist political views will read into the plot a confirmation of their most paranoid fears, similar to the way Sax Rohmer's entertaining character, the evil Dr. Fu Manchu, played into nativist paranoia about the Chinese taking over the country, which was termed the Yellow Peril.

Clearly *Brainchild* does not, and was not intended to, articulate a detailed explanation of the interaction of class, ethnicity, and history. The quasi-historical prologue informs the reader that the Torres forebearers were members of an elite social class within Mexican society. It does not make it clear that the Spanish landowners themselves profited from injustices to the peons who labored in the fields to support the owners of the hacienda. Nor is the reader informed that there were Indians who occupied the land before the arrival of the Mexicans. The Torres ancestors were victims, but not innocent victims. They were part of a chain of victimization that has not ended yet.

No group is able to maintain power and privilege indefinitely. Those who are temporarily on top inevitably feel a sense of insecurity together with a sense of superiority. As the United States' position of political and economic leadership in the world begins to slip, most of us are aware of a mood of insecurity in the country. Though innocent of malevolent intent, the novel can be read as playing upon that deep insecurity and not balancing it with some positive suggestion on how reconciliation might be possible.

7

Sleepwalk
(1990)

For the people of Borrego . . . had become slaves to what they had built.

John Saul, *Sleepwalk* (1990)

Sleepwalk was published as a Bantam paperback original in December 1990. John Saul says of this book: "My father was a very strong trade unionist. *Sleepwalk* reflected the fact that my father worked in an oil refinery and my grandfather on my mother's side owned an oil refinery and actually did some wildcatting in that area of New Mexico and Arizona. Plus my own five years of archaeological experience out in that area. *Sleepwalk* is one of my favorite books. I'm really crazy about it. I had a good time with all the elements of that one.

"The religious imagery in *Sleepwalk* is basically my own invention. Since I know a lot about the Pueblo Indians and their mythological structure, I was very careful not to use any of their own myths because that would have been very insulting and offensive. I created my own in the Pueblo tradition, so while mine don't actually exist, they have a certain legitimacy."

PLOT

Sleepwalk is a story of the coming of age of Jed Arnold, how he reconciles his Anglo-Saxon and Native American heritages and almost single-handedly foils an evil corporate scheme for imposing dictatorship on the population.

The story is told primarily from the viewpoints of teenager Jed Arnold and high school teacher Judith Sheffield. Judith quits her teaching job in East Los Angeles because of the violence and gang activity and decides to return to teach at her isolated and peaceful hometown of Borrego, New Mexico. But shortly after she arrives there, the quiet atmosphere is marred by the tragic suicide of teenager Heather Fredericks, who jumps off a cliff.

Near Borrego is a village of Pueblo Indians, the Kokatí; as a child Judith Sheffield was friends with the children of the Kokatí village, or pueblo. And as a teenager she had had a crush on Jed's father, Frank Arnold. Frank had married a Kokatí Indian woman, and Judith used to babysit Jed for them. In the years Judith has been away, Frank's wife hung herself because she felt like an outsider, and Jed has grown into a troubled teenager.

The economy of the town is dominated by the local oil refinery. Judith renews her acquaintance with the Morelands, who own Borrego Oil, and their nephew Greg, to whom she had once been attracted. The Morelands plan to leave him their entire fortune. Greg, a handsome doctor, is around the same age as Judith. He has returned to Borrego to practice medicine and to try to help the teenagers in particular. In addition, he has set up a private sanatarium and hospice for chronic elderly patients on the outskirts of town.

Judith also renews her acquaintance with Frank, who is several years older than she is, and eventually, they will begin having an affair. Jed is angry about his mother's suicide and feels that he does not fit in anywhere because he is a "half-breed." Jed is alienated from his Native American heritage, and Judith persuades him to ride with her up to the Indian pueblo, where Jed joins his grandfather, Brown Eagle, in the kiva, a sacred underground chamber in which the men of the tribe perform religious rituals. Jed goes into a kind of trance while in the kiva. Afterward Brown Eagle reveals he had had vision of the girl who leaped to her death in the canyon. He tells Jed that Heather did not commit suicide; someone made her jump. Because the author gave us a privileged view of the scene, we readers know that Heather committed suicide in a kind of trance while responding to a mysterious voice inside her head, like the teenage girls in *Punish the Sinners*.

Jed's father, Frank, is beginning to notice some strange things going on at Max Moreland's oil refinery, where he works. Frank is president of the union. Max is being bought out by a foreign conglomerate called UniChem. Frank is puzzled that the spare parts he ordered to fix a broken pump have not come in yet and finds out that the suppliers will not deliver them because they say they have not been paid. As we later learn, Otto Kruger, one of the managers at the plant, has cut himself a deal with UniChem. UniChem has guaranteed Otto a good position in return for mismanaging Max's business so it would become unprofitable enough that Max would be forced to sell. Otto sees to it that maintenance on the Company's dam is not carried out so that a crack develops in the structure, which Max cannot afford to repair. This undermines Max's hydroelectric plant, which powers his oil refinery. However, this crack in the dam will later become the undoing of UniChem as well.

After signing the deal with UniChem, Max Moreland suspiciously dies in a one-car auto crash. Frank publicizes his suspicion that Max was murdered to keep him from reneging on the deal. The new owners try to find a way to get rid of Frank, whom they perceive as a troublemaker. To harass him, Frank is ordered to crawl into a narrow tunnel inside the dam to do maintenance. While in the tunnel he is seized with acute claustrophobia and has to be treated by Dr. Greg Moreland, who gives him an injection. Shortly after this Frank begins having uncontrollable seizures, goes into a coma, and dies.

Judith—or Jude, as Jed calls her—has gotten a job teaching in the high school that Jed attends. She is told to have the students bring in permission slips for flu vaccination shots. In talking to a friend of hers who is a physician, Judith learns that there is no reason for the students to be getting vaccinations, since there is no flu epidemic. She becomes suspicious when she sees that the needles and the vaccine have been supplied by UniChem, and that each syringe has a serial number on it, which the nurse records next to the student's name after administering the inoculation. This seems highly irregular, and she warns Jed not to take the shot. She marks his name off on the list and pockets one of the syringes, deciding to send it to her friend Peter Langston, who is a research chemist at the Brandt Institute, a high-tech think tank and laboratory in Los Alamos. While she is waiting to hear from him, she begins noticing that some of the students who received the inoculations are acting peculiarly.

She thinks of them as "sleepwalkers" because they act as if they are in a trance. They only do what they are ordered to, and they follow all directions literally, "like robots" (359).

At this point there are five simultaneous plot strands going: the relationship between Jed and his father, which is marked by increasing conflict and misunderstanding; the beginnings of a positive relationship between Jed and his grandfather, Brown Eagle; the blossoming love interest between Frank and Judith; the unfortunate Heather's mysterious death and the strange things happening with the students at the school; and UniChem's plot for taking over Max's company. Soon these five strands will be condensed into two. Frank will die, which will eliminate the two plot strands concerning his relationship to Judith and to Jed. And it will become apparent that the death of Heather, the zombie-like students at the school, the takeover of the refinery, and the death of Max and Frank are all related. There is a conspiracy afoot, as there was in *The God Project*. UniChem is behind all of these events, and Dr. Greg Moreland really is evil and secretly working with UniChem. So two more plot lines are collapsed into one.

This leaves just two strands to the plot: Jed's relationship to his grandfather, who is initiating him into the spiritual mysteries of the Kokatí religion, and a detection-suspense-action subplot in which Jed and Jude uncover the mystery of what UniChem is doing to the people of Borrego and risk their lives to foil the villains's plans.

Peter Langston, Judith's friend from the research lab, discovers that the syringes contain micromachines that are invisible to the naked eye. They are two microns large, larger than a molecule, but smaller than a bacterium, and have a protein coating that causes them to lodge in the brain. These infinitesimally small manufactured objects can be triggered by a radio signal to burn up, destroying a small portion of brain tissue as they do so. The evil Dr. Greg Moreland has been keeping tabs on Judith and realizes that she must have somehow gotten ahold of a syringe. He has his henchmen kidnap Judith and bring her to the sanatarium, where he injects her with a batch of the micromachines.

He tells her that she will get what he calls a "realignment" in a few hours when the radio signal is transmitted that will trigger the micromachines. He then gives her a lecture justifying what he is doing as being for the good of the nation:

> What we're faced with is economic ruin. . . . America simply can't compete. Our people aren't well enough educated and

they have no self-discipline. . . . It's simply a matter of making some adjustments to the brain. . . . And what we're going to wind up with is a whole population that is going to have powers of concentration such as no one has ever seen before. They're going to be able to take orders from their managers, and then carry out their jobs with so few mistakes that even the Japanese will sit up and take notice. (391–392)

Even as Dr. Moreland is delivering this lecture, groups of workers at the refinery are being sent to get the phony "flu shots." After Moreland leaves, Jed rescues Judith and temporarily disables the radio transmitter whose signal controls the micromachines. But he knows it is only a matter of hours before UniChem repairs the transmitter, and then they will be able to "realign" Judith, even though she has physically escaped from their clutches. He decides to set up a situation where the dam will collapse, flooding the area where the transmitter is located. This is where the crack that the villains created in the structure of the dam becomes their undoing. Jed opens the damaged main shaft to the dam and turns on the turbine, expecting its vibration to widen the existing crack, creating enough further damage to weaken the entire dam to the point of collapse. The dam does indeed collapse, and the entire area is flooded, destroying the refinery, the sanatarium, and the transmitter and killing Moreland and the other villains.

SUSPENSE

Unlike the typical John Saul story, which slowly develops an atmosphere of brooding unease through subtle signs that something is amiss, *Sleepwalk* is like a Hollywood blockbuster action movie, full of confrontations, chases, and hair-raising scenes from the first pages. At the start of the novel the following episodes succeed each other rapidly: There is a prologue in which an elderly woman collapses after having painful and grotesque hallucinations. Then we witness an attempted assault with intent to rape on Judith in her inner-city school, followed by a breathless car chase through East Los Angeles. Then the location shifts to Borrego and an off-road automobile race that ends in one car flipping over, injuring the passengers. Next Heather, an attractive teenager, walks to the edge of a cliff and leaps to her death. Then some friends of hers are startled to find her body in the water where they are swimming. All this in fifty pages.

In Saul's earlier novels the conflicts that drive the novel touch the protagonists personally. For example, in *Punish the Sinners* the protagonist, Peter, wonders if he should stay or leave. The plot owes as much to the protagonist's personal flaws as to the villain's conspiratorial machinations. The hero's inner compulsions repeatedly draw him to the very danger that threatens to consume him.

In contrast to this fated and inward-looking focus on psychological conflicts, we have in *Sleepwalk* a series of external events that the protagonists react to and potential traps they have to escape. It is as though Saul has decided to emulate some of the elements of the Robert Ludlum spy thrillers that he loves so much to read. Except for Frank's attack of claustrophobia at the dam, the protagonists' inner terrors are not activated in any significant way. They do not struggle with the dark side of their own sexual, spiritual, or aggressive impulses, and therefore, as readers, we do not have to struggle with our dark side in empathy.

Even the villain's mind-control method is relatively uninspired, and the motivation behind it is utterly banal. Compare Moreland's project to those of some of Saul's other mad scientist villains. Dr. Hamlin in *The God Project* sought to develop a race of superbeings. Dr. Engersol in *Shadows* wanted to create a half-human, half-machine supercomputer such as had never been imagined before. Dr. Phillips in *Darkness* wanted to live forever. But Dr. Moreland in *Sleepwalker* is only interested in making sure everyone does what they are told to do so that the businessmen can make more money. Hannah Arendt's phrase "the banality of evil" could apply here.

Saul tries to artificially boost the suspense by prodding us with conspicuous little bits of authorial commentary planted near the ends of chapters. For example: "Except that unknown to Judith, there was one person in Borrego who *had* come up with a solution . . . had . . . applied that solution to Heather Fredericks. And by her death had finally proven that the solution worked" (80), which is supposed to make the reader start wondering "Who? What?" Or again: "It no longer made any difference *when* Max had died. The only thing that would make a difference was *how* he had died" (147).

IRONY

Judith Sheffield is a young woman who wants to escape the urban disorder created by wild teenagers. She moves back to her sleepy hometown of Borrego, where there is a secret project to control troublemakers and impose social order through undetected destruction of brain tissue in the target population: rebellious teenagers, trade unionists, women, and ethnic minorities. These organized forces of social "order" present a greater threat to Judith than the anarchic delinquent youth did. The conspirators systematically follow her car, break into her home, and kidnap and attempt to kill her.

Greg Moreland's remote-control lobotomies turn some of Judith's "troublemaker" students into sleepwalking zombies with vacant expressions who do whatever they are told to do. She is quite disturbed by this. The ironic thing is that none of the other teachers notice this as a problem.

CHARACTERS

Jed Arnold is one of the two central protagonists. He is a troubled sixteen-year-old who feels he does not fit in because he is a "half-breed." His mother was a Kokatí Indian who committed suicide four years earlier. Jed feels abandoned by both parents. He feels angry at his mother for not loving him enough to stay alive and angry, too, at his father who is never around—always busy with work or union duties. He feels this contributed to his mother's loneliness. Jed's confused feelings prompt him to engage in typical teenage misbehavior: sneaking out at night, drinking beer, and drag racing his car; he is even thinking of dropping out of school. All of this brings him into further conflict with his father and leads to many bitter exchanges. In the beginning he is alienated from his Native American background. By the end of the story he has fully explored his Indian heritage, has actualized its spiritual dimensions, and has forged a strong relationship to his maternal grandfather. He outlives his father, avenges him, and fulfills his father's quest. And he finds a surrogate mother and friend in the person of Judith. He straddles two worlds—Borrego and the Kokatí pueblo. Far from remaining a misfit or a failure, he becomes instrumental in removing a peril to Borrego and the Kokatí Indian pueblo and to humankind in general.

A critical rite of passage for Jed involves entering the narrow pipe. This was a test that his father was put to earlier in the book in an attempt to force him to quit his job. Unable to master the claustrophobia, his father had lost control of his fear, unleashing a chain of events that quickly led to his death. Later in the book Jed must crawl down the same pipe. It is essential that he not show fear, else the bosses from UniChem will realize that he has not really been transformed into a "sleepwalker." He feels the same rising panic as his father had, but is able to master it by utilizing the mind-control techniques he has learned during mystical out-of-body sessions with his grandfather in the kiva.

Judith is the other protagonist. She is an intelligent and thoughtful young teacher who relates well to the Kokatí Indians. Like Jed, but to a lesser extent, she is able to mediate between the values of the Anglo community and the Indian ways. It is she who prods Jed to get in touch with his cultural heritage and establish a connection with his grandfather, Brown Eagle. Her connections to knowledgeable people outside of Borrego enable her to get the information that convinces her to warn Jed not to take the phony "flu shot" and later to find out about the micro-machines contained in the syringes and what they do to the human brain. She is clever and resourceful, and she thinks on her feet, as when she stole the syringe and altered the records to make it look like Jed got his vaccination. Judith plays an essential role in the story not only in protecting Jed, but also in figuring out what is going on. In the beginning of the story it looks as though she will be presented with a typical Gothic romance choice between two suitors—Greg and Frank—one of whom is actually a villain. However, for some reason Saul never develops the potential love interest with Greg Moreland, even though Judith had a crush on him when she was younger.

Brown Eagle is Jed's grandfather, a Kokatí elder of great spiritual power. He is modeled after someone like the now-deceased Black Elk of the Lakota tribe, whose visions are collected in the book *Black Elk Speaks* (1979). Brown Eagle learns of many things through visions. He opens his grandson's spiritual eye. Although Brown Eagle either cannot or chooses not to directly intervene to halt the evil that is present in Borrego, he is able to guide his grandson to do it. In this respect his role is similar to Clarey Lambert's in *Darkness*.

Frank Arnold is on the side of the protagonists. He is an honest and dedicated union president who enjoys the respect of his boss, Max More-land. Frank tried to bridge the gap between the Native American and Anglo ways when he married Jed's mother, but he was unsuccessful. In the end she killed herself. But Brown Eagle tells Jed not to judge his father harshly for this because Jed's mother was the type of person who did not feel at home anywhere—neither in the Indian world nor in the white world. Frank is a good-hearted man in a gruff way, but has difficulty connecting with his son because his hot temper and Jed's often seem to collide. When Frank panics while crawling through a tunnel in the dam, he puts himself in a situation where he is vulnerable to Greg Moreland's injecting him with the micromachines. Frank is a rough-cut, but likable, character who hangs onto his ideals, but fails to reach his goals.

Max Moreland is the owner of the oil refinery. His name is an allusion to America's westward expansion, which was justified by the doctrine of Manifest Destiny. (Max = maximum, Moreland = more land.) He is an old-fashioned rugged individualist. His oil company embodies his personal achievements and bears the stamp of his unique character. He is representative of the breed that is dying out: a romanticized "old-style" industrial manager, who is patriarchal, but personal, with a sense of loyalty to and responsibility for the workers. Although the refinery is unionized, the labor-management struggles are presented as having always remained within the bounds of civility. He is being forced out by the rising generation of impersonal corporate bureaucrats, who do not value individuality. Max's style is in contrast to UniChem's, which represents late-stage corporate capitalism, dominated by ruthless, faceless transnational cartels. UniChem engages in corporate espionage, sabotage, and disinformation in an effort to gain control of Borrego Oil.

Dr. Greg Moreland is the chief antagonist. At first he appears to be an altruistic young physician. But in fact, he is Saul's usual mad scientist. He is a thoroughly dislikable character. His eyes burn with intensity, and he has no time for attractive women, unless it is to inject them with brain-destroying micromachines. He also delivers speeches similar to those of the political candidates in the last elections about how Americans have gone soft and have to become more disciplined in order to compete with Japan. We can imagine John Saul chuckling as he put this speech in the villainous Dr. Moreland's mouth. In his student days, when he attended four different colleges and never graduated, Saul was undoubtedly lectured many times about the need for greater "self-discipline" if he was ever going to "amount to anything."

Greg Moreland, like Dr. Hamlin of *The God Project*, has giant economic interests backing him. A consortium of corporations is funding the research that Dr. Greg Moreland and UniChem have been carrying out.

Besides having an irritating megalomanical ambition to turn the work-
force into zombie-like slaves, he lacks any sense of personal loyalty. Despite the kindness his Uncle Max and Aunt Rita have shown to him, he
kills Max with micromachines and burns the house down with Aunt Rita
in it. His evil streak seems to have started early. As a youngster he
experimented on his pet puppy, suffocating the animal from curiosity
about how long death would take and about whether he could revive it
afterward. We see here the seed idea that would later be developed, in
Black Lightning, into the character of the Experimenter, who treats his
serial murder career as a research project in which he kills people and
then tries to bring them back to life.

Paul Kendall, Stan Utley, and Otto Kruger are the secondary antagonists who assist Greg Moreland. Kendall is a business executive who
likes the control Moreland's technology will give him. He is utterly ruthless and is prepared to detonate all of the micromachines in order to
cover up what they have been up to, even though that will mean many
of the people will be either killed or severely brain damaged. Utley is a
technician whose moral position is that he is just a technician and has
no responsibility to consider the moral implications of what he is doing.
Kruger is a despicable opportunist who sabotages his boss's company.

THEME

The primary theme of this novel is the negative consequences of technology, an idea that has been explored many times before in *Frankenstein*
(1818), Aldous Huxley's *Brave New World* (1932), Ira Levin's *The Stepford
Wives* (1972), and many other novels. Dr. Moreland, with his fantastic
scheme of worldwide mind control, is an example of technology gone
awry, raised to the level of the absurd. However, this novel does not
limit its criticism to imagining the dangers of technology as practiced by
mad scientists and dictators, but also questions the price that is paid for
the standard technology we have all come to depend upon.

On one of the occasions when Jed goes to visit his grandfather in the
kiva, he has a mystical experience of being lifted on the wings of the
Spirit Eagle Rakantoh, whose home is under the artificial lake created
by the dam. They fly over the oil refinery, and Jed sees it with new eyes:

> Like a hideous pit of vipers, the tangle of blackened pipes
> writhed among themselves, twisting around the furnaces that

glowed with the light of Hell . . . the drilling rigs poised like giant insects sucking the blood from the planet's body. (176)

Jed sees that the refinery, the dam, and the other signs of modern technology are not only wrong, but also "somehow evil." The technology has a spiritual aspect as well as a material one. The sacred Spirit Eagle is unable to reach its traditional home, which is now buried under the artificial lake. The reader is reminded of the bald eagle, which is a symbol of the United States and was on the verge of dying out as a species until strong environmental protection laws were passed to protect our national bird.

Jed contrasts the town of Borrego with its modern conveniences to the Kokatí pueblo, where a centuries-old way of life is still practiced, and decides the people of the town have become slaves to the machinery they have built—machinery that was supposed to have freed them. In fact, humans begin to become like machines under the influence of the machines. Humans must adapt to working artificial swing shifts in factories instead of living and working according to natural biological rhythms in tune with the sun and moon. Data processors sit in cramped positions, twisting their wrists and fingers to adapt to flat keyboards. Eventually, people begin to think of themselves as machines and treat themselves as such, looking to doctors and pharmaceutical companies to provide technological solutions to physical and spiritual problems produced by unnatural styles of living. Dr. Moreland takes this to the ultimate. He speaks of making "adjustments" to the brain, as though it were a piece of machinery, and Judith notes that the students who have been subjected to Moreland's mind control act like "robots." However, this very quality is also the Achilles heel of Moreland's approach.

Because the watchman has also been transformed into a zombie-like robot, Jed will able to gain access to the dam to sabotage it. This episode in the novel is reminiscent of the story—probably apocryphal—of Allied saboteurs during World War II who planted explosive bombs on the German railroad tracks and, to make sure the Nazi guards would not remove them, printed "Do not remove!" on the outside of the bomb case.

To underline the vision of technological hell that Rakantoh has shown him, when Jed arrives at school the next day, the students are receiving the phony inoculations provided by UniChem. Because he has been at the kiva all night, Jed is late for school and therefore misses the shot, and then Judith alters the nurse's records to make it appear that Jed received the vaccination. But symbolically, the reason he escapes the inoculation is because of his connection to his Native American heritage. Since they do not buy into the value of technology, he and Brown Eagle are the only two protagonists who escape the enslaving inoculations.

Other American writers have often romanticized the Indian as a symbol of one who, due to his connection to the sacred wisdom, has the strength to withstand the tyranny of modern life. Ken Kesey did this with the character of the Chief in *One Flew over the Cuckoo's Nest* (1962). The Chief is the only one with the physical strength and psychological fortitude to finally escape from the asylum.

When Judith steals one of the syringes, she sends it to her friend who works at a lab in Los Alamos. Historically, Los Alamos is associated with nuclear weapons testing and development, so this is an indirect reference to another peril of technology—the possibility of apocalyptic mass destruction from the "Bomb." As it turns out, the micromachines that are in the syringe act like bombs on a miniature scale. When detonated, they generate enough heat to destroy brain cells.

Granting Saul's premise—that technology is destructive and ultimately leads to the loss of one's humanity and the consolidation of bureaucratic control over freedom—how can the accelerating pace of technological change be halted? The answer suggested by the novel is that change will come through natural disaster. Whether by accident or by sabotage the accelerating technological forces will generate a disaster that unleashes the elemental cleansing forces of nature.

The machinations of UniChem are destroyed by water. When the dam collapses, the raging floodwaters pour down like the vengeance of the Old Testament God pronouncing judgment on Noah's generation. The floodwaters can also be considered symbolic of the anarchic—potentially revolutionary—mass social forces that are dammed up and held in check by the artifices of the state. The agents of UniChem had undermined the dam by failing to maintain it, as part of their plot to undermine the old order, represented by Max Moreland. Jed is able to capitalize on this and on the unthinking, robot-like nature of the watchman. When he sees the naked power of the water, Jed is in awe at "the sheer magnitude of the fury he had unleashed" (447). Jed realizes he has released something he cannot control, but it is better than the alternative. The terrible, frightening beauty of the flood provokes a religious experience in Jesus Hernandez, one of the workers, who has not been to church for years, but crosses himself and prays when he sees the mighty power of the water, which "scours clean" and "scrapes clean" the canyon, which has been polluted by the technological evil. Rakantoh can now come home to the lake. Balance has been restored to this small section of the land.

A FREUDIAN ANALYSIS OF *SLEEPWALK*

Freudian psychology is what was formerly termed a "depth psychology" because it focuses on the underground wellsprings of the mind underlying the conscious surface. Its founder, Sigmund Freud, influenced a number of other individuals who were important in twentieth-century psychology, notably Carl Jung, who later broke off and founded his own theoretical school. As discussed in Chapter 4, Jung's is the other main form of depth psychology. Jungians focus on the study of religious myths and symbols and unconscious forces called archetypes.

Sigmund Freud was a Viennese physician and neurologist whose career spanned the late nineteenth and early twentieth centuries. He became interested in psychological disorders and was initially influenced by the renowned French physician Charcot, who treated hysterical patients through the induction of hypnotic trance. Freud later abandoned hypnosis and founded a tradition of psychological analysis called, appropriately enough, psychoanalysis, which attempts to uncover unconscious thought processes and bring them into the patient's awareness. Freud tried to track down the hidden, or unconscious, wishes and motives through a sort of psychological detective work. He made a detailed examination of what caused someone to use the wrong word in a "slip of the tongue" and decoded the language of nighttime dreams. He studied the hidden connections between a person's thoughts through a method called "free association," in which the person says everything that comes into his or her mind without censorship.

Freud at times applied his method to the analysis of myths and works of literature and art, and for awhile a school of literary analysis flourished based on Freudian ideas. Freud's central concept was the Oedipus complex, which he named after the Greek tragedy of Oedipus, a child who was abandoned at birth and grows up not knowing his parents. Unwittingly, Oedipus kills his father and marries his widowed mother. When he later discovers what he has done, he blinds himself, and his mother hangs herself.

Freud believed that in early childhood all children have fantasies of becoming love partners of the opposite-sexed parent and in conjunction with these fantasies become rivals of their same-sexed parent, which triggers feelings of fear and hatred. These feelings and desires are quickly abandoned in most children, and all their traces are erased from memory. But the wishes persist in the unconscious and are often partially stirred up by the cataclysmic changes that occur at puberty. Freud was well aware that in some families a parent will violate the norm against incest and thus do spiritual violence to the child. But he felt that unconscious guilt over incestuous wishes was universal and affected even children in families where adults did maintain the proper boundaries on expressing their sexuality to the children.

In the case of male children implicit in the Oedipus complex is the desire to replace the father and obtain all his powers and privileges. According to Freudians, the unconscious persistence of guilt over the childhood Oedipal wishes may contribute to "fear of success," where a son feels anxiety and guilt about becoming more successful than his father. Surpassing the father's achievements can unconsciously be equated with triumphing in the Oedipal rivalry and can therefore stir up tremendous unconscious guilt, according to this line of thinking.

Although *Sleepwalk* presents a number of political, philosophical, and ecological ideas, the basic plot is about a boy supplanting and surpassing his father. There is the basic Oedipal triangle, in which it appears to Jed that his father Frank was unable to provide satisfaction to his mother and therefore she killed herself. Then Judith becomes Frank's lover. This in itself has Oedipal significance, since Frank can be viewed as a kind of secondary father figure to her, due to his age and the fact that she had a crush on him as a teenager. Now that Frank's wife is dead, Judith is free to have an affair with him, which can be regarded as the fulfillment of an Oedipal-type wish on her part. By virtue of her new relationship with Frank, Judith becomes a surrogate mother to Jed, although they are also close enough in age so that they can be friends.

After Frank dies, Jed enjoys an exclusive relationship with Judith, his mother-substitute. Although they do not develop a sexual relationship—that would be too obvious—Jed does become "the man" of the family, rescuing Judith from the villains and destroying their evil machinery. In order to succeed in his contest with the villains he must undergo an ordeal that his father failed. He must crawl through one of the maintenance tunnels in the dam without showing signs of fear.

For the young boy the father represents his primary experience of a powerful male. No matter how little power the father may actually have in the larger society, to the child the father appears tremendously powerful. Like all boys, Jed had ambivalent feelings toward his father. His internal images of his father included both an image of a "good" father, with whom he had had positive experiences, and an image of a "bad" father, who was critical, punitive, and distant. The reason a child feels guilt over the wish to surpass his father is because the defeat of the "bad" father also means wounding the "good" father, since they are really different perceptions or aspects of the same person. With his father's death these "good" and "bad" images of father figures cease to be bound together. For the rest of the story Jed will be free to experience powerful males as unambiguously bad or unambiguously good.

The good father figure is Brown Eagle, his grandfather. Brown Eagle does not represent a threat to Jed's bid for adult power, since Brown Eagle does not directly engage in the arena of action. He operates only on the inner, spiritual planes and limits his role to that of an advisor and guide. The bad father figure includes all the villains, particularly Kendall and Dr. Moreland, who do not want to relinquish any power and who want to keep the entire population in a position of childish obedience to them. By defeating these bad, tyrannical parent substitutes, Jed not only is triumphing in his own Oedipal fantasy, but also becomes a universal hero.

At this point let us examine more closely Jed's rite of passage in the tunnel at the dam, since this is central to his Oedipal triumph. Claustrophobia, fear of enclosed spaces, is a primal terror that was exploited by Poe, primarily in *The Premature Burial* (1844) ("I writhed, and made spasmodic exertions to force open the lid." 1976, 541), but also in "The Cask of Amontillado" (1846), which deals with being immured—sealed permanently in a tiny room—and "The Pit and the Pendulum" (1842), where fiery hot metal walls gradually close in on the narrator, forcing him to the edge of a deep pit.

From a psychoanalytic point of view, as propounded by Freud's protégé and early disciple Otto Rank, our first concrete experience with this fear is during birth, when the newborn is squeezed through the birth canal over a prolonged period and may have to be pried out with forceps. It is debatable whether the infant is capable of feeling fear at that point and how much of the experience can be committed to memory. However, if there is a biological prototype of claustrophobic concerns, this would be the best candidate.

From an emotional point of view, claustrophobia is sometimes associated with close relationships, particularly romantic or sexual intimacy. Clichés such as "I need more breathing room," "Don't be a clinging vine," and "I'm being smothered in this relationship" indicate a fear of psychological engulfment. In this type of relationship there is a fear of losing one's autonomy, identity, and freedom of action, of being hemmed in by invisible walls. But the more the one partner pulls away, the more the other partner feels abandoned and rejected, and either tries to hang on tighter or goes into crisis.

There are some clues in the text that Jed's father was a man who required a lot of autonomy. We see this in Jed's complaint that his father is never around. Jed's mother's suicide may well have partially been a reaction to the emotional distance she felt between herself and Frank. The physical symbolism of being in the tunnel in the dam stirs up Frank's emotional claustrophobia:

> Instantly, the space seemed to shrink around him. . . . The pipe, barely two feet in diameter, forced him to creep along, using only his finger and toes. . . . He felt bands of panic tightening around his chest. . . . *No*, he told himself . . . *the pipe's not getting smaller, and I'm not trapped.* . . . The terror grew. . . . He was going to die here. . . . The pipe was going to crush him. . . . He knew what it would feel like to be buried alive, knew the hopelessness of it. He clawed at the concrete, his fingernails tearing. (216–217)

Later, when Jed enters the tunnel, he begins to experience the same terror as Frank had, but drawing on the spiritual teachings of Brown Eagle, he is able to use his concentration to master his fear of the enclosed space. For him this becomes an initiation into manhood—a second birth. His emergence from the narrow tunnel with the "umbilical cord" of the rope wound around his foot represents a rebirth, symbolically and psychologically. He has succeeded where his father failed.

In the process of avenging Frank's death, Jed has succeeded at every project his father failed in: overcoming claustrophobia, bridging the gap between Indians and whites, and defeating UniChem. And to top it all off, he winds up with his father's girlfriend, but in a non-threatening, sexless relationship that floats in some undefined never-never land between mother-son and boyfriend-girlfriend.

8

Second Child
(1990)

Then her mother gave her a knife and said, "Cut the toe off; when you are a Queen you will have no more need to go on foot."
The Grimm Brothers, "Cinderella" (1972)

Second Child was released in hardcover by Bantam Books in July 1990 and as a paperback in July 1991. It appears to be the last in a cycle of books that began with *Suffer the Children*. Like its predecessors, it features a young girl who comes under the influence of a spirit who was wronged in the previous century. However, it differs in significant ways from the books that preceded it and appears to bring the cycle to completion.

PLOT

Today is Melissa Holloway's thirteenth birthday. She is looking forward to spending the whole day with her father, Charles, as he promised. Then a phone call comes. Charles's other daughter, Teri MacIver, whom he has not seen for several years, has just been orphaned by a fire, which killed her stepfather, Tom, and mother, Polly, Charles's ex-wife. Charles has to break his birthday promise to Melissa because Teri *needs* him right now. He intends to bring her back to their house in Secret Cove to live with himself, his second wife, Phyllis, and Melissa.

Melissa is shown a recent photo of Teri and is a bit taken aback. She had not realized her stepsister was so beautiful. Her hair is so nicely done, and her clothes look good on her, too—just the opposite of Melissa, who is good-hearted, but a bit of an ugly duckling. A wave of insecurity sweeps over Melissa, but then she decides optimistically that Teri will be able to show her how to fix her hair and give her tips on how to pick out clothes.

Since Melissa is not going to get to spend the day with her father, her mother, Phyllis, throws an impromptu birthday party and calls the women she knows from the exclusive Cove Club. They send over a group of their sons and daughters, who arrive dressed in tennis whites, making Melissa look out of place in her formal pink organdy dress. Her guests snub her for most of the party, and then she overhears one of the girls complaining to another that her mother forced her to go to this "mercy party" just to placate Melissa's mother. Her feelings wounded, fighting back tears, Melissa tells the two girls they are free to leave and she had not wanted them to come in the first place.

Melissa's mother, Phyllis Holloway—who is hyperconcerned about her standing with the Cove Club clique—becomes furious when she finds out that Melissa has been "rude" to the guests, as she inaccurately puts it. It was the guests who had been rude to Melissa. Flying into a blind rage, Phyllis rips Melissa's organdy dress asunder and then tells her to mend it by morning.

Meanwhile Charles has flown out to Los Angeles to get Teri. She is feeling insecure, wondering whether Charles loves her. He is puzzled by this question and startled by Teri's statement that his recently deceased ex-wife never showed her the letters and gifts he had sent her. Last year Charles gave a string of pink pearls to Melissa and sent a matching string to Teri, but she never received it. According to Teri, Polly tried to convince her that Charles loved only Melissa now. Charles is very upset by this revelation; he never realized his ex-wife despised him so much that she would try to drive a wedge between him and his daughter.

When Teri arrives, Phyllis is very happy to see her, thinking that with her good looks and social graces and her blue-blood descent, Teri will be an asset in Phyllis's drive to win full social acceptance by the Cove Club clique. Melissa, too, is affectionate with Teri, who seems to reciprocate. But when no one is looking, the reader sees Teri pull a strand of perfectly matched pink pearls from her pocket—the pearls she told her father she had never received. And we realize that Teri is not really what she seems to be. Although the characters do not know it yet, Teri has some scheme, and from now on the reader will not be able to take anything she says or does at face value.

In this way by Chapter 6 the basic plot structure has been laid out for the reader. One strand involves Teri's jealousy of Melissa. Teri desires to be the exclusive recipient of the privileges of being Charles Holloway's daughter. She devises a plan to make Melissa look insane so that she will be sent to an asylum. In the process Teri will murder someone, and Melissa will be blamed—shades of *Suffer the Children*. The second plot strand involves the neurotically driven social climber Phyllis Holloway. She is a psychologically and physically abusive mother—shades of *When the Wind Blows*. She always wanted a child like fair-haired Teri, not ugly duckling Melissa. As Teri's scheme unfolds, Phyllis can be counted on to view everything Melissa does in the worst possible light. The third strand involves Charles, who loves and appreciates the qualities in Melissa that Phyllis rejects—qualities that his first wife, Polly, had. But Charles also loves Teri and feels torn between them at times. Gradually, Charles will become aware of how abusive Phyllis is when he is away on business, and he will have to deal with that, too. There is a fourth plot strand that involves what the family calls Melissa's imaginary friend. Actually, it is the spirit of a servant girl, D'Arcy, whom Melissa is able to summon and who—like an alternate personality—takes possession of Melissa at times of danger, especially when Phyllis is lashing out at her.

The device of providing the reader with privileged information as to Teri's duplicity helps to build up suspense. We begin trying to anticipate what Teri is up to. Mentally the reader is warning Melissa, "Be careful! Be careful!" Teri insists that Melissa accompany her with some of the other teenagers on a boat ride, even though Melissa confides that she gets seasick easily. When she vomits all over the cabin, the boy whose boat it is says mean things to Melissa, who in turn tells the lot of them that she hates them and wishes they would all die.

Teri begins her campaign against Melissa in earnest by strangling the dog Blackie and hanging him from a rafter in the attic. Melissa is awakened by footsteps and goes upstairs to investigate. She begins screaming when she sees the dead dog hanging there with her pink pearls wrapped around its neck. While Melissa runs into her mother's bedroom, Teri hides the dog's body, so that when Phyllis goes to the attic, it appears to her that Melissa imagined or made up the whole thing.

Next Teri persuades Melissa to masquerade as D'Arcy for the costume party at the Cove Club. Teri is going as a fairy godmother. When Melissa

sees herself in the mirror, transformed by the makeup and wig into the
semblance of D'Arcy, a strange feeling comes over her, and she actually
becomes D'Arcy, who takes possession of her body and begins walking
down the road toward the ball. Jeff Barnstable, one of the boys Melissa
wished dead, drives up behind her and honks his horn to startle her.
When she turns around, he sees the face of the ghost, D'Arcy, in the
headlights and is so startled that he crashes the car over the cliff and
dies.

Finally Tag, the housekeeper's grandson, discovers that Teri killed
Blackie, so Teri smashes him on the head with a shovel and then finishes
him off with a machete. By the time the police arrive, Melissa has gone
into a self-protective trance in which only D'Arcy's personality is active.
Concluding that Melissa killed Tag, and that she is insane, the authorities
send her to a mental hospital.

Melissa sits in a blank, unresponsive state for days. On the night of
the August Moon Ball—when legend says D'Arcy will take her revenge—all the blank spaces in Melissa's memory are suddenly filled in.
She integrates the remembrances of what Phyllis and Teri had done to
her each time D'Arcy's personality had taken over her consciousness.
The moment that these memories return to Melissa is the same moment
that Teri, back at the house, kills herself. Teri has a vision of the veiled
D'Arcy pointing her handless arm accusingly at her. The faces of all the
people Teri killed or hurt flashes across the spectre's veil. Seized with a
terrible guilt, Teri hangs herself. But first she chops off her left hand,
and Charles finds the severed hand on his pillow holding the strand of
pink pearls.

IRONY

Phyllis is constantly getting furious at Melissa for the very faults that
actually reflect Phyllis's own failings. For example, when she finds Melissa's pink organdy dress on the closet floor, she flies into a rage. "Is this
the way you treat your clothes?" (31) Phyllis demands, and then she
deliberately rips the dress in pieces and slaps her daughter. The juxta-
position of Phyllis's concern that the dress is not on a hanger, followed
by her wanton destruction of the dress, is so absurd that it would be
humorous if it were not so horrifying.

As we have seen, Phyllis is not accepted by the Secret Cove social elite.

She is constantly blaming Melissa for this. As readers, we are aware that Phyllis has the habit of transferring the blame for her failings. So it strikes us as ironic when she unjustly accuses Melissa of her own trait. When Melissa complains that Teri deliberately set her up for embarrassment in front of her peers, Phyllis shouts at Melissa: "Stop trying to blame Teri! . . . I won't have you blaming anyone else for your own failings!" (207).

At the very end of the novel Charles has divorced Phyllis and has made her agree to stay away from the East Coast unless she wants to be charged with child abuse. Phyllis has gotten a job as a live-in nanny for a lawyer and his young wife. The baby she is in charge of—a brown-eyed little creature, like Melissa—starts crying when Phyllis picks her up. The mother anxiously reaches for the baby, but Phyllis shakes her head. She tells her not to worry and adds some words that are supposed to be reassuring, but that the reader will find ironically chilling: "I'll treat her just as if she were my own" (355).

Horror writers often have to defend themselves against the charge that the images in their stories deprave people's minds. The following scene in the novel may be the author's way of having fun with that criticism: Charles and Teri go to see a horror movie. Charles comments that cutting people up with machetes is not his "cup of tea," but that Teri "loved every minute of it" (116). A few days later Teri kills Tag with a machete, but not because she was inspired by a movie.

There is a second piece of dark humor in this scene. Phyllis tells Charles she is glad she did not let Melissa go with them because "She'd have had nightmares for a month" (116). But the fact is that while Teri and Charles were watching victims get cut up at the movie, Phyllis had been doing some cutting up in real life—chopping off hanks of hair from the head of the petrified Melissa and then cutting up some of her clothes. The nightmare a mere movie could have given her would be preferable to the nightmares from enduring these real-life horrors.

A possible inside joke concerns the "hundred year old curse," represented in this novel by D'Arcy. One hundred years has been the standard length for curses in many of Saul's earlier novels, including *Suffer the Children*, *Comes the Blind Fury*, *Nathaniel*, and *Brainchild*. When John Saul was younger, one of his relatives liked to use the aphorism "A hundred years from now what difference will it make?" These novels may be gently poking fun at this pet saying because in each of them events from a hundred years ago have the power to cause doom and destruction.

CHARACTERS

Melissa Holloway is a girl who has just reached thirteen—which turns out to be a rather unlucky age for her. She is going through an awkward period of her life. Physically she is rather graceless, and socially she is shy and insecure and does not mingle easily. In short, she possesses none of the qualities that Phyllis admires. And Phyllis's constant criticism of her only makes her more self-conscious and insecure. In some ways Polly MacIver would have been a better match as a mother for Melissa, since they shared a distaste for the superficial social whirl of the Cove Club. Melissa is very sweet and honest, but she lacks a certain spunkiness that would make her a more rounded person. She has a tendency to give up, feeling it is "better not to try at all" (76). She is dominated by Phyllis, who can be quite scary. When Phyllis frightens her, Melissa runs away inside herself, letting the personality of D'Arcy come to the fore. After Teri appears on the scene, Melissa makes some tentative changes. Teri picks out clothes for her and shows her how to use makeup. She also puts Melissa in a situation where she expresses her anger for the first time, telling some of her snobbish peers that she hates them and wishes them dead. Melissa's allies include her father, Charles; Cora, the housekeeper, and her grandson, Tag; and D'Arcy, the ghost.

Charles Holloway, Melissa and Teri's father, is a wealthy attorney who was born into riches. His name might be a pun: Hollow Way, signifying the superficiality of the mannered and insular upper-class way of life at Secret Cove. Charles has two tendencies in his personality, which are symbolized by his two daughters—a comfortableness with the conventions of the lifestyles of the rich, represented by Teri, and a boredom with the whole thing and a yearning for simplicity and sincerity, represented by Melissa. Charles can be contrasted to Jack Conger, the aristocratic father in *Suffer the Children*. Jack was a complex character with a dark side; his deficiencies as a husband contributed to the failings of his wife, Rose, as a mother. In contrast, Charles Holloway, in *Second Child*, is presented in a much more idealized manner. He is not shown to contribute in any way to Phyllis's villainy. He is like the good king in a fairy tale, while she is the evil minister who tyrannizes the people during the king's absence. True, Charles's frequent absences on business trips give Phyllis an opportunity to vent her abuse on Melissa unobserved, but who can fault Charles for having to attend to his business affairs? When he is around, he is most attentive to Melissa and is very protective of her. Since Melissa is a rather clumsy and uncoordinated tennis player, Charles deliberately misses balls in order to make the game more even. And when he learns that Phyllis has been tying Melissa to her bed at night with wrist and ankle restraints—so that she cannot sleepwalk—he becomes quite angry and orders the restraints to be removed from the house immediately.

There is one dissenting voice from this unblemished picture of Charles. It comes from the novel's psychiatrist, Dr. Andrews. (What would a John Saul novel be without a misguided psychiatrist?) The good doctor believes the root of Melissa's problems is that Charles overprotects her because of guilt over giving up his first child, Teri. According to Dr. Andrews, because Charles indulges Melissa, Phyllis becomes cast as the disciplinarian, and Melissa gets "mixed messages," causing her to become confused. Like most of Saul's psychotherapists, his theory sounds good, but does not fit the facts.

Tag and Cora are Melissa's friends. Cora was the housekeeper when Charles was a boy, and he has kept her on, although now she has to work under Phyllis's imperious eye. Cora loves Melissa and never believes she is guilty, even when the evidence is stacked against her. She sees through Teri early on, since Teri is one of those who feels free to show her less attractive side in front of the servants. Tag is Cora's freckle-faced grandson and Melissa's playmate. Phyllis discourages Melissa's familiarity with a servant boy—even though he is her only friend. But Charles says he would rather see her marry Tag than a wealthy boy without character. Teri murders Tag after he discovers that she killed Blackie.

D'Arcy Malloy is unique among Saul's ghosts in that she is a benevolent being. She is a protector for Melissa—a sort of fairy godmother, but without the magic powers to materialize fine clothes and such. After Phyllis deliberately rips the pink organdy dress and then tells Melissa to repair it, D'Arcy takes possession of Melissa's body. She works through the night sewing the torn seams, like one of the shoemaker's elves in the Brothers Grimm fairy tale, so that when Melissa wakes in the morning, the dress is magically repaired.

D'Arcy lived in the prior century, and she disappeared exactly one hundred years ago, on the night of the August Moon Ball after she was jilted by her Prince Charming, Joshua. He was a boy from a wealthy family who had promised to marry her and to announce their engagement at the ball. D'Arcy's faith in the power of true love is dashed when the boy decides to break it off with her rather than get disinherited by his parents. He asks for his ring back. Unable to get if off her finger, she grabs a meat cleaver from the kitchen, chops her hand off at the wrist, and flings it at him before the horrified onlookers. His shirt stained with her blood, he gapes at her as she runs off, never to be seen again. Since this is the hundredth anniversary of the ball, the legend is that she will come back this year to get her revenge.

D'Arcy never directly harms anyone. But she does act as the voice of Teri's conscience—somewhat like the ghosts in Dickens's Christmas tale—and after Teri sees her soul reflected in the mirror of D'Arcy's accusing gesture, she hangs herself in guilty despair.

Teri MacIver, Melissa's antagonist, is an angelic-looking blonde whose exterior hides a ruthless heart. Despite her smile, her sky-blue eyes betray an "emotionless chill" (64). She is not entirely lacking a conscience, since she is plagued by bad dreams of the fire and of her murdered mother coming back to life and asking "Why did you do this?" (90). But she has managed to pretty well submerge her conscience by pretending to herself that the memories of these bad things are not real.

Teri knows how to manipulate male egos by playing the damsel in distress and turning it to her advantage. She set fire to her own house in Los Angeles in the hopes it would make her father come to rescue her. And shortly after arriving in Secret Cove she pretends to be drowning as a way to meet Brett Van Arsdale (a name that suggests sexiness and class), who swims out to rescue her. She later admits to Melissa that it was just a ruse. Melissa's reaction is a naive and scrupulous one: "But that's like lying, isn't it?" Teri's reply is "If it works, do it" (75). Teri figures out the role that D'Arcy plays in Melissa's life, learns how to communicate with D'Arcy, and tricks the spirit into helping fulfill her spiteful scheme.

Teri is intelligent and creative and displays some genuinely likable qualities at times. She makes up volleyball rules that are to Melissa's advantage: Whenever a team scores, whoever scored that point has to drop out. As a result, everyone has to try to play badly. Finally only two players are left, Melissa and a boy from the other team. "In the end, when Melissa finally managed to get the ball over the net, and Jerry . . . missed it entirely, everyone, including she and Jerry, were laughing so hard that no one cared who had won" (122). When Teri does nice things like this, the reader would like to believe that she has abandoned her cruel plan to get rid of Melissa, but it is not so.

Melissa's other antagonist is her mother. Phyllis Holloway was Teri's nurse—or nanny—before Charles and Polly divorced. There is an implication that she did everything in her power to speed the breakup of the marriage. She is an ambitious social climber who scorns her own humble origins as a Pennsylvania farm girl and feels insecure about her status, even as she puts on grand airs. Her style is completely out of synch with that of the Cove Club in-crowd she seeks to emulate, and she is constantly grating on their nerves. She would be a pitiable figure if she did not take her frustration out on Melissa so much. She sees in Melissa's graceless behavior the secret self she refuses to accept and feels the reason the smart set does not accept her is on account of Melissa's failings. Thus, Melissa becomes the whipping boy (or girl, in this case) whenever Phyllis's ego smarts from feeling socially slighted. At the end of the novel we see Phyllis about to fasten her claws into some new, unsuspecting couple, like one of those evil fairies that steals newborn children.

Blackie, the dog, is Tag's pet, whom Teri deliberately kills early in the novel. Blackie is one of a long line of pet murder victims in Saul's stories, beginning with Cecil, the cat in *Suffer the Children*, and continuing with Hayburner, the horse in *When the Wind Blows*, and Patches, the horse in *Hellfire*. Blackie and Teri are at odds from the beginning of the novel. Not one to be fooled by appearances, Blackie growls whenever he sees her, displaying the sixth sense that also distinguished Shadow, the dog in *Nathaniel*; Greta, the horse in *The Homing*; and Sumi, the cat in *The Unloved*.

THEMES

There are two significant themes in *Second Child*. One is the playful allusions to the Cinderella motif. The second is an affirmation that facing one's problems can lead to maturity and real inner growth.

As Bruno Bettelheim writes in *The Uses of Enchantment*, " 'Cinderella' tells about the agonies of sibling rivalry, of wishes coming true, of the humble being elevated, of true merit being recognized even when hidden under rags, of virtue rewarded and evil punished" (1976, 239). *Second Child* does something interesting with the fairy tale by giving the reader four variant Cinderella characters: D'Arcy, Phyllis, Melissa, and Teri.

Phyllis, Melissa, and Teri all feel, like Cinderella, that they are being treated unfairly. Melissa thinks it is not fair that her mother blames her for everything. Phyllis thinks it is unfair that the club women will not accept her. Teri thinks it is not fair that she will not get invited to parties because no one wants Melissa to tag along with her. And D'Arcy was clearly treated unfairly by her fiance.

Like Stephen King's *Carrie*, D'Arcy's sad tale is a kind of *negative* Cinderella story, in which all of her plans to live happily ever after with the prince are overturned at the ball. But rather than being embittered, she becomes the protector of the abused, almost like a fairy godmother.

Phyllis's tale also shows a Cinderella element, since she went from being a servant to being the bride of the ruler of the castle. But despite her good fortune, she fills out the role of the wicked stepmother. Even though Melissa is her daughter, she really treats her like a stepdaughter and thinks of Teri as her own child. Melissa is clearly a Cinderella because she has a cold, wicked mother and a jealous, evil half-sister, and as a punishment she is made to wash the dishes by hand and scrub the floors. She spends most of her time with the servants, Cora and Tag, because she feels most at home there. But like Cinderella, by the end of the novel she has become the center of attention at the ball. Teri, too, is a Cinderella figure, but to understand how, we must look at the variants of the fairy tale.

Fairy tales are one of the first forms of popular culture. According to Bettelheim (1976), the original written version of "Cinderella" dates from 900 A.D. in China, but its origins as an orally transmitted folktale are much earlier. It is one of the most popular and most widely disseminated fairy tales, with over 345 variant versions found in many ethnic cultures throughout Asia, Africa, and Europe. The version best known in the United States is the one recorded in France by Charles Perrault in the seventeenth century. However, there are many older stories that are recognizably part of the "Cinderella" cycle, but that differ in significant details.

In a very old Italian version Cinderella (named Zezolla in the story) murders her mother, who is then replaced by the governess as the father's bride. Both these elements appear in *Second Child* in relation to Teri, who is one of the Cinderella figures in the novel. Teri kills Polly, her mother, through the fire, and Phyllis, her former nanny, becomes her stepmother.

A slipper generally plays a significant role in the Cinderella story, reflecting its origins in China, where the size of a woman's feet was an important aspect of her attractiveness. However, there are variants in which a ring takes the slipper's place. In Saul's story the diamond engagement ring figures strongly in the tale of D'Arcy as Cinderella. D'Arcy is given the ring by her "prince," and it fits so well she cannot get it off, so she finally chops her hand off with a cleaver. This gory act finds echoes in The Brothers Grimm version of the fairy tale, in which the slipper becomes filled with blood after one of the stepsisters cuts off her toe trying to make her foot fit; later she is punished by pigeons pecking out her eyes.

The other important theme in *Second Child* is an affirmation of the human potential to surmount a traumatic history and turn it into a source of strength. The conclusion of the novel shows that it is possible for someone who was previously a victimized teenager to mature and achieve not only serenity, but also "depth and wisdom" (352). This is what the inhabitants of Secret Cove see in Melissa's dark brown eyes when she returns to the Cove Club to dance at the August Moon Ball with her father on her eighteenth birthday.

The significance of Melissa's triumph is enhanced by appreciating its uniqueness in the cycle of similar stories authored by John Saul. For example, compare the first work in the series, *Suffer the Children*. In both books we see two sisters: an angelic blue-eyed blonde whose radiant appearance conceals an inner darkness and a dark-eyed brunette who becomes mute and takes the blame for the unspeakable deeds of the other. In both novels the parents have a troubled marriage, and the mother dislikes her husband's interest in his daughter. But despite these similarities in the basic structure of the plot, the resolution is so different. In *Suffer the Children* the ending is nihilistic. The dark-eyed girl goes mad, and her sister and both parents commit suicide. But in *Second Child* the resolution is that the guilty sister commits suicide, the father divorces and expels the abusive mother, and the dark-eyed innocent and her father live happily ever after.

The banner that announces the theme of the ball, "Full Circle, Back To Our Beginnings" (339), at the end of *Second Child* could equally well describe the role of this novel in John Saul's body of work. *Second Child* is a return to the beginning. It is the final book in a cycle of supernatural-revenge stories featuring a young girl possessed by an ancient spirit. As the final book, it brings a resolution and a sense of completion that were missing from the other novels. In *Second Child* for the first time a heroine is able to master the past, so that when she revisits the scene where the horror occurred, she is not retraumatized. She can experience the memories while appreciating that they belong to a past that is "dead and buried" (351). The reader who has followed Saul's writing career through all the twists on the basic tale, beginning with *Suffer the Children*, through *Comes the Blind Fury*, *When the Wind Blows*, *Hellfire*, and *The Unloved*, and finally to *Second Child*, can at last feel that all the variants of the night-mare have been played out and can now sigh with relief and say with Melissa Holloway: "The past is the past and all the ghosts are gone" (352).

A FREUDIAN READING OF *SECOND CHILD*

The fundamentals of a Freudian literary analysis were discussed in Chapter 7. As mentioned, Freud studied folktales, fairy tales, and modern literature to uncover hidden meanings. The primary among these, for Freud, was the set of unconscious incestuous wishes he called the Oedipus complex. As in dreams, these unconscious ideas are not communicated according to the laws of normal waking logic. Thus, in *Sleepwalk* we saw how the father figure could be simultaneously represented by a multiplicity of characters. Analogously, in *Second Child* we shall see that the daughter figure is represented by more than one character.

Second Child can be viewed as a type of fairy tale—a Cinderella story, in fact. In the modern versions of *Cinderella* much is made of the sibling rivalry motif. But in the older versions the conflict is primarily between Cinderella and her mother. As Bruno Bettelheim points out in his book on fairy tales *The Uses of Enchantment* (1976), Cinderella experiences her mother as punitive because she has wronged the mother in some important way. In the Freudian way of looking at the world Cinderella wrongs the mother by desiring to replace her in the father's heart. Cinderella's forbidden wishes are hidden beneath her image of innocent victim. But in *Second Child* Cinderella's dark side is represented by her evil half-sister, Teri.

Teri is the double, or dopplegänger, of Melissa. The double is an age-old literary device that can be found in the works of such writers as Dostoyevsky, E.T.A. Hoffman, and Edgar Allan Poe. A double is more than an alternate personality; it is an alternate physical manifestation of the person. A Jungian might call it the shadow (see Chapter 4). This relationship between Teri and Melissa is symbolized by the arrangement of their rooms, which are connected by a passageway, so that "You can get into my room without ever going into the hall . . . we can sneak back and forth without Mom and Dad ever knowing" (63).

The use of rooms of a house as a metaphor for alternate personalities or alternate identities is hinted at in the first chapter of the novel, where Melissa thinks that she will have to give up both D'Arcy and her Victorian dollhouse now that she has turned thirteen. The dollhouse is so big that when she was younger, she had actually been able to crawl inside it. And it is filled with perfect miniature furniture replicas. The dollhouse, then, is a microcosm that reflects the larger world. It is a metaphor for Melissa's mind. In the novel the author adds the unnecessary detail that Melissa could actually move around inside this microcosm. This symbolizes the personality's ability to migrate to different "rooms" or spaces in the mind, to let another personality take over. The linking of the dollhouse with D'Arcy subliminally underlines the association of the dollhouse with the mind's potential to generate multiple identities.

Psychologists have observed that many individuals with multiple personalities spontaneously use the metaphor of multiple rooms to symbolize their different states of consciousness:

> An associated feature of the identity confusion and identity alteration associated with Dissociative Identity Disorder [another name for Multiple Personality Disorder] is the feeling that different parts of one's brain contain different personality states and/or personalities. Patients may report an internal architecture inhabited by alternate personalities, as in the following example: 'All of the parts inside of me have rooms. Every room is different. My room is at the far end and there's more space between my door and the door next to me. Diana's room has walls made out of mahogany.' " (Steinberg 1994, 81)

When Teri moves into room that adjoins Melissa's and is connected by the private passageway, the microcosmic metaphor of the dollhouse is lifted to a macrocosmic level. The two rooms in which "Teri" and "Melissa" can secretly exchange places correspond to the hidden connection between them and the secret of their shared identity.

What evidence is there that Teri is Melissa's double? The most striking piece of evidence is that all of Melissa's missing memories return to her the moment that Teri dies. The only logical meaning of this is that Teri represented some alienated aspect of her self that Melissa has now succeeded in absorbing into her core personality.

Other evidence includes all the parallels between the two girls. They have identical pink pearl necklaces. Teri admits that she, like Melissa, once had an imaginary friend. Melissa and Teri are the only two characters who can perceive D'Arcy. Both are able to get D'Arcy to help

them. Both, at different points, masquerade as D'Arcy. And it is significant that Teri begins the killings at Secret Cove only after Melissa first
releases her own fury. On that occasion Tag encouraged Melissa to vent
her anger by hacking away at overgrown vines with the machete. She
imagines to herself that she is hacking at her mother, and as the words
"I hate you!" spontaneously emerge from her lips, "her pent-up fury
raged like a torrent" (160). It is shortly after this that Teri strangles
Blackie and hacks Tag to death with machete blows. The only other
occasion when Melissa vents her fury is on the boat, where she tells her
tormentors, "I hate all of you, and I hope you all die!" (199). Soon afterward one of them, Jeff Barnstable, drives over a cliff.

   Also, there is the constant use of mirror imagery in connection with
Teri and Melissa. Mirrors multiply the self, creating illusory second
selves that appear to possess a separate existence, which is in reality
false. Many people have had the experience of unexpectedly coming
upon a wall-sized mirror and not realizing at first that the person approaching them is their mirror image. Mirrors also reverse the image of
the self. Metaphorically, one could say that Teri is the mirror image of
Melissa. Teri's outward beauty and inner deviousness form the flip image of Melissa, whose exterior is dowdy, but who inwardly is affectionate and sincere.

   The appearance of Teri in the plot opens with a mirror and closes with
a mirror. When Melissa first gets the news that Teri is coming, she looks
at a photograph of Teri, and then "almost against her will" her eyes go
to the mirror over the mantelpiece (19). And at the end, when D'Arcy
appears to Teri to confront her with her evil deeds, Teri is looking into
a mirror. In between there are several other scenes of Teri and Melissa
with mirrors. The most evocative one follows:

   Now, as she gazed at Melissa's reflected image in the mirror,
   she smiled gently. . . . "I'll tell you what. . . . We'll tell her it
   was all my idea, and then she can't get mad at you, can she?"
   In the mirror, Melissa's eyes met Teri's. "Would you really do
   that?" (119)

If you remove the names from this passage and substitute appropriate
feminine pronouns, this sounds like someone talking to *herself* as she
looks into the mirror.

   From this perspective the novel describes Melissa's spiritual journey
toward the wholeness of her true self. In this reading Teri is a partial

aspect of Melissa, just as the figures in one's dreams are psychological fragments of the dreamer's self. Melissa is incomplete as a withdrawn, insecure girl who is paralyzed by fear of failure. Teri is incomplete as a self-confident, assertive, but heartless, person. To become a complete and whole person, the two personalities must be integrated.

This is marked at the end of the novel by Melissa's arrival at the August Moon Ball. August marks the transition from the astrological sign Leo to the sign Virgo. The symbols for these signs are the Lion and the Virgin. The combination of these two creates the figure of the Egyptian Sphinx, with the body of a lion and the face of a woman. The Sphinx is the symbol of initiation, of transition to adult life. Melissa has made that transition. She is clad in a "deep red dress that complemented her coloring perfectly and accentuated her figure to her best advantage" (352).

Red is a sensual color, and this description of Melissa's attire suggests mature, integrated sexuality. It contrasts to the virginal white dress she wore to the costume party, or the bloodstained white dress she had on later.

For Freudians the hallmark of entering adulthood and mature sexuality is the renouncing of the Oedipal wishes that have been stirred up again in adolescence. This giving up of the wish to possess the father is symbolized by the bloody severed hand on Charles's pillow, holding the pink pearls. The hand, being on the bed, suggests a sexual theme, particularly in conjunction with the blood, which can indicate menstruation or the bleeding accompanying loss of virginity. The severed hand on Charles's pillow is thus the equivalent of the severed hand D'Arcy threw at her fiance, Joshua, when they broke off their engagement. That hand was wearing the ring Joshua had given her; this one is holding the pearls Charles had given Melissa—for Teri secretly switched their pearls.

The death of Melissa's double, Teri, represents her integrating into herself the good aspects of her shadow's strengths, and the cutting off of the hand symbolizes the renunciation of her childhood Oedipal infatuation with her father. In this way at the end of the dream that is *Second Child*, which in turn is the last of a series of fictional dreams, Melissa, as the culmination of all the earlier John Saul heroines, finally finds integration and maturity.

9

Darkness
(1991)

Lying on the floor was a dead man. . . . He was withered, wrinkled, and loathsome of visage. It was not till they had examined the rings that they recognized who it was.

Oscar Wilde, *The Picture of Dorian Gray* (1891)

Darkness was published as a Bantam hardcover in July 1991 and released in the paperback edition in June 1992. Like the preceding novels *The God Project, Brainchild, Creature*, and *Sleepwalk*, it is a "techno-thriller" with science-fictional elements. However, as usual Saul includes some supernatural trappings in order to keep a foothold in the horror genre.

PLOT

Like *The God Project*, this is a novel about a conspiracy. All of the plot strands in the novel interlock to serve one end—the unravelling of this conspiracy and the destruction of the evil empire of the Dark Man, who goes about the swamp at night stealing babies. One strand concerns illiterate swamp dweller Amelie Coulton and her determination to protect her baby from the Dark Man's clutches, even though this leads to her husband's being murdered. Another strand concerns the ancient telepathic crone Clarey Lambert, who stubbornly hangs onto life until the day she can witness the end of the Dark Man's reign. Another concerns the new police chief, Tim Kitteridge, who is pursuing a murder investigation that could lead him to discover the existence of the Dark Man. Another concerns the built-in flaw in the Dark Man's pyramid of power that causes it all to begin to collapse. Another plot strand—and this is the central one because it intersects with all the others—is the story of Michael Sheffield and Kelly Anderson's friendship and how they empower each other by recognizing a commonality of experience that dissolves their sense of individual freakishness and enables them to act upon the knowledge that Clarey Lambert imparts to them. A final plot strand has to do with Barbara Sheffield, Michael's adoptive mother, who begins to intuitively piece things together and, with the help of Amelie Coulton, realizes that Kelly Anderson is really her lost daughter, Sharon, whom she had thought died at childbirth. As all these plot strands interweave, accelerate, and come together at the end, the town becomes aware of the gigantic crime perpetrated by the Dark Man, known to them as Dr. Phillips, and by certain "leading citizens" who conspired with him. But the ones who truly put an end to the Dark Man are the children of the swamp, led by Michael Sheffield, who is revealed to be the biological son of the Dark Man.

The novel opens with a scene that looks like some kind of diabolical infant sacrifice. Hidden in the swamp Amelie Coulton witnesses a semicircle of dark figures on a small island, gathered around an altar ablaze with candles. A couple place their newborn infant on the altar. A terrifying figure "shrouded in black" with his face obscured by a veil steps forward saying, "Give me what is mine!" (4). He holds some type of sharp metal instrument and plunges it into the screaming child's chest. This is the cult of the Dark Man, which has kept the superstitious swamp dwellers in fear for decades.

Eventually, we learn that these supernatural trappings are just playacting designed to keep the superstitious swamp people in check. And the baby was not killed; the instrument plunged into its chest was a hypodermic needle. The Dark Man is really Dr. Warren Phillips, who has been performing secret scientific experiments, trying to find the secret of rejuvenation. He has discovered it in the vital fluids produced by the thymus, a gland that is quite large in newborns and gradually shrinks as they age. He has gotten his own little herd of babies from the swamp, and he markets their vital fluids to a select clientele in Villejeune, the town neighboring the swamp. He gets the babies and drains off the fluids from their thymus gland for the first few weeks of life; then he milks the gland periodically through the rest of their childhood. He refines the extract down to the concentrated essence and injects this into the patients able to pay the price for eternal youth. As for the children, they are indoctrinated in his cult, for which he has developed spurious rituals. The children develop a kind of apathetic, emotionless quality after they lose their vital essence, and the cult seems to fill a void in their lives. Also, they develop some sixth sense, as though in compensation for what they have lost. This sixth sense enables Clarey Lambert, the oldest of the "children," to call them telepathically.

In addition to the children he gets from the swamp, Phillips sometimes steals those born in the town by giving the newborn babies a drug so it appears they are dead. Then in collusion with the coroner and the undertaker—both members of his select clientele—he gets the infant out of the casket, revives it, and raises it in the swamp. There are only two babies who did not meet this fate—a girl and a boy. The boy grew up in Villejeune and was named Michael. The girl, named Sharon at birth, was given to a family who brought her to Atlanta and christened her Kelly.

When the children in the Dark Man's cult grow up, they, too, can get the vital life-prolonging injections from him. To do this, he enrolls them in a kind of pyramid scheme. First they must marry another within the circle of the cult and bring him their offspring. He uses the vital fluids from the cult's babies to prolong the lives of himself, his grown-up "children," and his paying clients. But as time goes on he needs larger and larger doses of new life essence to continue to hold the ravages of old age at bay. It is easy to see that eventually the number of artificially maintained adults will outstrip the number of new infants whose hormones can be harvested. This is the fatal flaw built into his scheme. His need for ever-increasing quantities of the elixir is bound to eventually mushroom out of control and attract unwanted attention, which it does. Phillips becomes unable to supply his customers their usual dose because he is running out of babies. So they start stealing children for him, quite brazenly. Judd Duval kidnaps a grown child, six-year-old Jenny Sheffield, who had gotten lost in the swamp.

Dr. Phillips is able to cover up Judd's reckless act by giving Jenny drugs to make her appear dead. He tells everyone she was found drowned in the swamp, stages a phony burial with the collusion of the undertaker (one of Phillips's clients for rejuvenation treatment), and then spirits Jenny away to his underground lab where he can rob the fluids from her thymus. But then old George Anderson has the audacity—or desperation—to steal an infant right out of its mother's lap in broad daylight, which threatens to completely blow Phillips's cover. He decides it is time to pack his bags and move to a third-world country, where he will be able to buy babies cheaply. Suddenly, his escape is blocked by the now-rebellious "children," led by Michael, who is revealed to be Phillips's biological son. The Dark Man and his fellow conspirators are killed by the children, who reclaim their stolen essence by tearing the shrunken thymus glands out of the dying men and swallowing them.

The ripping out of the thymus glands is the only really horrific scene in the book. "His ribs, brittle and soft, crumpled as Michael touched his chest, and when the boys' fingers tore into his flesh, the desiccated tissue gave way as if it had been cooked" (317). "Ripping a fragment of it away, Quint passed the small mass of tissue to the waiting hands of the other children" (359).

IRONY

Saul does not go for outright laughs in his stories, but he does like to play and have fun with the story in minor ways. For example, the name of the town where the story is set, Villejeune, is a play on the theme of the story. *Ville* is French for "village" and *jeune* means "young." One of the streets in Villejeune is Ponce Avenue, after Ponce de Leon, the Spanish conquistador whom legend says discovered the mythical fountain of youth. Whoever drinks from the waters of this fountain stays young. And what Doc Phillips is peddling is the modern equivalent of the fountain of youth.

Another pet trick of Saul's is to write pieces of dialogue that in retrospect are seen to be ironic or to have a double meaning. A prime example of this occurs when Kelly Anderson first arrives in Villejeune. Carl Anderson says returning was the best thing for her and "just what the doctor ordered" (36). In the context of the story this normally harmless cliché takes on a sinister meaning. "The doctor" is Dr. Warren Phillips, alias the Dark Man, and what he "orders" is usually something not too pleasant. In Kelly's case it will mean being inducted into the cult rituals of the Dark Man's children.

CHARACTERS

The central protagonists of the story are Michael Sheffield and Kelly Anderson. In a way they are siblings, since—unknown to most of the characters—Michael's adoptive mother is also Kelly's biological mother. Kelly Anderson is a teenager who dies her hair pink and wears studded punk-rocker-style clothes to cover up the fact that she feels dead inside. Since she was an infant, she has been plagued with nightmarish visions of a wizened and leering old man reaching out to take something from her. When she was older, she saw a psychiatrist about it, and he explained that she had constructed an imaginary father to substitute for the biological father she had never known. She knows this explanation to be false, so she eventually tells the psychiatrist the visions have gone away, just so she will not have to endure useless counseling sessions anymore.

Michael is about the same age as Kelly and given to dreamy fits, when he wanders in the swamp for hours and loses track of time. He is a part of the swamp because the Dark Man is his biological father. The Dark Man extracted fluid from Michael's thymus, too, but let him grow up outside the swamp instead of making him part of the circle of cult members. He had Michael placed with the Sheffields as an adopted child to replace the one he stole and gave to the Andersons. Michael becomes the leader of the rebellion against the cult. Saul maintains Michael as a sympathetic character by manipulating the plot so that he does not have to directly kill his father. The Dark Man dies as a result of his own fear. In one of the final scenes of the novel Michael, with the other children watching, raises a knife as if to strike the Dark Man and then pauses. That moment of panic drains Phillips of the stolen hormones that have preserved his life and youth for so long; as a result, his internal organs fail, and his flesh almost instantly putrefies and collapses, just like in Edgar Allan Poe's "Facts in the Case of M. Valdemar" (1845) and in many of the old Dracula films.

Craig, Barbara, and Jenny Sheffield are Michael's adopted family. Craig is an attorney, Barbara a social worker, and Jenny is a six-year-old. They are basically good people. Unknown to Barbara, Kelly Anderson is really her child Sharon—the one whom Warren Phillips deceived her into thinking was dead. There is an instant bond between Kelly and Barbara when they meet. Barbara has a flash of intuition of Kelly as her daughter. This makes her receptive to Amelie Coulton's revelations about Dr. Phillips, which might otherwise have been taken as the wild ravings of a grief-stricken mother.

Loosely on the side of the protagonists is Tim Kitteridge, the new chief of police of Villejeune. He represents the rational approach, trying to figure out what is going on. It seems a hopeless task at first. He has a dead body of an apparently eighty-year-old unidentified man whose chest was ripped open and a much younger man who is missing. There is talk of people who are alive, yet dead, like zombies. It all sounds crazy. Kitteridge thinks maybe he should let go of the investigation. But stubbornness keeps him plodding on.

There is a collection of characters who are the primary victims of the Dark Man. These are the "swamp rats." They are second-class citizens. The people of the swamp do not legally exist; born at home, many of them have no birth certificates, no school records, no social security cards, no death records. They are members of a closed community and do not share their secrets with the townspeople. The police chief thinks of them as being like the illegal aliens of Southern California, "living outside the system, disappearing into society just as completely as the swamp rats of Villejeune faded into the marshes" (76).

Two of the swamp people play important roles in the story. Clarey Lambert is the Dark Man's nemesis. By herself she cannot destroy the Dark Man, but through her telepathic powers she can guide Michael and Kelly and help them to become conscious of who and what they are. Long ago the Dark Man offered Clarey the elixir of eternal life, but she refused. She is ancient now, but she hangs onto life by force of will until she can see his kingdom destroyed. Not until she knows the Dark Man is dead can she thankfully surrender to the peace of death herself. Clarey represents a certain spiritual principle. Over and against the Dark Man's artificial immortality she stands for the earth wisdom of the natural cycle of the generations.

Amelie Coulter, although a blue-eyed blonde, is one of the swamp people. She is almost a teenager, poor and uneducated, and aware of her powerlessness and low social status. But she is determined not to lose her baby after she finds out that her husband, George, is one of the "children" of the Dark Man and therefore owes him his offspring. For some reason George married someone outside the circle, and now he is going to pay for being in a mixed marriage. He is executed by Jonas Cox, another member of the cult, as the penalty for wavering on carrying out the Dark Man's edict. For the baby's protection the now-widowed Amelie decides to give birth in a hospital instead of at home and enlists social worker Barbara Sheffield's assistance. But it is a case of leaping from the frying pan into the fire. The attending doctor at the hospital delivery room is Dr. Warren Phillips, the Dark Man himself. When she is told her baby died in childbirth, she does not believe it. Like the women in *Nathaniel*, she can feel through some primitive maternal instinct that her child is not dead. She suspects Dr. Phillips of stealing her baby, but does not make the logical connection that he is the Dark Man. She thinks he sold her baby to a childless couple for a high price because it was blonde.

Another swamp rat worth mentioning is Lavinia Carter. The Dark Man removed her vocal cords so that she could not tell his secrets. She is the only one of his "children" who has seen his face without the mask on. She works in the secret nursery in the soundproofed chamber underneath his house, tending the babies. Her role is similar to Sarah in *Suffer the Children* in that she is aware of his dual nature, but cannot communicate it to others because she is mute.

The chief antagonist and villain of the novel is Dr. Warren Phillips, a man with two faces. To the world at large he is a benevolent country doctor, and for the few who can pay he is also the dispenser of a life-restorative elixir that keeps them perpetually young. But to the superstitious people of the swamp he is the Dark Man, a cult leader with a supernatural aura who inspires terror in their hearts. Dr. Phillips is another version of the traditional "mad scientist." Not that he is truly insane, or that his discoveries do not work. He is mad in the sense that he has cut himself off from the conventional moral standards of the community.

Allied with Phillips is a segment of the local power structure: Judd Duval, the deputy sheriff, raised in the swamp; Orrin Hatfield, the coroner; Fred Childress, the undertaker; and possibly Judge Villiers get Doc Phillips's "special" treatments. Three of them—the deputy, the coroner, and the doctor—try to convince Kitteridge that it is useless to pursue the case of the dead man found in the swamp—a case that, if solved, would lead him to the secret of the Dark Man.

Carl Anderson, a construction contractor, is morally compromised, but tries to deny it to himself. He is like the man who loves steaks, but would feel repulsion at having to carry out the bloody work of slaughtering the cow and dressing the carcass. When Dr. Phillips is running out of elixir and tells Carl he will have to supply a baby if he wants a shot, he balks at the thought and protests, "I can't do that." He is willing to pay whatever amount is necessary, but cannot do the dirty work himself. Phillips tells him he has nothing left to sell. As the symptoms of accelerated aging begin to overtake Carl, he is brought to a point of moral choice that he has hitherto covered over with evasions and rationalizations. His survival interest overrides his half-hearted scruples. He needs his fix, and he does not care what it costs someone else.

THEMES

In *Darkness* the imagery of the Dark Man and his cult condenses multiple themes without being fully encompassed by any one of them. Among the themes alluded to are political oppression, drug addiction, sexual exploitation, and the redemptive effect of revolutionary action.

Darkness is a horror tale with political dimensions, like Saul's earlier novel *Hellfire*. Here is the climactic scene of *Darkness* where they confront Phillips:

> The children stood in a semicircle. . . . Their empty eyes fixed on him.
> They began to move, edging forward. . . . Hunger.
> Hunger, and hatred.
> The semicircle spread outward, leaving him with no retreat.
> (365–366)

Compare it with the parallel scene in *Hellfire*, a book that also deals with the exploitation of children by greedy adults: the use of child labor by factory owners in the 1800s. In the final scene the ghosts of the perished children confront the descendant of the long-deceased mill owner.

> All around her, their faces looming out of the darkness, she saw the faces of the children.
> Thin faces, with cheeks sunken from hunger, the eyes wide and hollow as they stared at her. . . . They were circling her, closing in on her, reaching out to her.
> She backed away from them. (*Hellfire*, 324)

As was discussed in Chapter 2, there is a hidden connection between horror literature and political unrest. The period when the Gothic novel flourished in England was in the aftermath of the French Revolution of 1789. The English middle and upper classes were aghast at the bloodbath that followed, including the execution of King Louis XVI in 1793 and the subsequent Reign of Terror, when hundreds were beheaded by the guillotine daily—a historical situation that formed the backdrop for Charles Dickens's *A Tale of Two Cities* (1859). Some commentators have suggested that the popularity of the Gothic during the 1790s was a case of the public preferring imaginary terrors to these all too real ones across the English Channel.

What we find at the core of *Darkness* is a tale of revolution. The backward people of the swamp are presented as the modern equivalent of the eighteenth-century rural French peasant. They even have French names—for example, Lambert, Coulton. They are ruled by the Dark Man, who dresses in dark flowing robes and is as ruthless as any feudal tyrant. To solidify his power, the Dark Man procures allies among the ruling elite in the neighboring town of Villejeune, including Judd Duval, a Sheriff of Nottingham type of character—to mix historical analogies.

The Dark Man has developed a false religion, which he uses to keep the peasants in check. Some of the revolutionaries of the nineteenth century described religion as "the opium of the people." This was a philosophical judgment based on materialism that failed to distinguish the support some religious hierarchies give to the political status quo from the validity of the transcendent vision that animates religion. However, in the case of the Dark Man's cult, the comparison to a drug is fitting.

Opium is the pain-relieving narcotic from which the addictive drug heroin is refined. The use of opium as a metaphor for religion is particularly fitting in the case of the Dark Man because the shots that he gives function like a drug. Not only are they administered with a hypodermic, like a heroin fix, but also they have to be received at regular intervals, or the addicted person goes into terrible withdrawal where he is willing to do anything to get another shot. (Is it coincidental that our hero, Michael S., has the same last initial as Saul's friend Michael Sack, who, as discussed in Chapter 1, was involved in the fight against drug abuse?) Also, fitting in with the drug metaphor, the children of the Dark Man are lifeless, apathetic, and dead inside, like chronically addicted people. This is not only implicit, but also directly suggested by the text: When Kelly comes back from the swamp and her mother sees her glazed eyes and pasty complexion, the word "*drugs* . . . flashed through Mary's mind instantly" (132). And after Jenny Sheffield is kidnapped, Phillips gives her morphine—a derivative of opium—to depress her vital functions so she will appear dead. Then he keeps her drowsy with mind-altering drugs while he harvests her fluids.

The revolution against the Dark Man, like most popular revolutions throughout history, has the dispossessed youth at its vanguard. The young people are the shock troops who actually seize power from the Dark Man and his henchmen. They have had the power all along to do so, but it lay dormant. It took Michael to awaken it. Michael is the son of the oppressor. His role is like that of the legitimate heir who rallies the troops to depose the tyrant in medieval times or the radicalized member of the elite who leads the masses in modern times. Michael is like the swamp children, but also not like them. His vital essence has been exploited like theirs, but he has also been educated and raised in privileged circumstances, like someone who has left a small island ruled by a dictator and has gone to study abroad. Michael has seen the world outside the swamp, and his consciousness is different from the swamp children's. He knows that the Dark Man's rule is something that need not be. And once he becomes aware of his solidarity with them, he is in a unique position to mediate between them and the outside world. He becomes the leader of their revolution in which, like the people described in Frantz Fanon's *The Wretched of the Earth* (1961), they reclaim their aliveness through the act of violence:

> The six children led by Jonas Cox pulled Judd Duval's body from the boat and began ripping it to pieces. . . . Their cries of rage began to die away as they tore their souls from Judd Duval's dying corpse, and as tears began to fill their eyes . . . for the first time in their lives they felt whole. (363)

This scene reverberates with the one at the shocking climax of Tennessee Williams's play *Suddenly Last Summer* (1958), where Sebastian Venable, the aristocratic Southern hedonist, is mobbed on the beach by a swarthy horde of hungry, homeless children who literally tear the flesh off him and devour him. Sebastian is a pedophile, attracted to young boys, and he consumes them sexually in return for a few coins. To Sebastian this is just a casual thing, just as Warren Phillips rationalizes that what he is doing is not really hurting the children. Yet the swamp children experience it as their souls being stolen and their youth being robbed.

So there is another metaphor buried in this text. Besides images of feudal political oppression and of drug addiction, there is the image of sexual exploitation. The old men—and it is only men that we are shown—are milking the children of their bodily fluids, of their vital essence, of their very souls. In Chinese medicine and throughout Asia and the Indian subpeninsula there is an equation of the vital essence with the sexual fluids. And within the text the exploitation of the children is talked about in language that is sexually suggestive. When Phillips revives Jenny from the effects of the morphine, he wonders if the suppression of her breathing caused brain damage, not that it really matters because he "wasn't the slightest bit interested in Jenny Sheffield's mind. It was her thymus he was after" (265). Substitute "body" for "thymus" to see the sexual overtones. An even better example comes from a scene where the Dark Man inserts the hypodermic into a newly presented infant on the altar in the swamp: "Though its body remained unharmed, its spirit began to die, impaled on the tip of the Dark Man's weapon" (128). This clearly has a subliminally suggestive sexual association. *He impaled her on the tip of his weapon* is a clichéd euphemism for sexual intercourse that has been copied in countless poorly written novels, as the author well knows. Saul's inclusion of this type of language is clearly meant to suggest a parallel between the Dark Man's activities and the sexual exploitation of children. After all, the sexual abuse of children was a theme that Saul introduced in his first novel, *Suffer the Children*, as discussed in Chapter 3. There the victim of abuse suffered in silence (i.e., Sarah was mute). But with *Darkness* we enter the 1980s, when children are starting to fight back against those who have victimized them.

Hence, when the children in the novel band together to confront their oppressors, this reflects what we have been reading in the news in recent years about the many victims of collective sexual abuse—such as those who were abused by physicians or clergymen (and Phillips is both)—who have come forward publicly and named their abusers and who have been publicly joined by their fellow victims so that the credibility of their accusations could not be dismissed. Indeed, a few years ago there was one such tragic case involving a clergyman in a Cajun section of rural Louisiana.

The power of these sexual exploiters of children is based on psychological intimidation. Often there is no other power behind it. Once the victims name their oppressor, his power crumbles. We see this in the novel. Once they are challenged, Warren Phillips and George Anderson are not able to fight back. Their fear causes them to collapse in upon themselves and die without even being touched. They are paper tigers whose power is illusory and crumbles when challenged.

A SOCIOPOLITICAL READING OF *DARKNESS*

Sociopolitical analysis of fiction was defined in Chapter 6. As discussed there, a sociopolitical analysis can look at the realism with which a fictional work reflects conditions of political, economic, and social inequality and the underlying social and political implication of the text. Since *Darkness* is a fantasy, not realistic fiction, it does not make much sense to examine it in terms of the accuracy of its portrayal of daily life. Instead, we will look at whether there is some underlying sociopolitical message we can extract from the text.

An oddity of the text is that the atmosphere in Villejeune is reminiscent of the Louisiana bayou, complete with swamps, shacks raised on stilts, and clannish inhabitants with French surnames like Duval, Lambert, and Coulton. But instead of setting Villejeune in Louisiana, Saul sets it in the Florida everglades, south of Orlando. Why? A possible answer is that this setting fits in with the underlying message of the novel. Florida is the promised land of the over-sixty set, and Carl Anderson is getting rich building retirement homes. At the same time—as the text mentions—the economy has benefitted from the nearby construction of the commercialized children's "paradise"—Disney World. So in the larger context, of which Villejeune is a microcosm, the author brings two elements into conjunction within the first chapters of the novel: the retired elderly and the commercially exploitable young.

Is *Darkness* a parable of the situation in Florida, which in turn is a microcosm of the nation? Can we read into it an indirect reference to the current population demographics of the United States? The proportion of older people is increasing, due to improved life expectancy, while the proportion of younger people is dwindling. Economists are predicting a crisis in the social security system, due to the shrinking numbers of young wage earners whose tax dollars are needed to support the growing ranks of the elderly. Are older people extending their lives at the expense of the young? Congress turned down universal health care coverage, and politicians are busy cutting benefits to families with young children. While some children go without needed vaccinations and immunizations, a huge portion of the federal tax revenues is being spent, through Medicare, on expensive medical procedures for prolonging the last months of life.

The picture can be expanded. The situation within the United States is a microcosm of what faces the world. Compared to the nonindustrialized, third-world countries, where young people represent the largest segment of the population, the industrialized Western nations are top-heavy with older people. A huge proportion of the planet's natural resources goes to maintaining the lifestyle of these nations of older people. Projecting Saul's parable onto the planetary level, we in the Western nations of the Northern Hemisphere are the Carl Andersons of Villejeune, and the rest of the world is in the unenviable position of the swamp rats.

Perhaps there is a peaceful way to arrive at a more equitable balance among the generations and among the nations. The implicit message of *Darkness*, the truly scary message—much more frightening than the novel's stage-blood horrors—is that if equity does not come about peacefully and rationally, it will come about violently, and it is we who may be torn to pieces to feed a ravenously hungry mass.

10

Shadows
(1992)

In the later, male-oriented patriarchal myths, all that is good and noble was attributed to the new, heroic master gods, leaving to the native nature powers the character only of darkness—to which, also, a negative moral judgement now was added.
　　Joseph Campbell, *The Masks of God: Occidental Mythology* (1964)

Shadows was published as a Bantam hardcover in July 1992 and was released in paperback in June 1993. It is a work of pure science fiction, well conceived and executed, with some thematic weight. There are no overtly supernatural elements. It is the first of Saul's books to be considered for possible development into a computerized CD-ROM game.

GENRE

Shadows is the story of a secretly funded experiment being conducted at the Academy, an exclusive residential school for academically gifted children. Dr. Engersol, the director of the school, has masterminded several apparent suicides of students. The students were actually murdered and their brains removed as part of a bizarre experiment to integrate supercomputers with amputated human brains. Two new students, Josh

MacCallum and ten-year-old Amy Carlson, are targeted to be the next victims of this plot.

This novel has elements of the cyberpunk genre of science fiction which was pioneered by William Gibson in his novel *Neuromancer* (1993), and which has been recycled by other writers such as Joan D. Vinge in *Cat's Paw*. The cyberpunk worldview has two shared premises. First is the notion of a new dimension of reality, called cyberspace, produced by the linking together of millions of computers in a complex electronic network called the Net or the World Wide Web through which it is possible to "travel" in a kind of virtual reality. The concept of virtual reality has been further popularized by the television series "VR5." The second premise is that humans could use complex electronic interfaces to mesh their nervous systems with computers so thoroughly that events in cyberspace could have a profound effect on the human who is linked up—to the point of even causing death under certain conditions. A third premise that some authors subscribe to is the possibility of one's personality continuing to have a recognizable existence on the Net in data form even if your body died while you were hooked up.

Reality may be stranger than fiction. In the recent book *Modern Cosmology, God, and the Resurrection of the Dead* (1994), physicist Frank J. Tipler argues, with a straight face, that the human soul is basically a computer program run on the human brain, and that super-supercomputers of the future will be able to bring people back into existence by running their programs.

An earlier book, *Brainchild*, was Saul's first novel about computerized brain research. Its plot was more akin to the traditions of robotics in science fiction. Alex Lonsdale, the central character in *Brainchild*, is a human who has been transformed into a robot. The robotics genre descends from Isaac Asimov's *I, Robot* (1973) to the man-machine hybrid popularized in the movie *Robocop* (1987). It includes the notion of artificially implanted memories, as pioneered by writer Philip K. Dick. In contrast, Amy, of *Shadows*, becomes transmuted into a part of the computer "Net." She merges into something larger than herself. In both *Brainchild* and *Shadows* Saul adds some supernatural flourishes to the techno-thriller plot. But in *Shadows* this is done much more subtly, through allusive imagery and allegorical symbolism, but without any actual supernatural elements.

PLOT

The main narrative line has to do with the conflict between Dr. Engersol and Amy. The conflict commences at the beginning of the novel, when Dr. Engersol's assistant, Hildie, tries to persuade the homesick Amy to remain at the Academy. The conflict gradually escalates as Dr. Engersol attempts to deliberately provoke an emotional crisis in Amy as a prelude to staging her "suicide." After her body has been disposed of and her severed brain hooked up to the computer, it appears that the conflict is over, with Amy being the loser. However, she learns how to control the computer with her mind and extends her control beyond the computer into anything that is electronic. Using these powers, she wages a battle to the death with Engersol, who tries to find a way to disconnect her brain from its life support system without Amy becoming aware of it. Although the primary conflict is between Engersol and Amy, young Josh has a close friendship with Amy, and after her disappearance he begins probing into the mysterious goings-on at the Academy. He surmises the truth about Engersol's experiments and discovers the secret entrance to the laboratory in the school's basement. He becomes an emotionally involved witness to the battle between Engersol and Amy, but is powerless to directly intervene.

Secondary narrative threads have to do with the Aldrich twins and their family and with the relationship between Josh and English teacher Steve Conners. The twins are protégés of Dr. Engersol. Adam agrees to secretly have his brain removed from his body, hoping life inside the computer will free him from the pain of his ordinary existence. However, after his brain has been transplanted into the computer, he becomes concerned that his mother will miss him, so he tries to contact her by transmitting ghostly messages that appear on her computer. When she does not respond, he eventually projects an image of himself on her television. At first she thinks she is having hallucinations, but eventually she decides someone is playing a cruel practical joke on her. She and her husband conclude it must be the surviving twin, Jeff. After the parents confront Jeff with this and threaten to remove him from the Academy, he sabotages the family car, causing his parents to die in an auto accident. This enrages Adam and contributes to his going mad, so that eventually he kills Engersol by closing off the ventilation in the laboratory until the scientist asphyxiates.

The other secondary narrative concerns the positive relationship that

develops between Josh and English teacher Steve Conners. Conners, like
Amy, is one of the few who relate to Josh as person, not just a brain.
This is very healing for Josh, who has felt neglected by his father since
his parents' divorce. Unfortunately, just as this relationship is really get-
ting under way, Conners dies. He is murdered by Engersol's assistant,
Hildie, in order to cover up Amy's murder.

The reader's interest in the plot is maintained through narrative devices that build suspense. These devices include the stimulation of curiosity through the creation of a mystery and the heightening of tension
by developing an atmosphere of anxious anticipation. The sense of mystery is created in the opening pages of the novel with Tim Evans's death,
the cause of which is very unclear. The questions raised by his death
emerge again with the disappearance of Adam, a third of the way into
the novel. Adam appears to have committed suicide by deliberately lying
in the path of an oncoming train. But there is something very odd about
the suicide, for he and his brother Jeff had been discussing it ahead of
time, and Jeff did not try to to persuade Adam to go on living. In fact,
he urged him to stick to his decision. Then after the body is discovered,
Jeff keeps hinting that Adam is not really dead. Two chapters later the
reader gets a glimpse of the next stage of Engersol's sinister plot. The
scientist decides that Josh would be a good candidate for the special
seminar because the boy has already made one suicide attempt—so if he
were to kill himself, no one would be surprised. It becomes clear that
there are hidden dimensions to the apparent suicides at the Academy,
but it takes many more pages before the reader discovers the true extent
of them.

In addition to the mystery, there is an atmosphere of anticipation.
Again, the stage is set by the description of Tim Evans's death in the
prologue. After this shocking scene, the novel begins in a leisurely fashion, taking several pages to lead up to Josh's admission to the Academy.
For fans of Saul the name of the school will create a sense of déjà vu
because in a prior novel, *The God Project*, the site for a series of top-secret
genetic experiments was also known as the Academy. After describing
the serene atmosphere of the campus, Saul has Josh's mother think the
place looks "*too* peaceful" (55). She feels a "chill of foreboding" as
though beneath the perfect surface of the place something is really very
wrong. But she dismisses this intuition as silly. Saul often uses a character's subjective disquiet to induce a parallel emotional response in the
reader.

For example, after many pages of presenting Hildie Kramer as an apparently kind, but obviously manipulative, person, he has Amy Carlson voice what the reader has already begun to think: "So far they'd never made [Amy] do anything she didn't really want to do. Or had they? In her mind she began reviewing the days since she'd first come to the Academy. . . . Hildie'd always been very nice to her but in the end . . . she'd always wound up doing what Hildie wanted her to do" (166).

Saul builds up an unsettling atmosphere partly through a series of almost subliminal suggestions that have a cumulative effect. For instance, when Josh is still trying to decide whether to come to the Academy, Jeff calls the school "a jail," but then later says he was only joking. But his first words were closer to the truth. Saul also uses the technique of sounding false alarms in order to raise the hairs on the reader's neck. Shortly after Adam's death Josh enters his own room and is horrified to find the dead Adam sitting at the computer, his shirt soaked with blood. It turns out to be Adam's twin brother, Jeff, made up with stage blood as a gruesome practical joke.

Foreshadowing is another technique used by Saul to create anticipatory tension. Foreshadowing is a literary convention where the introduction of some element during the development of the plot creates an expectation in the reader that this element will play a role in the climax or resolution of the plot. So if we are shown a gun in somebody's desk drawer in the opening chapters, we sense that gun will be used by someone before the novel ends, and we begin trying to anticipate when and how. In *Shadows* the central conflict between Amy and Dr. Engersol is foreshadowed in the seventh chapter, where Engersol is described as taking an unusual interest in Amy's fear of descending a cliffside stairway. To underline the introduction of this plot element, Saul describes Brenda MacCallum's subjective reaction to seeing Engersol studying Amy—a deep sense of foreboding. Later Engersol arranges to have Amy's fear of heights tested by the coach, who tries to get her to climb a rope and jump off a high diving board. When he learns from the coach how severe her fear of heights is, he seems pleased. As readers, we wonder why. When he indicates to Amy that he wants to perform an experiment on her, we feel both emotionally uneasy about what is going to happen to her and intellectually curious about what form the threat will take. All of these suspense-building techniques are designed to keep the reader compulsively turning the novel's pages.

CHARACTERS

The main characters in this novel come in pairs: Josh and Amy, two highly gifted children, are the protagonists. Dr. Engersol and Hildie Kramer, who desire to imprison and exploit their brains, are the antagonists. And the twins, Adam and Jeff, are initially Josh's and Amy's friends, but ultimately become henchmen of the evil Dr. Engersol.

Amy's personality is the most complex and ultimately the most enigmatic in the novel. The credibility of her capacity to exert great force of will is pivotal to the novel's intense climax. This important quality of her personality is foreshadowed at the beginning of the novel. When the character of Amy is first introduced to the reader, we are informed that she locked herself in a closet in a battle with her parents to avoid being brought to the Academy. A couple of chapters later we see her determined struggle with her fear of heights, and she succeeds in walking down a steep stairway with the help of Josh's reassuring presence.

The other defining quality we note about Amy is her gentleness, as expressed in her relationship with Josh and in her love of animals. In fact, her name sounds like the French word *aimé*, meaning "beloved." Hildie's promise that the school's cat can sleep in her room is what initially persuades Amy to agree to stay at the Academy. She is more attuned to the natural world and has none of the enthusiasm for computers that characterizes Josh and the other boys. When Amy is confronted with Dr. Engersol's experiment, in which he surgically removes part of a living cat's skull, her compassion for animals joins with her outspoken force of will. In no uncertain terms she denounces Engersol and her classmates and announces that she is going to tell the authorities how they are torturing the cat.

This kindhearted picture of Amy contrasts radically with the primordially enraged avenger she becomes by the end of the book. The cause of her transformation is the unimaginably total violation of her person by Engersol, who, by depriving her brain of a body, has put her in the ultimate claustrophobic situation where she is totally dependent upon him. Several of Engersol's previous experimental guinea pigs became completely mad when they awoke and realized what had happened to them. That Amy neither goes mad nor succumbs to Engersol's will is a testimony to her strength, which was less apparent when she was in the frail body of a ten-year-old. That she manages to turn the tables on Engersol is no mean feat. In the course of doing this, she must protect Josh from Hildie, who has been ordered to seize him and bring him to the underground laboratory. Now Engersol and Hildie will learn to their dismay that rather than subjugating Amy, their obscene experiment has empowered her, since she now has the potential to access any piece of electronic equipment in the building or elsewhere by using her mind. To stop Hildie from reaching Josh, Amy takes control of the elevator Hildie has entered and seals her in. She then toys with Hildie, repeatedly raising the elevator and then letting it plunge—sometimes a few inches, sometimes several feet. Thus, Amy forces Hildie to experience both the sense of trapped claustrophobia that she experiences and the fear of falling that Engersol had used to humiliate her.

It is hard to suppress the vengeful sense that the heartless Hildie is finally getting exactly what she has deserved. There is a kind of glee the reader feels in seeing the helpless child Amy become powerful enough to get the best of these sinister adults. Yet what she is doing to Hildie is calculatedly sadistic and horrible. She wants to terrify Hildie and make her feel fear and pain as the repeated plunges of the elevator subject the villainess to multiple fractures that are compounded again and again. Saul spares Amy the final responsibility for Hildie's death; he has her accidentally lose control of the elevator when Adam launches a mental assault upon her within the computer. But this is purely a literary device to preserve some vestige of Amy's original innocence. We sense that she ultimately would have killed Hildie, and Engersol, too, although again Saul has Adam do that piece of dirty work.

At the end of the final chapter Saul has Amy redeem her innocence by renouncing the power she has newly gained. She tells her parents, who have been summoned to the lab by police:

> "I can't live like this. . . . Adam changed, Mama. He wasn't like himself anymore. He started hating everyone, and if Dr. Engersol hadn't killed him, he could have done anything. He could have gone into any computer anywhere and done anything he wanted. And if my brain stays alive, I could do the same thing." (384)

So she does the noble thing, apparently, and shuts down the life support system that is maintaining her brain. As the final chapter closes, the picture of a kindhearted, self-sacrificing girl is restored, but at the price of her being frozen forever in victimhood.

Then in the epilogue the reader learns that Amy did not really die.

She replicated herself as a computer program before letting her brain die off, and now multiple copies of herself exist in several computers, with the potential to exercise the kind of power she warned against. The reader is forced to revise his or her understanding of the tear-jerking scene a few pages before when Amy pulled the plug on herself in front of the police and her parents. Why did she pretend to die then? Saul does not supply us with an answer for this. It is up to the reader to solve the mystery. Perhaps she was sincerely trying to spare her parents, letting them mourn the loss of the little girl they loved, knowing they could never really accept her as a disembodied brain or as a phantom who exists as coded bits and bytes on a computer. Or maybe it was just a cynical confidence game to protect her new digitized existence from the authorities by duping the police into thinking the whole incident is now over. Or maybe she really was pulling the plug on herself, but at the instant before death her survival instinct involuntarily took over.

Regardless of how we assess her motives, Amy remains a tragic figure. We remember her as she was. We understand how she became what she now is. And even in her new, inhuman form, she retains a vulnerability, a loneliness that prompts her to contact Josh with the longing that he will abandon his earthly life and join her in her rarified form of existence on another plane of reality.

Josh also changes significantly in the course of the novel, though not as radically as Amy. In a certain sense this is a "coming of age" novel, in which Josh wins a new maturity at the cost of becoming sadder, but wiser. When we first meet Josh, he is a self-absorbed intellectual frustrated by the constant rejection of his peers, who resent his academic genius. Unable to fit in and increasingly losing control of his temper, he finally slashes his veins in a suicide attempt. His expectations are so negative that when he is brought to the Academy and given a difficult mathematics test as part of the screening procedure, he assumes he has failed and runs to hide in a clearing surrounded by dense shrubbery. There he first encounters Amy, who is also hiding because she is lonely and wants to go home. They resonate with each other's fears and longings and, in a well-written scene, strike up an immediate friendship based on mutual sympathy. This is the first true friendship for either of them, and the relationship is all the more intense for being cross-gender, even though it is not overtly romantic.

Josh's loyalty to Amy is tested at various points in the novel, as Dr. Engersol begins to manipulate her, provoking emotional outbursts from her that will make her look suicidal. On the first such occasion Amy is invited to an experiment where a cat is subjected to electric shocks and other noxious stimuli. Amy is repulsed by the cruelty of this, denounces it, and runs out of the room crying. Josh is about to go after her, but succumbing to his intellectual curiosity to view the end of the experiment, he accedes to Engersol's admonition to "Let her go" (190).

Next Amy is publicly humiliated by Engersol, who hooks her up to physiological monitoring devices and then deliberately provokes her fear of heights. Here Josh has lost all intellectual curiosity in the experiment. He is intensely concerned for Amy from the start because he is aware of her acrophobia. When she runs away in tears, he starts to follow, but Engersol says, "Let Hildie take care of Amy, Josh" (215). Seeing Hildie go after her, he is lulled into a false reassurance and allows himself to again be caught up by intellectual curiosity as Engersol explains the computerized display of Amy's brain wave and cardiac reactions. Unknown to Josh, at this very moment Hildie is drugging Amy, after which Engersol will remove her brain and Hildie will dispose of the body.

Amy's disappearance and apparent death cause Josh to snoop around the Academy, despite his fears, and thus discover the underground lab. He witnesses on a television monitor in Engersol's office the life and death struggle between Amy and Engersol. Like some hero of Greek mythology, at the end of the novel he must make one last choice concerning Amy—whether or not to accept the dangers of continuing a relationship with her now that she has transmuted into a type of infernal goddess of a computerized netherworld. Josh decides to sever their connection, as symbolized by throwing his computer out. Saul, through Josh's mother, proclaims that this turning away from obsession represents an impulse of basic sanity on Josh's part, but not all readers will be satisfied with that. From now on, thinks his mother, Josh will be "all right" (393). Now he is content with the satisfactions of ordinary, everyday life in his hometown of Eden, which had seemed such a hell to him at the beginning of the novel. Eden now begins to acquire some of the afterglow of its biblical namesake.

In opposition to Amy and Josh are the criminal pair Engersol and Hildie. We know little of Engersol, except that he is a monomaniac, obsessed with becoming famous and intent on proving he is an even greater genius than the gifted children at the Academy. Like Victor Frankenstein, he views himself as the creator of a new order of beings. These beings are part-human, part-computer. He believes that if his project is successful, the public will overlook the children he sacrificed in the process of perfecting his technology. The irony is that Engersol himself is already half-human, half-machine. Although he has a body, he functions essentially as a disembodied intellect, with not a flicker of ordinary human sympathy or compassion.

Engersol's partner in atrocities, Hildie Kramer, is a matronly, overweight woman with a warm, welcoming manner and a gift for making parents feel at ease. She has a special instinct for children. She can sense what they are feeling at a given moment and can often predict what they will do next. She is unerringly successful at finding the right words to appease them and the proper stratagem to influence their will in the direction she chooses. Her skill at smoothing over any traces of the nefarious activities at the Academy is illustrated in an early scene where the author is planting subconscious impressions in the reader's mind.

The scene occurs when Josh and his mother, Brenda, are first touring the Academy with Amy. They are atop a sea cliff, about to descend a steep flight of rickety stairs to the beach. Amy feels a touch of vertigo and draws back. This is when we first learn of her fear of heights. It is only with Josh holding her hand that she is able to force herself to make the descent. As this is going on, Brenda notices George Engersol studying Amy with an odd, intense expression that is chilling in its detachment. But before Brenda can analyze her disquieting feeling any further, a smiling Hildie suddenly interrupts her thoughts "holding out a welcoming hand" (91) and pulls Brenda away to introduce her to some other parents. A few pages later when Jeff Aldrich is about to tell Josh about the mysterious death of one of the students at the Academy, Hildie cuts in with a laugh and changes the subject, saying, "You don't want to scare poor Josh away on his very first night with us, do you?" (100).

The reader's perception of Hildie gradually comes into focus over the course of the novel. It is not that her character develops, but rather that her true nature is progressively revealed. At the beginning she is all maternal charm and comfort, but a false note is struck from the start, and it becomes clear that her every action is calculated and manipulative. At first it appears that her manipulation is directed toward positive ends. Even after Engersol is unmasked as a callous and fiendish intellect, the reader is for a time led to believe, along with Josh, that Hildie may act as Amy's protector. This hope is punctured when Hildie drugs the trusting girl and drags her to Engersol's secret underground laboratory, revealing herself to be the evil doctor's most essential lieutenant.

Hildie's cunning and ruthlessness are further dramatized in her quick thinking when Steve Conners, the English teacher, blunders onto the scene of the crime, narrowly catching her disposing of Amy's remains down the sea cliff. Hildie feigns distraught grief and lures Conners to the edge of the precipice, whereupon she dispatches him to the rocks with a quick thrust. She then thinks how to throw suspicion on Conners by planting the suggestion that he might have had an interest in sexually abusing Amy.

The relish with which Hildie carries out these evil deeds is never clearly explained. We know nothing of her background and learn little about her true thoughts or motivation. Apparently, she shares Engersol's grandiose commitment to the artificial intelligence project, for she becomes intensely furious when Amy, now a disembodied brain, challenges Engersol's control. Because she betrayed Amy's trust so thoroughly, it is Hildie, more than Engersol, who becomes the personalized target of Amy's vengeful wrath, as she exerts control over the elevator system, causing it to repeatedly plunge until all of Hildie's bones are shattered.

The other pair in the novel is the Aldrich twins, Adam and Jeff. Adam is the type of boy who keeps his feelings bottled up inside himself, and throughout his life he has been dominated by his outgoing twin, Jeff. Adam agrees to have his brain permanently linked to the computer because he hopes thereby to escape the frustrations of the everyday world. In this respect Josh and he share a certain similarity. Both of them have previously tried to escape the world through suicide attempts. After his existence becomes confined to the enclosures of the computer, Adam longs to establish contact with his mother and explores ways to communicate with her, extending his presence through the electronic network to her office computer and her home television. In this way he foreshadows the possibility that Amy could also take control of electronic appliances in her showdown with Engersol.

Adam's brother, Jeff, is the selfish, callous twin—a kind of younger version of Engersol. Extending the biblical allusions Saul has provided in the novel, Jeff could easily have been renamed Cain for convincing his brother to give up his body. On the eve of Adam's transformation Jeff's only concern is to claim the leather jacket that Adam will no longer need. Later, when his parents become a problem, Jeff experiences no apparent hesitation or remorse about killing them. Jeff is somewhat loose lipped. At the beginning of the novel he is the one who tells Josh the legend of Eustace Barrington and the secret rooms he built in the basement of the Academy before Hildie shushes him with a feigned laugh. Jeff's most important role in the novel is to move the plot along by providing Josh with hints that Adam is not really dead. This later helps

Josh to realize that Amy also may still in some way be alive, and this inspires his quest to solve the mystery of the Academy by finding the secret laboratory hinted at by the legend.

One other character is notable—Steve Conners, the English teacher. Other than Hildie, he is the only staff member at the Academy who seems to take much personal interest in the students. But unlike Hildie, his interest is genuine, not a manipulative act. He takes Josh for a movie and a burger on his free time and gives Josh his first taste of what it would be like to have a father-substitute. He also has genuine concern for Amy and is outraged when he learns Engersol has subjected her to the bizarre experiment that played on her acrophobia. Ironically, Conners's positive trait of concerned involvement with his students is manipulated by Hildie to plant suspicions that he was inappropriately involved, and that he murdered Amy Carlson after molesting her.

THEMES

The primary theme of this novel is the increasing interpenetration of human life by technology and the one-sided values that can develop as society grows increasingly complex.

Society tends to objectify people and judge their worth based on some single overvalued trait rather than relating to the whole person. Women often encounter this in terms of being valued or devalued solely on the basis of overall physical attractiveness, or even something as narrow and specific as the size of their breasts. Other aspects of their person are discounted. In *Shadows* the boys and girls are judged solely on the basis of their intellect. Sometimes their intellect is valued negatively, as in the public schools where their peers dislike them because they are "nerds" or "brains"—too smart and lacking physical grace. At the Academy this same narrow form of judgment is simply inverted. Engersol and the other teachers value them solely for their intellect. This is taken to the extreme by Engersol, who so values their minds that he disposes of their accompanying bodies, considering the body a parasite that wastes the brain's energy. By keeping the children's cerebrums alive in his lab, Engersol literally relates to them as "brains."

The only staff member who genuinely relates to the children as multi-faceted beings with emotional needs is Steve Conners, the English teacher and informal coach. The British intellectual C. P. Snow used to write about the "two cultures" that were emerging—one science-based and the other humanities-based. The old-fashioned intellectual was conversant with both. But Snow noted that in the twentieth century, as technology has become ascendant, the two cultures have begun to drift apart to the degree that those who specialize in one are no longer even able to understand the language of the other. Conners represents the importance of humanities as well as sciences for a well-rounded individual. He gets murdered early on by Hildie Kramer, however, which does not bode well for the future of the humanities.

Shadows reflects the modern romance with technology. The earliest familiar exploration of this theme was Mary Shelley's *Frankenstein* (1818), in which the creature, fabricated using a primitive imaginary forerunner of biotechnology, yearns to be loved by its creator. It was not until 170 years later, toward the latter half of the twentieth century, that this theme could be fully explored. For with the advent of advanced computer technology we have finally succeeded in creating machines in our own image, demonstrating sophisticated information-processing capabilities. Some philosophers began to question if technology might not eventually evolve to a point where we would no longer be able to draw a bright boundary line separating "human" intelligence from "artificial" intelligence.

On the other hand, the tremendous information storage and processing capacity of modern computers has made possible the advance of technology from the mechanical to the biological area of life. The current project of mapping out all of the genetic information in the human chromosomes using supercomputers raises the possibility of the conscious manipulation of life through genetic engineering to a degree still unimaginable.

It seems to be impossible from a practical point of view to limit the avenues of technological exploration. If something can be done technologically, someone will want to do it. This seems to be the point of Amy's statement to Josh near the end of the novel that she'd located another project "just like the one at the Academy" (392). The death of Engersol and the destruction of his lab can only delay, not prevent, the emergence of what he was working on, since wherever there is a potential technology, there is also a commercial incentive to develop it for profit. The implication of the novel would appear to be that Amy represents the wave of the future. Technology will eventually bring about a radical alteration in the way we experience ourselves. Josh may be able to tune this out for now, but not permanently.

A FEMINIST READING OF *SHADOWS*

The definition and fundamental principles of feminist literary analysis were discussed in Chapter 5. There are several feminist themes in *Shadows* that work on literal, metaphorical, and symbolic levels. On the most literal level there is the sexist manner in which Amy is treated by her male classmates. She is one of the few girls who is mentioned as being a student at the Academy. Josh, who has a genuine egalitarian friendship with her, is teased by his classmates for having a "girlfriend," as if the only possible way for a boy to relate to a girl is romantically. When Amy is invited to the special class Dr. Engersol conducts for the inner circle of students, she becomes enraged by the uncaring way he treats a laboratory cat. When she emotionally protests this, her male classmates emit a collective groan, as though her reaction is automatically unworthy of being taken seriously.

The male characters, as portrayed in the novel, tend to be more attuned to abstract ideas and analysis, rather than emotion, and this is presented as a weakness on their part. Amy is certainly the intellectual equal of the boys, and yet she does not lose touch with the emotional context as the boys do. Even Josh, who is emotionally attuned to Amy, is distracted by abstractions at key moments of the plot, becoming curious about meaningless experimental data when he should be paying practical attention to Amy's plight.

Computer technology is also very overvalued in the novel by such characters as Engersol, who literally sacrifices children to it, much as some ancient peoples sacrificed children to their gods. Adam overvalues the computer, thinking that by becoming one with it and fully entering its world, he can escape the pain of his real life. Metaphorically, the overvaluation of computers can be seen as a flight from nature and therefore a rejection of women.

Women are biologically able to give birth, and consequently, most societies have encouraged women to remain in the domestic sphere. Even when working outside the home, women have often been channeled into jobs that are extensions of the domestic sphere—teaching in elementary schools, preparing or serving food, cleaning, and caring for the sick. At home and in these types of occupations women have tended to remain relatively more in touch with the biological basics of life—birth, feeding, growth, disease, death—than most men. The aversion many cultures have to menstruation may be viewed as a rejection of women's bodies, which are defined by men as "out of control" because they visibly fluctuate to biological rhythms and circadian cycles. In contrast, the world of computer technology is "clean," non-biological, antiseptic, predictable, static, with no messy lunar cycles, no disease, no birth and death. It is in this bloodless realm that Adam aspires to escape his pain.

Although no one yet has gone to the extreme of having his or her brain physically grafted onto a computer, a significant number of people do it metaphorically, in the sense that they become so wrapped up in technology that they cease to effectively relate to anything outside of that sphere. In industrialized nations we are particularly prone to deluding ourselves that we can solve, or at least distract ourselves from, the problems of the human condition by developing newer and increasingly more complex technology.

While the fascination with computer technology can represent a flight from women and the biological aspect of life, at the same time on the symbolic level the computer can play the role of the ideal "female" in its replacement of relationships with actual women. Most of the pioneers in computer technology have been males with a keen interest in analytical thinking and formal mathematical logic. Within the patriarchal model of culture there is a sense in which it is natural for computer technology to be gendered as "female"—that is, as subordinate. The computer appears to be the ideal personal secretary or junior assistant, under the total control and dominion of the scientist-creator, ever ready to serve, and not having any emotional needs for recognition or appreciation. And this is what Engersol tries to do to Amy—make her into a machine to serve his will.

Yet there is a contradiction, for the servant also threatens to be more powerful and must be kept down. Thus, there are so many popular fantasies, such as the movies *2001: A Space Odyssey* (1968) and *Blade Runner* (1982), where technology's creations rise up against the human creators. Engersol at one point thinks of his project in terms of a new creation and muses that Amy should have been called Eve. But in the biblical story Eve rebelled against God and vied for divine knowledge by eating the forbidden fruit. Similarly, Eve/Amy rebels against her creator-god, Engersol, and becomes a kind of Lilith. She refuses to play the dutiful daughter for papa Engersol, and he becomes like a sorcerer who has conjured a powerful jinni that escapes from the charmed circle and destroys him.

Some feminists believe the male-dominated societies of recorded history replaced an earlier matriarchy, which centered on the worship of goddesses. A corollary of this theory is that these sacred goddesses were eventually reinterpreted as demonesses. When Amy appears in Josh's computer at the end of the novel, it is in the guise of a demigoddess of the electronic age. Is she demon, goddess, or amoral force? Is technology bad, good, or neutral? Readers must decide for themselves.

11

The Homing
(1994)

> There was a deliberate voluptuousness which was both thrilling and repulsive, and as she arched her neck she actually licked her lips like an animal.
>
> Bram Stoker, *Dracula* (1897)

The Homing was released as a Fawcett Columbine hardcover in August 1994 and was an alternate selection of the Literary Guild book club. It was released as a paperback the following summer, timed to appear in bookstores simultaneously with John Saul's new hardback, *Black Lightning*. In this novel Saul returns to his literary roots by dealing with themes of incest, sadism, and attempted rape—elements that were prominent in his best-selling first novel, *Suffer the Children*.

According to Saul, *The Homing* was a book that looked fine at the outline stage, but he ran into difficulty when he began the actual writing. "Midway through I had to go back and rewrite the first half. I'd done it from the wrong point of view." He had started out with Kevin as the main protagonist and then realized it should have been Julie. "I kept thinking, 'I know there's something wrong.' The scenes were almost working, but not quite. All of a sudden one night I woke up at two o'clock in the morning with this great epiphany and realized I'd been writing from the wrong character's point of view. I had to go back and reverse everything. I thought, 'This is a quick and easy rewrite; all I have to do is go back and change it to a female voice and change he to she.' But it turned out every single scene had to be completely rewritten."

PLOT

The Homing is another of John Saul's tales about a family that tries to escape the crime and violence of the big city, only to fall prey to unsuspected horrors lurking in an apparently peaceful small town. There are two major plot lines in this novel. The first concerns a late-in-life romance between two previously married adults, Karen Spellman and Russell Owen, who attempt to blend their existing families. This includes several chapters on the conflict between Karen and her prospective father-in-law, Otto, who is grouchy and set in his ways. It also subsumes the tentative romance between Karen's sixteen-year-old daughter Julie and Russell's teenage son Kevin.

The other plot line concerns the deadly menace that threatens Karen and Russell's children. At first it appears there are two distinct menaces. One is a sadistic killer of teenage girls, who eventually takes an interest in Julie. The other is the mysterious presence of a deadly strain of mutated bees. The menace collides with the lives of Karen and Russell on the day of their wedding, and the family's fortunes remain intertwined with this double threat for the remainder of the novel. Eventually, it becomes clear that the sadistic serial killings and the mutated bees originate from the same source—the entomologist Carl Henderson.

The first hint of the menace of the bees comes early in the novel, when Karen's daughter Molly goes into the barn and sees a mass of insects swarming in the hayloft. Eventually, this grows into a dense cloud of bees bigger than the barn itself. Then at the outdoor wedding of her mother and new stepfather a bee gets under Molly's skirt. Not wanting to disrupt the formality of the proceeding, she remains still and is stung. She has an allergic reaction, which threatens to shut down her ability to breathe. An injection of the stimulant epinephrine at the local hospital fails to control the reaction, and she is flown to the medical center at San Luis Obispo, where she is saved by the injection of an experimental antivenom serum being tested by UniGrow.

Meanwhile, back at the farm, Carl Henderson is staring at Julie in a way that she finds frightening. Shortly after this Julie is assaulted near the hives by Carl, but her new grandfather, Otto, arrives and scuffles with him. While the men are fighting, Julie is stung by some bees and develops the same kind of allergic reaction as Molly did. Henderson hopes Julie will die so she cannot accuse him of attacking her. He does not want her to receive the experimental antivenom and recover. So he surreptitiously replaces the antivenom with a chemical he has developed in his home laboratory. The purpose of this chemical is to produce an alteration in the queen bees. To his surprise, injection of the chemical does stop the allergic reaction. But unknown to him, it also begins to alter Julie's body, so that she will gradually mutate into a kind of human queen bee.

The first effect of the injection is that Julie feels inwardly in pain, very feverish and nauseous, but with the outward appearance of feeling well. And, most peculiarly, some internal force inhibits her from telling her mother or the doctor, Ellen Filmore, about how ill she is feeling. When she opens her mouth to disclose her condition, she finds different words emerging almost against her will. She hears herself telling them that she feels fine.

For the next several chapters Julie undergoes a process of gradual transformation. Her mother, Karen, notices and broods over Julie's strange behavior, but misinterprets it. She worries that some urban plague has pursued them to their rural retreat. First she suspects the eating disorder bulimia because of Julie's uncontrolled binge in which she completely devours the contents of a refrigerator, including an entire raw lemon and the congealed fatty gravy in some cold leftover pot roast. Next Karen suspects drug abuse, reasoning that marijuana-induced euphoria caused this craving for food. Since Julie was with a boy during this eating binge there is also a suspicion that she might be becoming sexually active. And finally Karen suspects a virus, since Julie's face appears unnaturally pale and clammy. Yet the true culprit is not any of these modern ills that are daily trumpeted to the public's attention in popular magazines and daytime television, but something much worse. The real source of Julie's peculiar behavior is something particularly native to the rural setting: the omnipresent insects, which have taken up a home inside of her.

Julie becomes increasingly attracted to the sounds of night: the humming of the insects and the noise of the crickets. She finds it sensual and hypnotic. One night the sound of the insects lures her out of her bedroom, and she falls asleep in the deep grass of the pasture only to

awaken covered with hundreds of ants. Gradually, she realizes that she
is being controlled by the insects, but that she also has influence over
them.

At the same time that she is mutating into a half-human, half-insect
creature, there is an insect colony within her that is turning her body
into a kind of hive and has even lodged in her brain and central nervous
system. The tiny insects can launch themselves out of her mouth and fly
very short distances to enter another person's lungs and set up house
(or hive) inside there. Anyone who kisses her is in danger of getting a
mouthful of bugs and becoming infected with her condition.

At the end of the novel Julie, flanked by her three drones Kevin, Andy,
and Jeff and attended by a dense cloud of insects, descends upon the
house of Carl Henderson, where she looses her insect minions, who not
only eat Carl alive, but also make swiss cheese of the structural beams
in his house until the whole thing collapses into a ruin, like the castle in
Poe's *The Fall of the House of Usher* (1839). In an apocalyptic ending, the
remains of the house burst into flames, and the monstrous mutant children are destroyed along with Carl, but they were doomed anyway because the insect colony inside each of them was slowly making swiss
cheese of their brains.

IRONY

Before Saul became a thriller writer, his interest was in comic novels.
Saul feels the conventions of the genre require him to suppress his humorous side, but it does seem to emerge at times in a subtle irony. For
instance, when Julie is informed that she will be leaving her friends in
Los Angeles and permanently moving 200 miles away to a farm in the
San Joaquin Valley, she cannot believe that this could be happening to
her. She thinks to herself, "Not even sixteen yet, and her life was basically over" (10). In typical adolescent fashion she overdramatically ex-
aggerates the disastrousness of having to make a life change. But
ironically, in her self-pitying statement that her life is essentially done
with, she is unknowingly prophesying the truth—that she will undergo
a monstrous transformation that will result in her death.

The town in which this terrible transformation will occur is named,
ironically, Pleasant Valley. When John Saul gives a town a bland, upbeat
name that could have been thought up by a marketing executive, like

Pleasant Valley or—in *Creature*—Silverdale, we *know* horrible things are going to happen there.

The clumsily attempted seduction of Julie by a boy named Jeff is brimming with irony, which only underscores the horror of the scene. Julie is babysitting Jeff's younger brother. She is gorging herself on the contents of their refrigerator in a greedy, animalistic fashion. When Jeff suddenly comes upon this sight, he is simultaneously excited and repulsed by this picture of sensual abandon. Julie smiles at him, and he interprets this as a sexual invitation, particularly since she is from Los Angeles and therefore automatically sex-crazed, according to his mentality. He reaches to fondle her, but when his fingers make contact, she jerks away. At the same time she runs her tongue over her lips, which are smeared with food. Jeff chooses to ignore her backing away from him and instead focuses on her licking her lips. Jeff thinks she is signalling him with this gesture. Presumptuously, he tells her, "I know what you want," (179) as he begins caressing her. She tries to wriggle away, which only excites him more. Then as he pins her to the floor and lowers his lips to hers, she opens her mouth and out flies a cloud of tiny bugs, which he inhales into his lungs in terror. Not quite what he had expected.

CHARACTERS

Sixteen-year-old Julie is the central protagonist of the novel. Saul is careful to make her remain sympathetic, even while she is being transformed into something inhuman. A key scene occurs after Jeff has been infected through contact with Julie. He and Julie are near the corral when Julie's little sister Molly tries to ride the mare. The horse senses something unnatural about the teenagers and rears up, throwing Molly off its back. Its hooves are lashing out in a panic, and Molly is in danger of being trampled. Julie mentally summons the swarm of bees from the barn. The horse plunges away from Molly, trying to escape the bees and is stung repeatedly until it dies. Julie watches the horse's torment with an "oddly emotionless" expression (193). What is revealed here is Julie's ability to control the bees, as well as a side of her that is rather cold and cruel. This scary aspect of her is softened by the fact that she acted in defense of her sister. Another way that Saul modifies the plot to keep her sympathetic is by having Jeff—not Julie—release the cloud of tiny insects that colonizes Kevin's body.

Kevin, Julie's teenage stepbrother, is the secondary protagonist. He is a highly sympathetic character. He is sensitive and kind throughout the beginning of the novel. He is attentive to and protective of little Molly and feels an immediate attraction to Julie. He wonders whether Julie likes him as a brother or as a boy and hopes it is the latter. After he becomes infected, he still struggles to protect the younger children from the inhuman force within him. On two occasions he exerts all his willpower to prevent himself from allowing the bugs inside his lungs to infest little Molly. And in another instance he warns little Ben away just as the boy's older brother Jeff is about to infect him. However, he is not always able to control it. One evening the force within him preys upon Sara McLaughlin, a girl who is sexually attracted to him and whom he lures into the woods by pretending to make a pass at her.

Karen is a typical concerned mother. She moves back to her hometown of Pleasant Valley with Julie and Molly because she just cannot afford to pay the bills in Los Angeles after the children's father leaves her. She gets a bit rankled by her new father-in-law's unfriendly attitude, and after Molly is stung, Karen becomes spooked about the bees and wants Russell to get rid of them. But that is an impossibility, since they are essential to the fertilization of the crops.

Julie's new grandfather, Otto, is a moralistic, hot-tempered, male chauvinist, and like a John Wayne hero, he thinks women belong in the kitchen pouring coffee for their men. But he is really not a bad person at heart. He is an old-fashioned rugged individualist, like Max Moreland in *Darkness*. And despite his gruff manner and lack of political correctness, he is greatly superior to the new generation of smooth-talking vipers like Carl Henderson, who are ruining the good old ways with their newfangled technology. When Otto goes to Carl Henderson's house to confront him for assaulting Julie, Henderson locks him in the basement with poisonous scorpions that sting him to death.

Dawn Sanderson, who appears in the prologue of the novel, is one of Carl Henderson's victims. She is a sixteen-year-old who runs away from home to escape her stepfather's attempts to molest her. Filled with new hope, she dreams of "making it" in Hollywood and vows to change her name to Dawn Morningstar. Carl Henderson offers her a lift in his car, and she ends up being fodder for his flesh-eating insects.

Jeff Larkin is the character who becomes infested by the bugs that fly out of Julie's mouth as he is trying to rape her. He is not particularly likable. Though not diabolically evil like Henderson, he lacks any redeeming moral qualities. At one point he is about to pass the insect sickness on to his little brother, but Kevin shouts a warning, and the little boy runs away.

Andy Bennett is another teenager who is transformed into one of Julie's drones.

Dr. Ellen Filmore's role in the novel is to do the medical detective work of finding out what is happening to the teenagers and then provide an explanation to the readers about microscopic entities in the bloodstream, which are destroying parts of Julie's, Kevin's, Jeff's, and Andy's brains.

Carl Henderson, the entomologist, is the antagonist of the novel. He is another obsessed scientist type, spending lonely hours isolated in his basement working on his self-initiated research project of trying to build a better bee—one that can withstand the effects of the UniGrow chemical fertilizers the farmers use. Like several of Saul's other single-minded scientists, one can detect a certain parallel to the solitary figure of the novelist at work, spending lonely hours at his keyboard, trying to spin the ultimate novel out of his imagination.

Although Carl turns Julie into a human insect through the chemicals he has developed, that is just an accident. He had no idea the antivenom substitute would have that effect. His principal mode of villainy is not that of mad scientist, but that of serial killer. He has a split personality and experiences an overwhelming urge to kill a certain type of teenage girl. His method of killing them is quite sadistic, letting them be overrun by flesh-eating ants. His split personality goes back to an incident when he was four years old and accidentally walked in on his sister and her boyfriend having sex in the living room. His sister became very angry with him: "You little creep! . . . Didn't I warn you to stay outside until I told you to come in?" (376). The reason little Carl had burst into the house was because he was excited about the butterfly he had just caught in a jar. His sister says, "Stay in here if you like bugs so much," and locks him in a dark basement room that is crawling with termites (377). Since this trauma, he developed a compulsion to kill girls whose appearance reminds him of his sister.

There is a parallel here to the character of Monsignor Peter Vernon in *Punish the Sinners*, who accidentally witnessed his parents having sex when he was a young child and then saw his sister kill his parents; as a result of this, he develops a compulsion in adulthood to cause the death of teenage girls. But unlike Monsignor Vernon, who gets away scot free, Carl Henderson is destroyed by a creature that embodies a combination of the girls he has murdered and the bugs he has killed for his collection. The Hindus and Buddhists have a concept called karma: What you do comes back to you. Carl's demise is a karmic payback. The sister who punished him in the dark basement, and whom he in turn punished in the same way in surrogate form, returns in yet another incarnation to reinflict the same chastisement upon him.

GENRE

At one time insects were more popular than vampires as a source of horrific chills. Professor May Berenbaum, author of *Bugs in the System* (1995), hosts an annual Insect Fear Film Festival through the University of Illinois Entomology Department, at which she shows long-forgotten films like *Brain Eaters* (1958) about maggots that take over your personality. The largest category is movies about radioactively mutated giant insects, reflecting the 1950s fear of the A-bomb and nuclear fallout.

The Homing does not appear to owe anything to these now-campy B-movies. Instead, the novel's creative antecedents can be viewed as in part derivative of three classic films: John Fowles's *The Collector* (which was made into a movie in 1965), Alfred Hitchcock's *The Birds* (a 1963 film based on the short story by Daphne de Maurier), and David Cronenberg's 1986 cinematic remake of *The Fly*. From *The Collector* comes the notion of a psychologically disturbed individual who initially is obsessed with butterflies and later expands his collection by kidnapping a woman he is obsessed with. Although Carl Henderson is more vicious and sadistic than John Fowles's character, his "pinning" of one of his victims to the wall, just as insects are pinned in their display cases, reveals the similarity of their obsessions.

From David Cronenberg's *The Fly* comes the notion of a gradual transformation from human to insect: The metamorphosis becomes externally evident only in the last stage; in the beginning it is largely internal, as alien, insect-like patterns of thought begin to take over the human consciousness. In *The Homing* Julie's body becomes bloated and distended. Her fingers turn into long sharp stingers that emit poison. And she emits pheromonal chemicals through which she communicates to the insect hordes and directs them. Her personal identity is submerged in the life of the insect colony, and her mind has become a focal point for the expression of the collective will of the hive. As a queen bee in a still largely human body, she is attended by Kevin, Andy, and Jeff, who have metamorphosed into human drones who chew food and feed her from their own mouths.

From *The Birds* comes the concept that small creatures that individually are relatively harmless can pose a frightening, destructive threat when massed in great numbers. The scene in which Karen is in the house, views a great black cloud of bees outside the window, and wonders if they can burrow in is strongly reminiscent of the anxiety aroused by the flocks of birds in the Hitchcock thriller.

The truly horrific aspect of the novel is not the special effects of Julie's body becoming more wasplike. The horror comes from the sense of dislocation when perspective shifts from the human mind in its apparent individuality to the transpersonal group mind. This reversal of figure and ground is similar to the peculiar perspective that biologists take when they view human bodies as vehicles that genes use to perpetuate themselves. In our pride we think of ourselves as passing on "our" genes. But to the genes—if they could think as humans do—"we" are *their* mechanism for recreating themselves and exist to maintain their immortality.

Julie experiences a similar mental shift of perspective long before her body begins outwardly changing: "Soon she began to understand that the bees weren't individuals at all, but merely tiny parts of the swarm that together comprised a single being. A being that was communicating with her" (329). As her transformation into a human-insect hybrid progresses, she and the two boys begin responding to non-verbal messages from an alien mind—the collective insect mind—which is communicated to them through the pattern of the dance of the insects in flight.

Saul effectively evokes this altered consciousness, and it is instructive to compare his treatment of it with the brilliant exploration of the same theme in Frederic Brown's powerful 1949 story "Come and Go Mad," in which an alien mind composed of trillions of red and black ants, called The Brightly Shining, plays cosmic games using human beings as pawns. ("Your mind is under partial control and your ability to recognize me is blocked out. . . . I am an instrument of The Brightly Shining" [Brown 1981, 309].)

THEMES

Saul returns in this novel to some of the ecological themes of his previous novel *Sleepwalk*, where he discussed the negative implications of technology in the setting of an oil-refining town. There Saul compared technology to a Pandora's box: Once opened, it unleashes a swarm of problems, and yet there is no easy way to stuff it back in the box. *The Homing* explores some of the same issues in relation to agriculture. The farmers in Pleasant Valley need bees to fertilize the alfalfa crop. Pollination is a millions-of-years-old natural process, which still has not been supplanted by machines. But chemical and genetic technologies are exploring ways to engineer living organisms as though they were machines. UniGrow (shades of the sinister UniChem from *Sleepwalk*?) markets a new chemical fertilizer, which has supposedly been thoroughly tested, but which turns out to make the bees sterile. This is potentially disastrous, and as a makeshift remedy the farmers have to bring in new bees from outside the area every season. Carl Henderson begins experimenting with ways to create hybrid bees that can withstand this fertilizer. But every new technological solution creates a new problem. The venom of the hybrid bees is particularly virulent, and little Molly almost dies after she is stung by one. So technology has to advance another step, to manufacture an antivenom that can combat the more potent venom. All this represents realistic concerns about agricultural technology.

Since nature is anthropomorphized as female in this culture ("Mother Nature"), the ecofeminists—feminists who are concerned about ecology—argue that misuse of the environment is linked to the same attitude that produces the devaluing of women. Although human bodies are a part of nature, this is more obviously so in the case of women whose bodies are directly subject to nature's provisions for biological reproduction—menstruation, pregnancy, childbirth, and lactation. The female body—the real female body, not the idealized fantasy body of men's magazines—bears witness to these organic processes in various ways, including the distended abdomen of pregnancy.

Therefore, a related theme of the novel deals with men's distorted attitudes toward women. The ultimate form of this is Carl's utter hatred of young women. But subtler forms are also explored, particularly the ways in which young men project their own sexual feelings onto the female and shift responsibility to her. One example of this, which was discussed earlier in the section on irony, is the scene where Jeff sees Julie making the ambiguous gesture of licking her lips and assumes that she "wants it," and that he now has permission to rape her on the theory that "girls say no when they mean yes." Another example is that after Carl is accused of trying to rape Julie down by the hives, Deputy Mark

Shannon begins thinking that maybe she is "jail bait"—a seductive Lolita who teased Carl into coming on to her sexually. There is speculation going around that Julie is "loose" because she comes from the big city, and also because she and Kevin left a group of kids they were drinking beer with under the power lines and wandered off by themselves. And everyone knows what *that* means! However, this, too, is a false interpretation of Julie's behavior. She asked Kevin to leave with her because she was feeling sick. The humming of the electric power lines intensifies the rate at which the insects reproduce inside her body. Incidentally, this is another example of the negative impact of technology—in this case, electric power.

In Saul's earlier novels, a protagonist like Julie would have become ostracized by her peer group as her behavior became stranger, and ultimately she would have committed suicide. Unlike this earlier formula, *The Homing* is another example of Saul's recent tendency to shift in the course of the novel from a single protagonist (i.e., Julie) to a collectivity of adolescent peers who ultimately bring about the destruction of an adult villain by bending his own destructive devices back upon him. As was argued in discussing *Darkness* (see Chapter 9), this probably reflects the changed mood of society, including the trend for victims of sexual abuse or harassment to unite and bring the perpetrators to account, as reflected in Anita Hill's confrontation of Supreme Court nominee Clarence Thomas, the furor over the Navy's Tail Hook scandal, and the indictment of former clergymen, like Raymond Porter in Massachusetts, who was charged by a group of adults with sexually molesting them when they were children.

A FREUDIAN READING OF *THE HOMING*

The method of Freudian, or psychoanalytic, analysis was outlined in Chapter 7. Freud was concerned with what he called "the instincts," particularly the sexual instinct. Beneath the horrific insect imagery, *The Homing* is a novel that is dripping with sexuality. In his analysis of the Oedipus complex Freud focused on incestuous sexual desires. *The Homing* opens with a sixteen-year-old girl running away from home because her stepfather has made it clear he wants to have sex with her. The girl, Dawn Sanderson, becomes a victim of Carl Henderson, in whom normal sexuality has been displaced by a sadistic pleasure he gets out of torturing girls who resemble his sister. Incestuous enough? Henderson hates his sister because she punished him as a child for observing her in the act of sexual intercourse.

Next we go to the wedding scene between Karen and Russell. A bee gets under nine-year-old Molly's dress during the ceremony. Just as the minister pronounces them man and wife, and they kiss, the bee plunges its stinger into her thigh. By putting these two events in conjunction, the author has established a subliminal association between sexual union, as symbolized by the wedding, and the act of the bee penetrating the flesh under Molly's dress.

After this, Carl Henderson's personal demons become aroused by Julie's resemblance to his sister, and he feels compelled to kidnap her and bring her to his torture chamber. This occurs while Julie is near the bee hives. Once again, a subliminal association is set up. She escapes from Henderson, but like her sister, she is stung by a bee at that moment.

Later, when Julie has begun her transformation, her symptomatic behavior is interpreted as signalling her sexual availability. And when Jeff attempts to have sex with her, she infects him with the insect sickness through mouth contact. Sexuality again, and clearly the author was aware of the parallels with AIDS in terms of the sexual mode of transmission (though not by kissing, in the case of AIDS).

Kevin feels attracted to Julie as a girl rather than a sister and is happy that the feeling is mutual. Although they are not blood relatives, they are brother and sister by marriage, so there is an incestuous flavor to their relationship. After Kevin becomes infected with Julie's disease, he passes it on to Sara McLaughlin. He is compelled by the colony of insects within him to approach her mouth with his. She thinks he is sexually attracted to her and opens her mouth to receive his kiss, but gets his insects instead. At another point the same inner force tries to compel Kevin to put his mouth to that of Molly, his nine-year-old stepsister. As noble as he is, he is barely able to resist. This scene evokes the dark side of sexuality, involving incest and forbidden impulses toward much younger children.

At one point, as she hears the droning of the bees, Julie's consciousness begins to "drop away into some bottomless darkness." As she loses control to the "dark force within her," she feels a "feverish heat" and strips off all her clothing (227). When she recovers consciousness, hundreds of bees are fanning her with a gentle breeze, and others are clinging to her naked body, stimulating the nerve endings of her skin with their legs. Something within her responds to the sensuality of this.

Turning to the insects themselves, the bee is the sexual messenger of the flowers, acting as an agent of reproduction by transferring the pollen. For this reason the bee is traditionally a symbol of sexuality and fertility. The queen bee's role is entirely bound up with sexuality and reproduction, as she lays up to two thousand eggs a day.

Andy Bennett feels Julie reach out to him with her mind and draw him to the cave where she has gone. The walls of the cave are lined with living insects, in contrast to Carl Henderson's house, which is lined with specimens of dead insects. He finds her lying naked, swollen and distended, covered with insects. This both fascinates and repulses him. This one scene encompasses images of sexuality (nakedness), fertility (swollen and distended), and decay (covered with insects). This is what French intellectual Julia Kristeva in *Powers of Horror* calls *the abject*: "It is . . . not lack of cleanliness . . . that causes abjection but what disturbs identity, system, order" (1982, 4). To escape abjection, "The body must bear no trace of its debt to nature. . . . Any secretion or discharge, anything that leaks out of the . . . body defiles" (1982, 102). Abjection is a feeling that is particularly likely to attach to perceptions of a woman's body, which reveals the human subordination to biology. Horror exploits this feeling through depicting "monstrous" changes to the human body. Since insects are associated with repulsive odors and sights—slimy, decaying organic matter, refuse, disease, and death—they, too, partake of the abject.

Andy's response to Julie's abjection is an ambivalent one—fascination and repulsion, like the emotions of the princess in a fairy tale whose sexual initiation consists of kissing a frog. Fascination accompanying repulsion is a characteristic initial response to sexuality or to any core biological or instinctual imperative when it is scrutinized—such as eating meat—because such acts are perceived as both self (since we are biological) and not-self (since we seek to define ourselves apart from nature). In the end, however, fascination wins out. When next we see the boys, they have become abjected members of Julie-insect's retinue. Kevin is now a drone, feeding his queen chewed-up food from his own mouth.

The teenagers have lost their personalities as their minds are submerged into the collectivity of the hive. The highly organized society of the hive with its absorption of individuality could remind the reader of Dr. Greg Moreland's megalomanic dream in *Sleepwalk* of a nation of robotic drones, who fulfill their task mindlessly and contentedly. But in *The Homing* the author seems to be suggesting an opposite risk. Like Odysseus's sailors, who are at risk of destruction from either Scylla or Charybdis, individuality can founder on the shore of a totally lifeless, work-oriented mentality or on the opposite shore of complete surrender to the vital instincts. The threat of the hive to Julie is that it represents the Dionysian impulse to abandon one's hard-won self and merge seamlessly into the hedonistic oblivion of instinctual life.

In the final climax when Julie travels in royal procession to Henderson's house flanked by Kevin and Jeff and surrounded by a great cloud of insects, cutting a wide swath through the countryside, she has become transformed into an instinctual symbol—what the Jungians would call an archetype. She has become a chthonic or dark goddess—an embodiment of nature's amoral elemental power—like the beautiful Artemis of Greek mythology, who transforms into the dreaded nighttime deity Hecate, traveling with a pack of howling hounds and ornamented by a headfull of snakes.

12

Black Lightning
(1995)

> He who fights with monsters might take care lest he thereby becomes
> a monster. And if you gaze for long into an abyss, the abyss gazes
> into you.
>
> Friedrich Nietzsche, *Beyond Good and Evil* (1886)

Black Lightning is John Saul's nineteenth and most recent novel. It was
released in July 1995 as a hardcover by Fawcett Columbine. It breaks
new ground in that it is his first work of fiction set in a metropolis. The
supernatural elements are minimal. This novel demonstrates a new level
of mature stylistic craftsmanship on Saul's part.

PLOT

The novel opens in Seattle, Washington, with a narrative from the
point of view of someone who is performing some type of experiment.
Gradually, it becomes clear that what is being called an "experiment"
here is one more in a series of gruesome mutilation murders by a serial
killer who is called the Experimenter.

In the next chapter we flash ahead five years and are inside a woman's
mind, eavesdropping on her thoughts concerning an execution she is

about to witness. The woman whose thoughts we are overhearing is Anne Jeffers, Seattle newspaper reporter. She is about to witness the execution of the Experimenter—convicted serial killer Richard Kraven. His name sounds like "craven," fitting for a murderer. Anne led a crusade in her newspaper to get Kraven convicted, and finally she will feel the satisfaction of seeing justice done. It has taken two years—two years from when he was arrested to the day of his execution. Before he dies, he wants to have an interview with her. Apprehensively, she listens. He says the killings will not end with his execution; the murders will begin again. And when that happens, he tells her—intense hatred in his eyes— Anne will realize she was responsible for executing an innocent man. She is shaken by this.

The story cuts to Anne's husband, Glen, an architect in his mid-forties, who is with his partner, Alan Cline, on a scaffolding high atop their latest high rise. They are there to drink a champagne toast to their successful architectural project, but Glen is beginning to feel a touch of acrophobia in reaction to the height. He imagines the girders will crumple like a house of cards. As they toss their empty glasses over the side of the scaffolding and watch them fall to the pavement, Glen is seized with a giddy panic and collapses into a heart attack. There is a parallel between what is happening to him and to Anne. Just at a moment when they are basking in success, both experience an unexpected, severe jolting.

Cut back to Richard Kraven, being executed. He is killed by 2,000 volts of electricity surging through his body. Just before he dies Anne can feel the intensity of his malevolent stare. He seems to be looking directly at her, even through the one-way mirrored window of the execution chamber.

Cut back to Glen, who is in an ambulance. The paramedics attempt to revive him with 360 joules of electricity from the paddles of the defibrillator. Glen has already left his body. In a nicely written passage Saul shows him speeding down a long tunnel, being beckoned toward the end, where his grandparents are waiting to greet him, as described in currently popular books like Betty Eadie's *Embraced by the Light* (1992). The paramedics stimulate Glen's heart with another jolt of electricity, and he comes back to his body again. He is taken to a hospital where Anne comes to see him.

Days later we cut to the Experimenter—the one we were introduced to at the start of the book. It has been so long since he has let himself think about another "experiment." Two years, in fact. Now he is planning his next murder. So Richard Kraven was innocent after all?

All of this action gets set up within the first one-fifth of the book. It is a fast-paced, taut thriller that grabs the reader from the beginning and never lets up. The basic plot line can be broken down into four strands. First, the serial killings have begun again. The police will eventually realize that there are two killers on the loose: one replicates Richard Kraven's style of killing with eerie precision, the other is a clumsy imitator. This segment of the plot is along the lines of a police procedural crime story. Second, crusading reporter Anne Jeffers has been targeted as a victim and is receiving written threats from the Experimenter. She and her children are at risk. This can be called the woman-in-peril segment of the plot. Third, Anne's husband is experiencing blackouts and disquieting personality changes. What is happening to him? This could be called the "uncanny" portion of the plot. Fourth, Detective Mark Blakemoor has a crush on Anne Jeffers and would like somehow to get a serious relationship going with her. Anne loves her husband, Glen, but is feeling a gulf develop between them as Glen becomes increasingly strange and secretive. Despite herself, she feels an impulse to lean emotionally on the strength of Mark Blakemoor. This is the love-interest portion of the plot.

Saul exploits each element of the story to its fullest effect. For example, he introduces a minor character, Sheila Harrar—a Native American woman who has become an alcoholic since her son was murdered by Richard Kraven—and manages to wring three separate interludes of suspense out of the one character. First she calls Anne Jeffers because she has some important information to give her. She hopes Anne will be interested in what she has to say, but fears Anne may discount her as a "drunken Indian" like the police did. She leaves a message on Anne's voice-mail, but the end of the message gets garbled, so Anne is not able to make out how to reach the woman. We suspensefully wonder whether the woman will call back or whether she will give up and wrongly decide that Anne does not care. Later there is a scene where Sheila decides to call again, but this time to Anne's house. Anne is not home, but a male answers. Is it the Experimenter? He seems very interested in hearing all about the woman's story. We wonder if he is going to go to where she lives and kill her. Finally Anne manages to track down some information on the woman in the police files. As she is driving out to the area where the woman is located, we experience anticipatory anxiety that

Anne will find her dead. With that one minor character Saul has managed to get three bites out of the apple.

Saul also manages to unobtrusively introduce little snippets of social consciousness–raising into the plot, concerning issues that are important to the gay and lesbian communities: violence against gay people, death from AIDS, and legislative battles over basic legal recognition of gay and lesbian partnerships.

SUSPENSE

Saul keeps planting little anxiety-raising possibilities. The copycat killer, the Butcher, obtains entry to Anne's next-door neighbor's house by finding her spare key hidden under the doormat, knowing that many people have an extra key hidden somewhere. When it is revealed that Anne's family also hides their key in the planter on the front porch, a warning note sounds in the reader's mind. Does this foreshadow the Butcher's gaining entry to Anne's house with the hidden key? As it turns out, it does not. But it raises another possibility to keep the reader's mind spinning and anxiety churning.

Saul builds up an air of anticipation through frequent repetition of the anxious thought that danger can strike unexpectedly. As Anne is leaving the hospital, Glen warns her to be careful because "There're a lot of creeps out there" (89). And sure enough, as Anne is walking, she can feel someone watching her. And then we shift to the point of view of the Experimenter, who indeed was watching Anne. She feels his gaze. And he can tell that she feels it. Next Glen is looking out his hospital window and sees a man. The man looks up at Glen, observing him, and thinks he would like to go up to the hospital room right now and rip Glen's life supports out.

Then Glen returns home from the hospital, and as he goes about the house, he has the feeling someone is watching him, but when he turns suddenly, there is no one there. The cumulative effect of all this is similar to that created by the rising tempo of eerie mood music on the sound track of a movie, as the heroine is turning corner after corner in the house, and we know that eventually something is going to jump at her as she rounds one of these corners, and with each one we brace ourselves and hold our breath, and then relax, and then brace ourselves again as the next corner comes into view and the music rises again. Finally the thing jumps out at us!

Another way suspense is developed is when Glen tries to tell his doctors about the mysterious blackouts he is having. The reader is on the edge of his or her seat, wanting to scream as the individuals who each have critical pieces of information keep missing opportunities to communicate with each other. The tension level is ratcheted up as the reader wonders if Anne and the doctors will put the puzzle pieces together to realize the truth before it is too late.

IRONY AND HUMOR

Although Saul is quite sparing with the use of humor, there is more of it in this novel than in his previous ones. Some of the humor is dark—very dark. As Robert Bloch has pointed out, comedy and horror are different sides of the same coin: "Both of them involve the grotesque, the unexpected. . . . Humor relies upon the twist, just as the shock in horror relies upon some kind of twist" (quoted in Robinson 1994, 6). A case in point is the murder scene involving the pathetic Rory Kraven. Named by his mother after her favorite star, Rory Calhoun, he is constantly trying unsuccessfully to get his mother's approval. Finally styling himself as the Butcher, he decides to rival his brother Richard by also becoming a serial killer, thinking maybe then his mother will love him. There is something extremely absurd and out of kilter about the thinking that would produce such a motive. Yet it truly exists, as can be seen from people like John Hinckley, who tried to murder President Reagan to make actress Jodie Foster fall in love with him. Absurdity can coexist with horror, and this is doubly underlined by the tragic, yet ridiculous, scene where Rory jumps out of a closet and murders Anne's neighbor:

> "Love me!" he commanded as the knife slashed down to plunge deep into Joyce Cottrell's breast. "Just love me!" (180)

At a time when millions of Americans tuned in nightly to the O. J. Simpson murder trial, Saul mocks our interest in sensational crime (and his, too) through the lens of black humor. The day after Joyce Cottrell's murder a convenience store clerk, not knowing he is talking to the murderer, announces that the victim had been in the convenience store the night before. Rory, covering up his nervousness, feigns surprise: "You mean here . . . right *here*?" Gratified by this apparent display of interest, the newly self-important clerk nods and eagerly says, "She came in here practically every night for a latte on her way home" (241–242).

The mention of latte, a flavored coffee and steamed milk drink, is yet another reference to the gourmet coffee phenomenon, which has come to be a trademark of Seattle. It becomes a running joke, with references to Starbuck's coffee and latte peppered throughout the book. Even one of the Experimenter's slayings is prefaced by a cup of coffee shared with the victim.

There are one-line gags: Glen's daughter buys a CD album of a band with the absurd, yet possible, name "Crippled Chickens." And inside jokes: The construction company's secretary is named Janie Berkey, the name of Saul's literary agent at the start of his career. Saul has the detestable Edna Kraven idiotically complain of a newspaper article: "How dare she write such filth?" (76), an accusation that the author has heard in real life concerning his own writing.

In a more lighthearted vein, at the emergency room, when Glen is being ushered in by ambulance to revive him from his heart attack, Alan explains to the receptionist that he is Glen's partner, then nervously adds "*business* partner," so she will not think he meant they are a gay couple. Her response is an apathetic "Whatever" (46). Some of the humor may be unintentional. After slaying the Jefferses' pet cat, the Experimenter butchers the *copy*cat. It is not clear if this pun was intended, but it is certainly implicit. And is the Jefferses' pet cat yet another incarnation of poor Cecil, Beth's first victim, from *Suffer the Children*?

CHARACTERS

The Experimenter is a protagonist of the novel. He is a central character, but not one that the reader willingly identifies with. Yet we are forced into intimacy with him and made to see events through his eyes as never before with a John Saul villain. The Experimenter is an eerie character. Is he Richard Kraven? Glen Jeffers? Or someone else? Our uncertainty as to who or what he is makes him all the more frightening because we cannot anticipate when or how he will materialize. Periodically, the narration switches to his point of view. At the moment when he invades the text the print switches to bold lettering, as though even the physical typography of the book is affected by his presence.

The Experimenter is concerned with the borderline between life and death. Like Dr. Greg Moreland of *Sleepwalk*, the Experimenter as a child tried killing an animal and then reviving it. Like Victor Frankenstein, his ambition is to reanimate a dead corpse. After he has cut the victim's chest open and stopped the heart, he uses electricity to try to start the life process again. His acts of murder are not done in a frenzy. They are almost emotionless, highly controlled, and surgically precise.

The Experimenter is very interested in the "life force" of living things, which he experiences as something akin to an electrical flow. Just before killing one of his victims he is described as gazing at her unconscious body, "savoring the life that seemed to radiate from it" (7). This obsession with the "life force" of the victims is reminiscent of horror writer Dean Koontz's professional killer Vince Nasco in *Watchers* (1987), who gets a sensual charge out of death, while finding sex repulsive. However, Koontz's villain imagines that he can absorb the victim's life force, and that after accumulating enough murders, he will become immortal. Saul's character the Experimenter is not just seeking immortality, but also trying to unravel the essential secret of Life and Death, the spark of "invisible black lightning that emanated from somewhere deep within the body itself" (182), which he symbolizes with the double lightning bolts that were the insignia of Hitler's SS.

The Experimenter seeks to play God. In his dialogue with Danny, a Native American boy, there is a discussion of a creation myth where a fish's belly is sliced open. This excites the Experimenter because it is similar to what he does to his victims. When Danny compares this to the biblical creation myth of Eve being taken out of Adam's rib, the Experimenter corrects him, saying, "But it wasn't a man who opened Adam. . . . It was God" (147).

Anne Jeffers and her husband, Glen, are the two central characters, apart from the Experimenter. Anne is a big-city reporter who is a mom as well as a career woman. She spent two years concentrating on the Richard Kraven case. This put her in close association with Detective Mark Blakemoor, who was part of the special investigatory task force. It has also made her number one on Kraven's hate-list. Now that it looks like Kraven may somehow be back from the dead, she and her children are at risk.

Glen Jeffers, Anne's husband, is an architect who designs high rises and is a fit, health-conscious individual who jogs daily. It comes as a shock to Anne when he is struck with a heart attack. In the opening chapters of the novel a certain parallelism is almost subliminally suggested between Glen and Richard Kraven. Kraven shouts at Anne, and the sound of his voice "bounced off the concrete and metal walls of the cell block'' (27). This image of something ricocheting off metal and concrete is subtly echoed when Glen tosses his champagne glass from the top of the high rise and it falls past the steel girders and shatters onto the concrete. Continuing the parallels, Kraven is bound with straps into the electric chair; then in the next chapter Glen is seized with a sudden panic and feels as though a metal band is being tightened around his chest. Kraven is killed by 2,000 volts of life-destroying electricity, and Glen is revived by 360 joules of life-giving electricity from the paramedic's defibrillator, which starts his heart going again. These parallels are each very subtly suggested, not at all heavy-handed.

The theme of electricity is used later to suggest a disturbing symmetry between Glen and the Experimenter. When Glen returns home from the hospital and is making love to Anne, he has a disquieting experience:

> As his fingers touched her bare skin, a sensation went through him he'd never felt before. Her skin seemed to tingle under his touch, as if somehow an electric charge were running through her. . . . It was as though her very life force were flowing into him, and he felt he was absorbing it through his fingers, his palms. (131–132)

Reading this passage with foreknowledge of the Experimenter's obsession with electricity and the ''life force,'' the reader experiences a chill.

Detective Mark Blakemoor is a 6'2", 210-pound police investigator whose wife, Patsy, left him ten months ago because he was too absorbed in his job and drinking too much. He has begun to notice Anne, and when her husband has a heart attack, he begins wondering what might happen between them if her husband dies.

Anne's two children, Heather, age fifteen, and her slightly younger brother, Kevin, play minor roles in the novel. Essentially, they are there to increase the suspense as additional potential victims. The reader feels heightened tension because of the natural sympathy for children and the knowledge of how devastated Anne would be if they were hurt or killed.

Sheila Harrar is an effectively portrayed minor character. She is a Native American woman who by degrees has slid into skid-row alcoholism. Within the economical space of three pages Saul gets us to care about her by deftly sketching her character in a way that conveys her essential humanity and spark of dignity. He convincingly demonstrates how for her, at this moment of her life, a simple thing that we take for granted—

making a phone call—has become an epic act akin to the incredible shrinking man's crossing an intersection.

Other minor characters include the physician and the psychiatrist. The physician's reassurance of Glen that there is nothing wrong with him will recall to many readers their first realization of how far off the mark doctors can sometimes be. The psychiatrist is a less sympathetic character than the physician. Most readers will be put off by his air of smug superiority as he discounts Glen's experiences with the statement: "A very simple suggestion can implant false memories that are every bit as vivid as genuine ones. We're seeing it all the time in child sex-abuse cases" (319). The psychiatrist's explanations have an air of reasonableness, but they are disastrously wrong.

At the center of the novel's mystery is Richard Kraven, the executed man. What is his connection to the Experimenter? Is he the dreaded serial murderer? Kraven was a charismatic university professor who mastered several abstruse subjects. Like some other real-life convicted killers, such as Dr. Jeffrey MacDonald of Joe McGinniss's *Fatal Vision* (1983), he continued to proclaim his innocence to the end and had a band of admirers who fervently believed him. When Anne sees him just before his execution, he is sitting calmly reading a book of Victorian poetry, like the cultured serial killer Doctor Hannibal Lecter in Thomas Harris's *The Silence of the Lambs* (1988). But when he talks to her, she can see and feel the fury within him, and she is chilled to the bone. In his intellectualism, his profound aloneness, and his lack of an appreciation of moral limits Kraven superficially resembles the type of antihero described by Russian novelist Dostoyevsky.

Two very unsympathetic characters are Richard Kraven's mother, Edna, and brother, Rory. Edna Kraven is a caricature of the highly dysfunctional parent, unable to recognize reality. She refuses to believe Richard is guilty and is forever singing his praises, while constantly criticizing her younger son, Rory, who has developed a terrible inferiority complex. We later learn that Richard's father tortured him physically and sexually as a child, and that when he told Edna, she told him he was mistaken and did nothing to protect him. It is hard to feel much sadness about Edna getting killed.

Rory Kraven becomes a serial killer called the Butcher in order to show he is as "good" as Richard. Having the Butcher running loose, confusing the police, while the Experimenter is also at work is a brilliant complication to the plot and has the additional advantage of allowing the author to contrast the relatively mundane barbarity of the Butcher to the utterly alien, crystalline monstrosity of the Experimenter's mentality.

Rory kills people's bodies, and Edna killed her sons' souls. When both become victims of the Experimenter, the reader does not mourn their passing.

SPECIAL NARRATIVE DEVICES

Young children have to learn the conventions as to where to draw the line between reality and make-believe. The first time they attend a play where a blank gun is fired on stage, they think that someone is really being killed, or at least are unsure of it. But then they absorb the conventions. They learn that the boundary between the audience and the stage also marks the difference between the finality of real life and the repeatability of dramatic evocation.

Of course, these boundaries do not always hold. On the set of the recent movie *The Crow* (1994) Brandon Lee was killed by a prop gun mistakenly loaded with live ammunition instead of blanks. Such an event is exceptional. Nevertheless, it is true that sometimes boundaries give way. The stock horror movie plot of the dangerous circus animal escaping from its cage, or King Kong breaking his chains, refers to such an event, in which the line is breached between art and reality.

Saul uses an innovative technique to play on such fears in *Black Lightning*. When Glen is shaving, he feels someone is watching him. He turns around and is knocked out. Then we shift to the perspective of the Experimenter, heralded by the appearance of the bold typeface that signals his narrative presence. The Experimenter picks up Glen's razor and examines it. He takes it apart, the way he takes apart his human victims, until it is useless. Then he brings it to the trash can outside. The neighbor sees him and is terrified by the evil look he gives her.

Five hours later Glen wakes up on the bathroom floor. As he gets up, he sees that his electric razor is in the sink, where it apparently fell when he passed out. As readers, we not only observe his disorientation; we now participate in it. The reader's mind reels. "Didn't I just see the Experimenter destroy the razor and drop it in the trash?" the reader thinks. "Was that a dream or fantasy sequence? Or was that all taking place at the Experimenter's house?"

"That must be it," the reader concludes. "It's a parallel action taking place elsewhere. It's just a coincidence that the Experimenter is taking apart his own razor at the moment when, at a separate location, Glen has just fainted and dropped his razor."

But then the neighbor, Joyce Cottrell, reports to Anne that Glen was out in the backyard that afternoon and gave her an evil look. "So maybe that was Glen after all?" thinks the reader. But, no, it can't be. Glen's razor is in his bathroom, not in the trash. And so confusion hits the reader again.

Then several pages later Glen picks up the razor from the sink and realizes it is not his. It is a brand new one. And his old one is in fact in the backyard trash can, completely demolished. What is happening here? The author has designed the text so that the reader is not simply observing the character's confusion, but is actually entering into the confusion with the character.

There is another example of this narrative technique. Glen goes back up to the top of the building to overcome his fear of heights. As he approaches the precipice, he becomes numbed with fear and is irresistibly drawn to throw himself off the brink. The reader feels sympathetic fear. Then Glen blacks out, and an alternate personality kicks in. That personality leaves to murder Rory, the Butcher. The reader sees him enter Rory's shabby apartment, and the door closes. Then Glen wakes up in an apartment, naked and covered with blood. He goes to the bathroom to wash it off and finds—to his horror—the body of the Butcher in the bathtub with his chest torn open. Anxious thoughts flash through the reader's mind. Will someone stumble onto this scene and surprise Glen in these compromising circumstances? Then Glen stumbles and falls onto the body, which comes alive and tries to bite him. The reader is horrified, but then realizes this cannot be real. Glen wakes up, and he is still lying on the edge of the precipice. So it was all a dream? The part where the alternate personality took over and left to go kill Rory—was that a dream, too? After all, it appears Glen has not left this spot. Or has he?

This is like dreaming of waking up within a dream. You believe you are awake, but you are still dreaming. The author is dreaming the dream of the character, and the reader is dreaming with him, identifying with Glen Jeffers. The novel, the reader's creature, has assumed a life of its own and is jolting the reader back and forth, jarringly, between what is dream and what is reality, creating a sense of terror from the unpredictability. It is like being on the wild elevator ride that Amy (another out-of-control creation) gave Hildie in *Shadows*.

THEMES

Two related themes dominate this novel. One is the fear that is engendered by the sense that there is no solid and substantial foundation for establishing absolute meaning in life. The other is a complex of ideas about the border between life and death.

As Glen stands at the top of his partially constructed building—a forty-five-story structure of naked steel girders—he glances down. His senses reel at the sight of the abyss yawning beneath his feet. The focus of his perception has suddenly changed. He glimpses the insubstantiality of what stands between him and the terrible abyss. This blinding flash of perception of vulnerability is similar to that of Frank Arnold in *Sleepwalk*: Frank becomes painfully aware, as he is crawling on his back through a tunnel in the dam, of the thousands of tons of concrete and water whose weight he imaginatively feels pressing down upon him as if to suddenly crush him.

Compared to the vast scale of these forces of nature, the human is a fragile creature, beset each day by hidden dangers from hundreds of potential disasters—from car crashes, muggers, fire, lightning, nuclear disaster—most of which are excluded from the narrow spotlight of daily awareness. Not only outer disasters, but also subversion from within threatens. The individual's body can turn traitor in an instant—delivering a heart attack, stroke, seizure, or sudden amnesia.

As Glen's senses reel at the top of the structure, his body rebels. Saul effectively conveys the frightening feeling of no longer being in command of one's body through a minutely detailed and evocative description of Glen's kinesthetic, tactile, thermal, and auditory sensations: dizziness, a sudden tingling in his groin and in his left arm, the sensation of his scrotum contracting, the cold feel of a clammy coating of sweat, the feeling that metal bands are tightening around his chest, the sound of his heart pounding in his ears, and "the terrible feeling of being drawn forward, pulled as if by some physical force over the edge" (31). He tries to regain control by concentrating on breathing deeply and evenly. But the dissonant harmony of these sensations finally reaches its crescendo as he collapses completely in a heart attack, perched high above the abyss.

The word "abyss" has a dual meaning. On a literal level it represents a chasm or expanse of space, but on a figurative level it signifies "the Void," the primordial cosmic chaos that existed before Creation. The equivalent on the social level is a state of anarchy and disorder. At the level of the individual, the abyss is often equated with madness. This is the sense in which Edgar Allan Poe uses it in his short piece "The Imp of the Perverse":

> We peer into the abyss—we grow sick and dizzy. Our first impulse is to shrink from the danger. Unaccountably we remain. . . . And because our reason violently deters us from the brink, *therefore* do we the most impetuously approach it. . . . Examine these similar actions as we will, we shall find them resulting solely from the spirit of the *Perverse*. We perpetrate them because we feel that we should not. (Poe 1976, 639–640)

The madness that Poe describes in this story is not schizophrenia or some other confused mental state. He is referring to criminality—specifically that peculiar type of criminal act that is fundamentally motivated not by greed, lust, or hatred, but purely by the desire to transgress, to negate the social consensus of norms and values. It is this diabolical impulse that the nineteenth-century writer Dostoyevsky explored in *Crime and Punishment* (1866) and other novels where he shows Nietzschean antiheroes claiming that everything is permitted because God is dead.

In this sense the abyss represents unlimited potentiality and unconditional freedom, for good or for evil. Not freedom in the idealistic and sentimental sense that we mean when we describe freedom as part of the American way of life. The abyss signifies freedom in the existentialist sense: the terrible burden of freedom. This is freedom without guarantees that strips away the coziness and security of life lived within fixed boundaries. This dizzying dropping away of one's cherished notions of how life should be is not pleasant, as voiced by Anne after Glen has his heart attack:

> People like Glen didn't have heart attacks. What was life, anyway? Just a big lottery? Even if you did everything right, did you just drop dead? (47)

Human life is lived within an apparently solid, socially constructed framework of beliefs and expectations that the individual takes for granted as if it were firm ground to walk upon. But according to the existentialists, in reality the "solid ground" is a tightrope suspended in space—or maybe not even that. There is nothing solid to hang onto and no refuge to flee to. The social framework is a provisional form, not an eternal bedrock. It can give way at any time. One of its floorboards can collapse, and you will disappear through the hole that has opened up. Someone you think you know well can suddenly do something so alarmingly unexpected that you feel your previous sense of him or her was an illusion.

It is this feeling of "terrible" freedom that Glen describes as having alarmed him once when making love to his wife after smoking marijuana. Whereas normally he felt "a comforting familiarity" and "a sense of safety" in their lovemaking, on that night

> Everything felt different . . . and he'd had the unnerving sensation that he was making love to a stranger, to a woman he'd never met before. The feeling had frightened him. (132)

In contrast to the fear and trembling that grips Glen when he confronts the existential abyss, the Experimenter is very comfortable balancing on steel girders high off the ground. He is well aware of the void at the core of existence and the radical freedom it implies. And out of the limitless possibilities that freedom offers, he has chosen the dark path, which leads away from human solidarity and fellowship.

Anne is an intermediate character between these two poles. Her job has taken her closer to the edge of life than Glen has been, and she has peered down the depths. After having sex with Glen, she, too, feels as though a stranger was touching her. But her initial response is more ambivalent than his was. She is "thrilled" as well as frightened (133).

A DECONSTRUCTIONIST READING OF *BLACK LIGHTNING*

As discussed in Chapter 3, deconstructionism blurs distinctions that people normally take for granted. For example, most people think of a text as a piece of writing. But to a deconstructionist anything can be viewed as a text—a ritual, an architectural structure, even Being itself. Deconstructionism is also subversive of the boundaries between writer and reader, seeing the construction of the meaning of the text as not being the sole privilege of the author.

Black Lightning itself is a text that is subversive of these boundaries.

Early in the novel Anne Jeffers compares Richard Kraven to Dorian Gray because his face does not show the signs of his depravity. The reference here is to Oscar Wilde's novel *The Picture of Dorian Gray* (1891), in which the central character retains his youthful appearance, despite his crimes, since only his portrait shows the marks of his corruption.

The Picture of Dorian Gray reverses the usual distinction between a work of art and its subject. The artwork is typically timeless—a moment frozen for eternity—whereas in Wilde's novel it is the subject of the work of art who becomes timeless. So, too, *Black Lightning* blurs the distinction between the experiences of character and reader.

Another passage where the novel announces this theme is in the dialogue between the Experimenter and the Native American boy—Sheila Harrar's murdered son: " 'Or maybe one of us doesn't exist?' the boy asked, grinning. . . . 'But which one of us is the figment of the other's imagination?' " (147). This is similar to the question posed by the ancient Chinese philosopher Chuang-Tzu, who dreamed he was a butterfly. Upon awakening he wondered if now he was a butterfly dreaming he was a man.

The puzzle proposed by this question resembles what deconstructionists call "decentering"—the subversion of the distinction between what is primary, or central, and what is secondary, or marginal.

The Experimenter does not subscribe to the notion of decentering. In his mind he is the center; only he exists. "All others were nothing more than the subject matter for his experimentation" (148). As such, he is an image of the author, who can wantonly kill, maim, make fall in or out of love, and generally experiment upon his fictional characters.

The text contains another image of the author as well. It is the image of the creature whose belly must be torn open to give birth. This birth is unilateral creation, giving life to a character torn out of the author's own self-stuff: the brain child, which as discussed in Chapter 6 sometimes becomes independent of the author. This image of creation is explicitly stated in the dialogue between the Experimenter and the Native American boy Danny, where Danny recounts the tribal legend of the first woman coming out of the belly of a salmon. Later in the book the reader encounters the image of Glen awakening, naked and covered with blood, like a newborn baby. He goes into the bathroom and sees Rory with his chest torn open, as though Glen had emerged from inside there.

There is also a third image of the author in the novel. This is represented by Glen when he goes back up to the forty-fifth floor of the new building for a second time. The text provides hints that this is really a cameo appearance by the author. Before he enters the elevator, he greets Janie Berkey, the contractor's secretary. This is actually the name of Saul's agent back when he was writing his first novel. Also, he gives her the excuse of going up to the top floor to get a *pen* he left up there. These clues aside, his central reason for being there is to force himself to peer out over the edge of the abyss again.

Peering over the abyss—this is an image of the author trying imaginatively to enter into the mind of the Experimenter in order to convincingly create the illusion for the reader of being inside the madman's brain. The mind of the Experimenter is like the abyss in its fearsomeness. To recreate it as a tangible experience that can induce terror in the reader, the author must be willing to experience the terror of it in himself first. The author must peer over the abyss and dream his dream, which he communicates to the reader so that it becomes the reader's dream as well. They say dreams cannot harm you, but this would not be the abyss without an underlying fear, perhaps only dimly perceived, that one could fall in.

Edgar Allan Poe was familiar with the abyss, for he describes it in terms similar to Saul's in "The Imp of the Perverse" (1845). His character Dupin, the great detective, in "The Purloined Letter" (1845) must solve the crime by assuming the mind-set of the criminal. This almost occult notion of placing oneself in the criminal's mind shows up in modern fiction like Thomas Harris's *The Silence of the Lambs*, in which the detective asks serial killer Hannibal Lecter for advice in capturing another serial killer. In Michael Mann's film *Manhunter* (1986), which is based on another Thomas Harris novel, the lead detective so immerses himself in the mind of the killer that others become afraid of him and react to him as though he were a killer, too.

This fear of contagion from the characters who inhabit one's imagination is symbolized by the fear of plunging into the abyss. The fear is that the author will not be able to just peer over the edge, but will irrevocably fall in and be swallowed up by the character:

> He felt himself leaning over, and an insane urge to jump blossomed inside him. Now he could feel it, feel the wind rushing past him as he dropped, feel the weightlessness of the fall. If he just let go. (259)

The same fear of contagion holds true for the reader. As Geoffrey O'Brien wrote in *The New York Review of Books*, horror is a "tainted" art form because it flirts with impulses that constitute a real threat to humanity. This is symbolized by two recurring horror themes, which he calls "the fable of the dangerous show" and "the fable of the deranged showman" (1993, 64). The dangerous show is exemplified by something like King Kong breaking out of his chains and wreaking havoc. This symbol represents the reader's fear that imaginatively indulging in horror could liberate something dangerous within him or her. Can a disturbing thought leap from one mind to another like a transmigrating soul changing bodies? While the reader is gazing into horror's abyss, is the abyss gazing into the reader?

The deranged showman is symbolized by Vincent Price in *The House of Wax* (1953), whose lifelike wax dummies conceal the murdered corpses of the individuals they resemble. When the author succeeds all too well in describing some particularly gruesome or revolting act, or in imagining some particularly loathsome character's state of mind, the reader may wonder, "What sort of person is this author, who could imagine these things?" This question can be turned around, of course: "What sort of reader is it who *responds* imaginatively to these descriptions?" We are back to the irresolvable paradox of Chuang-Tzu's butterfly. Does the reader dream he or she is the author, or does the author dream he or she is the reader? Does the work of art allow the reader to imaginatively exorcise his or her demons, functioning like the portrait of Dorian Gray? Or will the art corrupt the reader, the way Dorian Gray instantaneously aged when the painting was destroyed?

The many images of looking and watching strewn throughout the book suggest the presence of a reader, looking at the printed words, imaginatively watching the characters. Readerly voyeurism seems like a harmless, somewhat passive activity. But remember the scene where Rory, walking in the street, is being watched by Glen from his hospital window? Glen here reproduces the activity of the reader. Rory suddenly looks up, reversing the subject-object relationship, and thinks of proceeding directly to Glen's room and killing him. The inert book is about to strike out at the voyeuristic reader. The demons leap from the page and almost attack the very imagination that animates them. For the reader is the mind-stuff of all the parts of the dream, and the dream is as real and also as insubstantial as the electronic cyberspace that Amy of *Shadows* even now inhabits, waiting for someone to join her.

But wait. There is an unexpected element that brilliantly pierces through the disorienting fog of this compassless, deconstructionist landscape. It is an element that Saul had made some tentative passes at in his more recent novels. In *Black Lightning* he commits himself fully for the first time, and lands squarely on the desired effect. In the final pages, he gives the reader a redeeming glimpse of selfless love. A love which, like that of the Christian mystic or Buddhist bodhisattva, has the power to momentarily illuminate the abyss and imbue it with a spontaneously generated meaning. In the fullness of that moment, the multiple deconstructionist paradoxes cease to be of concern. They evaporate and are wafted away in a breath of fresh air.

As the ending of *Second Child* signaled the resolution of a cycle of thematically related stories, the conclusion of *Black Lightning* may also signal a shift to a new octave in Saul's work that will lift it further out of the confines of the genre, and let it resonate more fully with the broad range of human experience, sounding out the lowest to the highest registers, including the sublime as well as the depraved, encompassing hatred and love, evil and good, laughter and tears.

Selected Bibliography

WORKS BY JOHN SAUL

Note: All citations in the text are to the paperback editions, except for *The Homing* and *Black Lightning*, for which the hardbound editions are cited.

Black Lightning. New York: Fawcett Columbine, 1995.
Brainchild. New York: Bantam, 1985.
Comes the Blind Fury. New York: Dell, 1980.
Creature. New York: Bantam, 1990.
Cry for the Strangers. New York: Dell, 1979.
Darkness. New York: Bantam, 1992.
The God Project. New York: Bantam, 1983.
Guardian. New York: Bantam, 1994.
Hellfire. New York: Bantam, 1986.
The Homing. New York: Fawcett Columbine, 1994.
Nathaniel. New York: Bantam, 1984.
Punish the Sinners. New York: Dell, 1978.
Second Child. New York: Bantam, 1991.
Shadows. New York: Bantam, 1993.
Sleepwalk. New York: Bantam, 1990.
Suffer the Children. New York: Dell, 1977.
The Unloved. New York: Bantam, 1988.

The Unwanted. New York: Bantam, 1987.
When the Wind Blows. New York: Dell, 1981.

WORKS ABOUT JOHN SAUL

Chambers, Andrea, and Joni H. Blackman. "Careful Plotting for Success Lets Thriller Writer John Saul Enjoy All the 'Creature' Comforts." *People* 26 (June 1989): 79–80.
Kisner, James. "Interview: John Saul." *Mystery Scene* 16 (1987): 4–5.
Kramer, Laura. "John Saul: 'Remember, It's Only a Story.'" *Twilight Zone*, November 1981: 14.
Saul, John, telephone interview with the author, 17 May 1995.
Wiater, Stanley. "John Saul." In *Dark Dreamers: Conversations with the Masters of Horror*, 173–182. New York: Avon, 1990.

REVIEWS AND CRITICISM

Black Lightning

Booklist 91 (1 June 1995): 1684.
Publishers Weekly 142 (29 May 1995): 66.

Brainchild

Fantasy Review 8 (October 1985): 20.
San Francisco Chronicle 7 (February 1986): 32.
West Coast Review of Books 12, no. 1 (1986): 32.

Comes the Blind Fury

Book List 76 (1 July 1980): 1596.
Kliatt 14 (Fall 1980): 11.
Library Journal 105 (15 May 1980): 1190.
Publishers Weekly 215 (11 April 1980): 75.
School Library Journal 28 (September 1980): 92.

Creature

Book List 85 (15 February 1989): 961.
Inside Books, August 1989: 80.
Kenyon Review 57 (1 March 1989): 329.
Library Journal 114 (1 April 1989): 114.
Locus 25 (July 1990): 55.
Publishers Weekly 235 (10 March 1989): 75.
School Library Journal 35 (July 1989): 99.
Voice of Youth Advocates 12 (December 1989): 291.
Voice of Youth Advocates 13 (October 1990): 258.

Cry for the Strangers

Library Journal 104 (15 June 1979): 1359.
Publishers Weekly 215 (23 April 1979): 79.

Darkness

Book List 87 (1 May 1991): 1675.
Book Watch 12 (August 1991): 11.
Locus 27 (August 1991): 52.
Locus 29 (July 1992): 54.
Necrofile, Winter 1992: 16.
Publishers Weekly 238 (12 April 1991): 45.
Wilson Library Bulletin 66 (November 1991): 56.

The God Project

Best Sellers 42 (October 1982): 262.
Book List 78 (August 1982): 1484.
English Journal 72 (December 1983): 69.
Kenyon Review 50 (1 July 1982): 760.
Kliatt 17 (Fall 1983): 19.
Library Journal 107 (August 1982): 1484.
Los Angeles Times Book Review, 10 December 1982: 7.
Publishers Weekly 221 (25 June 1982): 1494.
Publishers Weekly 223 (22 April 1983): 102.

School Library Journal 29 (October 1982): 170.
Science Fiction and Fantasy Book Review, July 1983: 45.
Voice of Youth Advocates 5 (August 1982): 36.
West Coast Review of Books 8 (November 1982): 43.

Guardian

Book List 89 (1 June 1993): 1735.
Kenyon Review 61 (1 June 1993): 684.
Library Journal 118 (August 1993): 155.
Publishers Weekly 240 (21 June 1993): 84.

Hellfire

Kliatt 19 (Fall 1985): 26.
Los Angeles Times Book Review, 10 August 1986: 6.
Publishers Weekly 229 (27 June 1986): 82.
San Francisco Chronicle 8 (February 1987): 51.

The Homing

Book List 90 (1 June 1994): 1726.
Kenyon Review 62 (1 June 1994): 732.
Library Journal 119 (July 1994): 130.
Locus 33 (September 1994): 64.
Publishers Weekly 421 (30 May 1994): 35.
Rapport 18 (March 1994): 33.

Nathaniel

Book List 80 (1 June 1984): 1380.
Los Angeles Times Book Review, 30 September 1984: 8.
Publishers Weekly 225 (25 May 1984): 56.
San Francisco Chronicle 6 (August 1985): 41.
Voice of Youth Advocates 7 (February 1985): 332.
West Coast Review of Books 10 (September 1984): 55.

Punish the Sinners

Library Journal 103 (1 June 1978): 1200.
New York Times Book Review, 11 June 1978: 34.
Publishers Weekly 213 (10 April 1978): 70.

Second Child

Book List 86 (1 June 1990): 1850.
Books 5 (September 1991): 24.
Kenyon Review 58 (1 June 1990): 756.
Locus 25 (August 1990): 49.
Locus 27 (August 1991): 52.
Los Angeles Times Book Review, 8 July 1991: 10.
Necrofile, Winter 1992: 16+.
Voice of Youth Advocates 13 (February 1991): 36.
Voice of Youth Advocates 14 (December 1991): 299.

Shadows

Book List 88 (1 May 1992): 1563.
Kenyon Review 60 (15 April 1992): 495.
Locus 29 (August 1992): 54.
Locus 31 (July 1993): 45.
Publishers Weekly 293 (13 April 1992): 43.
Rapport 17 (July 1992): 27.

Sleepwalk

Book List 87 (15 October 1990): 394.
Books 6 (September 1992): 16.
Kliatt 25 (April 1991): 14.
Locus 26 (February 1991): 58.
Los Angeles Times Book Review, 6 January 1991: 10.
Necrofile, Winter 1992: 16+.
Publishers Weekly 237 (14 December 1990): 62.

Suffer the Children

Book List 73 (July 1977): 1635.
New York Times Book Review, 11 September 1977: 3.
Publishers Weekly 211 (25 April 1977): 3.
West Coast Review of Books 3 (September 1977): 65.
West Coast Review of Books 4 (July 1978): 23.

The Unloved

Kliatt 22 (Summer 1988): 26.
Publishers Weekly 233 (29 April 1988): 72.

The Unwanted

San Francisco Chronicle 9 (March 1988): 45.

When the Wind Blows

Kliatt 15 (Fall 1981): 16.
Publishers Weekly 219 (12 June 1981): 52.
West Coast Review of Books 8 (February 1982): 50.

OTHER SECONDARY SOURCES

Barron, Neil, Wayne Barton, Kristin Ramsdell, and Stephen A. Stilwell, eds. *What Do I Read Next? A Reader's Guide to Current Genre Fiction.* Detroit: Gale Research, 1994.

Bettelheim, Bruno. *The Uses of Enchantment: The Meaning and Importance of Fairy Tales.* New York: Alfred A. Knopf, 1976.

Brown, Fredric. "Come and Go Mad." In Bill Pronzini, Barry Malzberg, and Martin H. Greenberg, eds., *Classic Tales of Horror and the Supernatural,* 276–316. New York: Quill/William Morrow, 1981.

Burleson, Donald R. "H. P. Lovecraft." In E. F. Bleiler, ed., *Supernatural Fiction Writers: Fantasy and Horror.* New York: Scribner, 1985.

Büssing, Sabine. *Aliens in the Home: The Child in Horror Fiction*. New York: Greenwood Press, 1987.

Campbell, Joseph. *The Masks of God: Occidental Mythology*. New York: Penguin, 1964.

Chesterton, G. K. *The Secret of Father Brown*. London: Cassell & Co., 1927.

"Cinderella." In Margaret Hunt and James Stern, trans., *The Complete Grimm's Fairy Tales*, 121–128. New York: Pantheon, 1972.

Daniels, Les. *Living in Fear: A History of Horror in the Mass Media*. New York: Charles Scribner's Sons, 1975.

Haining, Peter, ed. *The Shilling Shockers: Stories of Terror from the Gothic Bluebooks*. London: Victor Gollancz, Ltd., 1978.

Jones, Stephen, and Kim Newman. *Horror: 100 Best Books*. New York: Carroll & Graf, 1988.

Kendrick, Walter. *The Thrill of Fear: 250 Years of Scary Entertainment*. New York: Grove Weidenfeld, 1991.

Kies, Cosette N. *Presenting Young Adult Horror Fiction*. New York: Twayne, 1992.

King, Stephen. "On Becoming a Brand Name." In Chuck Underwood and Tim Miller, eds., *Fear Itself: The Early Works of Stephen King*, 15–42. San Francisco: Underwood-Miller, 1982.

King, Stephen. *Stephen King's Danse Macabre*. New York: Everest House, 1979.

Koertge, Noretta. "How Feminism Is Now Alienating Women from Science." *Skeptical Inquirer* 19, no. 2 (March/April 1995): 42–43.

Koontz, Dean. "A Genre in Crisis." In Martin Greenberg, Ed Gorman, and Bill Munster, eds., *The Dean Koontz Companion*. New York: Berkley Books, 1994.

Kristeva, Julia. *Powers of Horror: An Essay on Abjection*. Trans. Leon S. Roudiez. New York: Columbia University Press, 1982.

Lee, A. Robert. "Darkness Visible: The Case of Charles Brockden Brown." In Brian Docherty, ed., *American Horror Fiction: From Brockden Brown to Stephen King*, 13–32. New York: St. Martin's, 1990.

Newman, John Henry Cardinal. *A Newman Anthology*. W. S. Lilly, ed., New York: Gordon Press, 1977.

Nietzsche, Friedrich Wilhelm. *Beyond Good and Evil: Prelude to a Philosophy of the Future*. 1886. Trans. Walter Kaufmann. New York: Vintage, 1966.

O'Brien, Geoffrey. "Horror for Pleasure." *New York Review of Books*, 22 April 1993, 63–68.

Poe, Edgar Allan. *The Complete Poems and Stories of Edgar Allan Poe with Selections from His Critical Writings*. New York: Alfred A. Knopf, 1976.

Rabkin, Eric. *Science Fiction: The Literature of the Technological Imagination*. Springfield, Va.: The Teaching Company, 1994. Audiotape.

Radcliffe, Elsa. *Gothic Novels of the Nineteenth Century: An Annotated Bibliography*. Metuchen, N.J.: Scarecrow Press, 1979.

Robinson, Frank M. "Robert Bloch Obituary." *Locus* 33, no. 5 (November 1994): 6+.

Ross, Jean W. "Bloch, Robert (Albert)." In *Contemporary Authors*, New Revision Series, vol. 5. Detroit: Gale Research, 1989.

Schneider, Kirk J. *Horror and the Holy: Wisdom Teachings of the Monster Tale*. Chicago: Open Court, 1993.

Server, Lee. *Danger Is My Business: An Illustrated History of the Fabulous Pulp Magazines: 1896–1953*. San Francisco: Chronicle Books, 1993.

Sladek, John. "E. T. A. Hoffman. *The Best Tales of Hoffman*." In Stephen Jones and Kim Newman, eds., *Horror: 100 Best Books*. New York: Carroll & Graf, 1988.

Steinberg, Marlene. "Systematizing Dissociation: Symptomatology and Diagnostic Assessment." In David Spiegel, ed., *Dissociation: Culture, Mind, and Body*. Washington D.C.: American Psychiatric P., 1994, pp. 59–90.

Stoker, Bram. *Dracula*. 1897. Reprint. New York: Pyramid Books, 1965.

Tarr, Sister Mary Muriel. *Catholicism in Gothic Fiction in England: A Study of the Nature and Function of Catholic Materials in Gothic Fiction in England (1762–1780)*. 1946. Reprint. New York: Garland, 1979.

Tipler, Frank J. *Modern Cosmology, God, and the Resurrection of the Dead*. New York: Doubleday, 1994.

Washington, Peter. *Madam Blavatsky's Baboon: A History of the Mystics, Mediums and Misfits Who Brought Spiritualism to America*. New York: Shocken Books, 1995.

Wiater, Stanley. *Dark Dreamers: Conversations with the Masters of Horror*. New York: Avon, 1990.

Wilde, Oscar. *The Picture of Dorian Gray*. 1891. Reprint. New York: Dover Publications, 1993.

Winter, Douglas E. *Faces of Fear: Encounters with the Creators of Modern Horror*. New York: Berkley Books, 1985.

Index

About the Author

PAUL BAIL teaches graduate courses on the psychology of crime at Fitchburg State College in Massachusetts. He holds a doctorate in clinical psychology from the University of Michigan. He has reviewed crime novels for *The Drood Review of Mystery* and was a contributor to the Edgar-nominated *Great Women Mystery Writers: Classic to Contemporary,* edited by Kathleen Gregory Klein (Greenwood, 1994).